Understanding Anxiety

Understanding Anxiety

*Our Invisible Handicap
to Happiness and Success*

CAROL KING *with* SEAN KELLY

Jefferson, North Carolina

ISBN (print) 978-1-4766-8838-1
ISBN (ebook) 978-1-4766-4641-1

LIBRARY OF CONGRESS AND BRITISH LIBRARY
CATALOGUING DATA ARE AVAILABLE

Library of Congress Control Number 2022016324

Front cover photograph of woman (Shutterstock/fizkes)

Printed in the United States of America

Toplight is an imprint of McFarland & Company, Inc., Publishers

*Box 611, Jefferson, North Carolina 28640
www.toplightbooks.com*

Table of Contents

Acknowledgments   vii

Preface   1

Introduction   5

One. What Is Anxiety?   13

Two. Social Anxiety   52

Three. Specific Phobia   77

Four. Obsessive Compulsive Disorder (OCD)   92

Five. Generalized Anxiety Disorder (GAD)   110

Six. Anxiety and Underachievement Across the Life
        Span   129

Seven. Managing Your Anxiety   147

Eight. Children, Anxiety, and Parenting Behaviors   176

Conclusion: Revealing and Confronting the Hidden
        Handicap   201

Appendix: Resources for Further Reading   203

References   205

Index   213

Acknowledgments

I have many people to thank for making this book possible. My clients, from whom I learned a tremendous amount, form the basis of the book. I particularly appreciate their courage to seek treatment and their openness in sharing their deepest fears with me.

I would never have had the knowledge, writing skill, or confidence to write a book had it not been for two of my professors at the Pennsylvania State University who had confidence in my ability and offered tremendous support. Ted Huston taught me to think like a psychologist in researching and writing. Indeed, he taught me to write. Ted and Graham Spanier saw my potential when I arrived at Penn State, a naïve young woman of 23 who had been raised in a small Midwestern town. Because of them, and the rest of the faculty in Individual and Family Studies, this graduate program was exceptionally nurturing. I look back on those years as being among my best experiences.

Thanks to my supervisors in a number of positions that I held after I completed my doctorate. Their support allowed me to flourish in applying what I had learned in graduate school. Initially, Linda Peterson encouraged me to pursue a clinical route when I worked with her at the Counseling Center, Inc. Later Ed Crane, George Krolick, Steve Flannigan, Thomas Guthrie, Lee Salter, Mike Bachman, and Tara Pressley all were extremely supportive of my clinical work.

My husband who is also my best friend has provided unconditional love and support as he endured many months of my preoccupation with this book. He looks at me through rose colored glasses and has never doubted that I could do whatever I set out to do. My four boys have always been the center of my universe no matter what I was trying to do professionally. From the age of three when we moved across the country for me to attend graduate school, Greg, my oldest, has been a part of my adventures. While most young children emulate their parents cooking, cleaning or doing carpentry around the house, my Greg spent several hours one day highlighting his Richard Scarry book with a yellow

Acknowledgments

marker as he had seen me do with my textbooks. With his engaging and ever enthusiastic personality, he forced me to relax and have fun when I wasn't on campus. In adulthood, Greg has inspired me to face my fears by mastering a number of potentially dangerous sports such as back country skiing and kite boarding. I can't begin to thank my second son, Sean, who was born on a weekend between my Friday and Monday statistics class and helped author this book. Working together on this project has been an amazing and satisfying experience that not every parent gets to enjoy.

Jeff, son number three, seems to have completely conquered any anxiety that he might have had. Not only is he an avid rock climber, which terrifies me, but he has traveled the world, exploring approximately 80 countries often by bike. My youngest son, Tyler, has encouraged me at every step along the way in writing this book. He is probably my biggest fan and cheerleader. His faith in me, his enthusiasm and encouragement for me to write, and his pride in my finishing the book has been extraordinary.

This book is dedicated to my two treasured grandchildren, Phillip and Evelyn. May they conquer stress and overcome anxiety throughout their lives.

Thank you to C. Deborah Laughton for encouragement to pursue this book. Thank you to Professor Jessica Collett at UCLA for reviewing draft materials and providing helpful feedback. Thank you to Kelly Anderson for her enthusiastic reading and edits.

Sean Kelly: It was fun to work with my mom on this book. We both love all things social science and enjoy putting ideas down on paper. The many years of clinical work that generated the vignettes and insights in this book represent a lifetime of work. I am so glad my mom is sharing that impressive work here in this book from McFarland.

Preface

This book deals with anxiety disorders and the many forms they can take. We hear a great deal about anxiety today, yet our understanding of it is more limited than we realize. Depictions of anxiety are often hazy, as in "she had a nervous breakdown." Everyone seems to have their own idea of what anxiety looks like; our understanding of it is limited by our own experiences. For example, some people would say anxiety is "stress," while others would say "it's worrying." These are both forms anxiety takes, but they fail to capture the true scope of Anxiety Disorder in all its forms. This book provides a comprehensive portrait of anxiety, from Panic Disorder to Specific Phobias to Social Anxiety to Generalized Anxiety Disorder and beyond. The vignettes presented in the book will not only show the range of anxiety disorders but also the profound consequences anxiety can have.

The primary purpose of this book is to illuminate the form, scope, and effects of anxiety so that readers can better understand its pervasive role in modern life. I address all of the major Anxiety Disorders and discuss the role of anxiety across the life course, from infancy through retirement. The focus of the text is not self-help, although I do include two chapters at the end on ways in which readers can deal with their own anxiety and minimize anxiety in their children. Throughout the book I reference resources readers can use to learn more about anxiety and its treatment.

In its milder but more pervasive forms, anxiety is, I will argue throughout, often "hidden" from full view. Anxiety is hidden in part because it is so diffuse in form and because it ranges so dramatically in its severity. Anxiety is fundamentally different from many conditions for which individuals seek help; for example, whereas overweight individuals may have been trying to lose weight their whole lives, anxiety sufferers are often unaware of the root cause of their problems. People with anxiety may assume that they lack courage or that a failure to achieve stems from a lack of ability. Anxiety is also hidden because

1

many people are still reluctant to talk about their own experiences with it. Anxiety still appears to carry a stigma when compared to depression and seems to be taken less seriously than depression and other medical illnesses.

The consequences of anxiety are far reaching. Not only does it cause much day-to-day misery and limit a person's enjoyment in life, but it accounts for underachievement in school and work. Additionally, it can interfere with a person developing and maintaining fulfilling relationships and enjoying leisure pursuits. As I will show using vignettes of anxiety sufferers, the hidden nature of anxiety often compounds its effects. Thus, understanding the different forms that anxiety can take is an important first step toward addressing and conquering it.

I am writing this book from a personal perspective. The more that I have researched anxiety, the more I have come to realize that there has been much anxiety in my own life and that of my family. For example, my father, a 1932 MIT graduate, gave up his engineering career early to help my grandfather run the family farm. While this decision was, in part, a lifestyle choice, I now believe that stress and anxiety played a role. His work likely wasn't the only aspect of my father's life that was affected by his anxious temperament. Even though he had traveled extensively in his younger years, my father barely left our hometown after he retired from engineering, and he seldom socialized with anyone outside of our extended family.

I hope this book will save or spare readers from the pain and waste that many people with anxiety disorders experience and that I have seen in my patients and my own family and friends. I began my career in psychology at a time when many psychologists started their professional work at local or regional psychiatric hospitals. While many of my colleagues were fascinated by the chronically mentally ill, I found that I was more interested in the lives of ordinary people with "normal" worries. The nuances and subtleties of their behavior seemed endlessly interesting. Anxiety is especially intriguing in that things are not necessarily what they seem. It takes some detective work to figure out what is really going on. Anxious people look just like everyone else. Indeed, we all experience anxiety to different degrees, and it sometimes affects us and our loved ones more than we realize.

I began to develop the specific thesis of this book in the 1990s while, after having worked in a variety of clinical settings, I was in private practice. Realizing that anxiety seemed to be far more prevalent than most people realized, largely because it was hidden and not well understood, I began looking more closely at my clients. Most of the people who sought treatment had come in complaining of another problem. It sometimes took a number of sessions to tease out the fact that anxiety was often at the root.

I was surprised to find that many of the people who came to me felt that they were failing to live up to their expectations because, for the most part, my clients happened to be the high functioning people who seemed to have everything figured out. It takes a certain amount of confidence and much courage to seek professional help. Yet many of these high achievers suffered from anxiety that interfered with them accomplishing even more. No one meeting many of these clients would have imagined the extent of their suffering. On the other hand, some of my other clients who were bright and appeared competent were not achieving anything close to what they appeared capable of doing. It became more and more clear that anxiety in its various forms was the common factor that was standing in the way of many of my clients' happiness and success even though, as I mentioned, very few of them had come to me complaining of anxiety.

Even more amazing to me was my realization that my clients were only the tip of the iceberg. I began to recognize the extent of the hidden anxiety within the general community. There were many far more handicapped people than my clients who were functioning too poorly even to seek help that I heard about from their friends or family. These anxious individuals are our neighbors and co-workers.

In describing the many dimensions of this hidden handicap to success I draw on the scientific literature on anxiety as well as my forty-plus years of working with anxious patients of all ages in a variety of settings. The vignettes of anxiety sufferers come from life histories of my clients in psychiatric hospitals, mental health centers, a university counseling center, and my private practice. I have also consulted in elementary, middle, and high schools as well as nursing homes. My patients included men and women of diverse racial and ethnic identities and sexual preferences. Not only did almost all of them appear very normal, but many were considered highly successful by any measure. As is standard practice in psychology, any potentially identifying details of these individuals have been purposefully altered to maintain confidentiality. Importantly, this book is not a substitute for professional mental health care.

Introduction

Anxiety is the most pervasive mental illness in the country. According to the Department of Health and Human Services (2019) approximately 40 percent of women and 20 percent of men suffer from anxiety at some point. Among young adults, stress is ubiquitous; an astounding 91 percent of those age 18–21 ("Generation Z") reported at least one physical or emotional symptom due to stress in the preceding month (American Psychological Association, 2018). Despite the fact that we have an incentive to view ourselves positively, only 45 percent of individuals under age 21 and only 56 percent of those age 22–39 describe their overall mental health as "excellent" or even "very good." As a result, much has been written about mental health and anxiety and discussions of anxiety emerge regularly in the media and popular press. Yet, with all of the scientific research on anxiety, and even celebrities discussing their own struggles with it, anxiety is still often not fully understood or even recognized. Publicized anxiety is only the tip of the iceberg. Much anxiety is "hidden." In their most severe manifestations, Anxiety Disorders are difficult to miss, but the more subtle and far more common forms anxiety takes are another story. While anxiety is responsible for a great deal of silent suffering and failure to achieve, even the anxious people themselves often don't understand the true nature of their struggles. They don't necessarily recognize that anxiety is their underlying problem. They may assume that they are just not as bright or competent as they were thought to be or that they lack courage.

For example, Sharon, a client of mine, had so much difficulty concentrating on her reading that she comprehended only a small portion of what she read and failed English in her first year of college. Since she had put a lot of time into this class, she concluded that she wasn't very bright and began to wonder how she had made it through high school. Another college student decided that he lacked courage because he started missing a class after he gave an embarrassing answer to a professor's question. James assumed that most of his peers would have had no problem returning to the class.

Considering that the anxious individuals themselves don't fully understand what is limiting them, it's not surprising that their family and friends have even less understanding. Anxious people are often misunderstood. Family and friends don't realize the real reason that their loved ones don't seem entirely happy and aren't living up to expectations. They often assume that their underachieving family members or friends lack motivation and aren't making an effort.

In Chapter One you'll meet Helen who had been a straight A student in high school but received highly inconsistent grades her first semester in college with As in some classes and Ds and Fs in others. Her parents assumed that Helen had been partying too much when in fact she had been missing her small group classes because anxiety had caused her not to enter the classrooms even after she had walked to the buildings.

Anxiety problems are driven further from view because there is still a stigma attached to anxiety compared to depression or bipolar disorder. Men tend to perceive anxiety as a weakness and no woman wants to be described as "nervous." In one study in which high school students were presented with a vignette describing a peer with classic symptoms of Generalized Anxiety Disorder (GAD), 15 percent of respondents described the symptom as "a sign of personal weakness" and believed the person did not suffer from "a real medical illness" (Hanlon & Swords, 2020).

In contrast, anxiety is often depicted in literature and film, and in these mediums, imagined characters struggle openly with various anxiety disorders. I use fictional examples throughout the text to illuminate specific anxiety disorders in part because these are familiar to readers. Indeed, in many ways, iconic characters provide cultural models of anxiety, simplified narratives that we use to understand anxiety. For example, just as Hilary Swank's character in *Freedom Writers* provides a cultural model of excellent, student-centered teaching (Kelly & Caughlan, 2011), Jack Nicholson's character in *As Good as It Gets* provides an example of severe Obsessive-Compulsive Disorder. I find depictions of anxiety in films and books are, for the most part, quite realistic. However, importantly, remember that the degree of self-realization of anxiety in fictional texts frequently goes beyond what we see in real life.

Returning to real-world anxiety, the fact that many anxious people "self-medicate" with drugs or alcohol makes it even more difficult to recognize the true nature of their struggles. As we know, misusing drugs and excessive drinking offer only temporary relief and are completely ineffective in the long run. Consider the well-known relationship between substance abuse and suicide. The prevalence of substance abuse, suicide, and the co-occurrence of the two was summarized by the Substance Abuse and Mental Health Services Administration in 2016. Almost 25 percent of individuals in the United States over the age of 12 engaged in binge drinking in the past month. At the same time, each year more than nine million people in the United States have serious thoughts of suicide. More than 41,000 people go on to commit suicide each year, making it the tenth leading cause of death. A staggering number of suicides and suicide attempts each year involve drugs and alcohol, leading to hundreds of thousands of emergency room visits.

In addition to arguing that anxiety is a particularly hidden mental health condition, another central insight from research on anxiety is that individuals differ in their predispositions to anxiety. People who aren't particularly anxious have difficulty understanding how much those with anxiety suffer and the extent of their difficulties functioning in the world. There is tremendous person-to-person variability in susceptibility to anxiety. Some estimates indicate that about 5 percent of the population will experience GAD during their lifetime (Wittchen & Jacobi, 2011). Yet, that risk is not evenly distributed, and problems of anxiety are, to a non-trivial extent, clustered in families and have a hereditary component (Bandelow et al., 2013). I have encountered patients who have a high vulnerability to anxiety time and again in my own work, and it is *useful* to individuals suffering from anxiety to know that some people really do have a heightened sensitivity to anxiety. While acknowledging a proclivity for anxiety entails some risk of creating a self-fulfilling prophecy, not taking anxiety seriously enough is a much greater risk. For example, in discussing parenting in Chapter Eight, I will emphasize that parenting anxious children requires strategic action that isn't necessarily required with less anxiety-prone children.

At the same time, an equally important insight you will see throughout this book is that, quite apart from any predisposition to anxiety or effect of heredity, anxiety is created, triggered, precipitated, etc., by real life events and the need to adapt to changes. These events are sometimes unanticipated, such as being assaulted or having a serious car accident. Other times, anxiety is triggered by regular or anticipated life events (e.g., getting a new job, getting married, etc.) that can

7

nevertheless be difficult. Consequently, the extent of a person's anxiety tends to wax and wane over their lifetime. This insight is central to understanding the origins of anxiety, to its remediation, and its prevention. This theme is carried throughout the book, but is especially central to Chapter Six, where I discuss the challenging transitions that occur throughout the life course and how anxiety can manifest at each stage.

Turning to the effects of anxiety, I will show that it contributes to much unhappiness and underachievement, ultimately resulting in failure to live one's best life. Fear causes the anxious to avoid many necessary and pleasurable activities. In an attempt to minimize the panicky feelings that characterize anxiety, sufferers naturally begin to avoid the situations that produce these feelings. Consequently, anxiety handicaps a person in every area of life, standing in the way when they are trying to complete their education, pursue a career, and develop and maintain fulfilling relationships. More formally, beyond arguing that anxiety leads to unhappiness, throughout the book I provide examples of the comorbidity or co-occurrence of anxiety with other mental health disorders such as depression and alcoholism. Since these disorders often present in a more striking way, the underlying anxiety may be overshadowed. Along the same line, while the many physiological symptoms that characterize Generalized Anxiety Disorder (GAD) are likely to be brought to a general practitioner's attention, the underlying anxiety may not be. Since a patient often complains about one symptom at a time, the doctor usually doesn't understand the full picture and the root cause of the symptoms for some time, if ever.

Anxiety has long been recognized not just as an individual psychological condition but as a major social problem. That anxiety may be due, in the aggregate, to social conditions dates at least to W.H. Auden's Pulitzer Prize–winning poem "The Age of Anxiety" (1947) and Dale Carnegie's still famous *How to Stop Worrying and Start Living* (1948). Sociologists and psychologists began writing even more about this in the '60s and declared that decade the "official" age of anxiety. A *Time* magazine issue published on March 31, 1961, featured Edvard Munch's *The Scream* on its cover.

Writers attributed this growing anxiety to basic features of American society, including the growing population in busy cities and suburbs and rising geographic mobility. Even more intrinsically, this increasing level of anxiety may be at least partially attributable to our having a greater number of choices than we've ever had throughout history. Once they reach adulthood, people of the Western world are at least theoretically free to choose where to live, what kind of work to pursue, and whom to marry, while in past generations, a sizeable proportion of people stayed in their hometowns, worked in their father's professions, and married someone they had known since childhood. Americans are now forced into making more choices per day with fewer "givens," more ambiguous criteria, less environmental stability, and less social structure and support than any people in history. Barry Schwartz, writing about this phenomenon in his 2004 book *The Paradox of Choice: Why More Is Less*, argues that as the freedom to choose increases, anxiety does as well.

Our worries may also be fundamentally more complex than they used to be. Scott Stossel (2013) wonders whether anxiety may be "an emotion that we can afford to indulge only when we're not preoccupied by real fear." He cites the fact that people in developing countries have lower rates of clinical anxiety. This makes sense, given that people in these countries need to put all of their energy into surviving. I would add that, in some sense, we Americans have built our own house of anxiety, since many of us lack a true sense of community which could mitigate stress. Our families are scattered, and friends don't stay in one place. In Chapter Six, I make the argument that even the retirement years, which were once conceptualized as stage of "winding down," have become another proving ground with a whole new set of expectations.

Almost everything that writers described about previous decades is even more problematic today. We continue to live in the age of anxiety. While geographic mobility has finally begun to fall somewhat (Current Population Study, 2020), the information age has brought us new sources of anxiety like the burgeoning identity theft occurring online. Additionally, social media has made it almost impossible not to compare ourselves to others who seem to be more successful or to be living fuller lives. Social media can have an especially stressful effect on teenagers. Indeed, Robert Leahy, writing in *Psychology Today* (April 30, 2008), declared that "the average high school kid today has the same level of anxiety as the average psychiatric patient in the 1950s."

When the Covid pandemic hit in spring of 2020, not only did people have a serious new health risk to be anxious about, but the need to isolate made it much harder for us to obtain support from family and friends or mental health practitioners. In a more positive way, the Covid era seems to have brought anxiety out in the open and to have made it more acceptable. Some people came forward to discuss their fears. It was suddenly OK to be anxious when the whole world was grappling with a very real threat. Yet many individuals were reluctant to admit that they were always prone to anxiety even when they didn't have an "excuse."

Scientific Grounding of the Book

The arguments in this book are an extension of the rich body of research in psychology and other disciplines that sought to explain the sources and consequences of Anxiety Disorder. In my view the seminal text on anxiety, and the most comprehensive work to date when it was published in 1988, is David Barlow's book *Anxiety and Its Disorders: The Nature and Treatment of Anxiety and Panic*. This excellent book was primarily geared toward researchers of Anxiety Disorders and mental health practitioners and built on decades of research on anxiety. Going back even earlier, important early studies of anxiety include Hamilton's (1960) work on anxiety from the late 1950s and Holmes and Rahe's (1967) research on life stressors. Ideas from those lines of research remain useful today and are referenced in this book. Several more recent books have done an excellent job bringing anxiety to the public's attention and are also scientifically robust. Two of my personal favorites are *Worry: Controlling It and Using It Wisely* by Edward Hallowell (1997) and *My Age of Anxiety: Fear, Hope, Dread and the Search for Peace of Mind* by Scott Stossel (2013). Hallowell's book focuses on worry in particular, and Stossel describes his own experience with anxiety while interweaving relevant literature on the topic. I reference ideas from both these texts throughout this book. I also draw on the most recent research published in scientific journals including *Frontiers in Neuroscience*, the *American Journal of Psychiatry, Social Indicators Research*, and many others. In addition, I direct readers to the Anxiety and Depression Association of America for further information. The appendix contains works on selected topics for additional reading.

Organization of the Book

The book is organized according to the Anxiety Disorders identified in the *Diagnostic and Statistical Manual (DSM)* published by the American Psychiatric Association. Chapter One begins with Panic Disorder because panic is the very essence of anxiety. Panic has its origin in the fight or flight response which evolved so that animals can react quickly to danger. However, in Panic Disorder the sufferer experiences fear and panic even when not in actual danger. Then I move on to Agoraphobia which sometimes follows from panic and to PTSD which involves panic in its most severe form. You'll meet Jill, who dropped out of college after having panic attacks on her way to class, and Nancy, a retired attorney, who hadn't left her house in two years.

In Chapter Two, I introduce Social Anxiety which involves fear and panic in a wide range of social situations. Social Anxiety can impact every aspect of a person's life because we are social animals and need one another to survive and thrive. The avoidance strategies individuals use to cope with Social Anxiety can be especially damaging to building relationships and careers.

In Chapter Three, I focus on Specific Phobia. Collectively, phobias such as the fear of crowds, flying, enclosed spaces, or heights are relatively common. While these might be viewed as just a nuisance, I show that even very specific phobias can be surprisingly debilitating. Highly competent and successful people can be derailed by phobias that they realize are completely irrational. I describe one of my clients, Maureen, who ended up selling her beloved historic home over a fear of spiders. Friends and family often don't realize that an individual is making such excessive accommodations due to a phobia.

Chapter Four discusses Obsessive Compulsive Disorder (OCD), characterized by obsessive thoughts and worries which can lead to compulsive behaviors, like excessive cleaning. Additionally, some people with OCD hoard worthless objects, filling every room of their homes.

Chapter Five introduces Generalized Anxiety Disorder (GAD), which is characterized by anxiety and excessive worry that may not be as intense as it is in some of the other anxiety disorders but is chronic and pervasive. GAD sufferers experience physiological symptoms such as fatigue, headaches, gastrointestinal problems, and insomnia, and they seek help for these discrete symptoms often without realizing they are due to anxiety. Joanne first had symptoms of GAD in early childhood and still struggles with it in retirement, in spite of having had a highly successful career and raising three children.

Chapter Six discusses anxiety disorders over the life course from birth through old age. Surprisingly, although we think of retirement as a time when our lives are relatively stress free, this is often not the case. Certainly, life changes that precipitate or trigger acute anxiety occur in *all* phases of the life course.

Introduction

Chapter Seven moves to addressing treatment for anxiety disorders. Although treatment is not the core focus of this text, I discuss general principles of treating anxiety along with some specific strategies for managing each of the major anxiety disorders. Managing anxiety entails attention to your overall health and involves finding ways to reduce stressors in your life. Another key theme is that treatment can be approached incrementally; it takes time and deliberate effort to overcome anxieties that may have been building for a lifetime.

Finally, Chapter Eight addresses what parents can do to address an anxiety-prone child's unique needs, which begin the minute the baby leaves the hospital. A key principle here is that parents can prevent many problems associated with anxiety by taking careful action early, before the effects of anxiety snowball into School Phobia or other serious problems.

ONE

What Is Anxiety?

We have all known people who don't appear to be living their best lives. We call them underachievers. Examples include the seemingly bright student who obtains Cs and the middle-aged man "who never made anything of himself." All too often, friends, family, and even the underachievers themselves attribute their problems to an all-encompassing but vague shortcoming: they just don't have what it takes. But this commonsense diagnosis is naïve and robs the individual of the agency to make changes in his or her life. What can explain why some people seem to be such obvious underachievers? I argue that achievement in modern life is often undermined by a pervasive but subtle enemy of success and happiness—anxiety.

In this chapter I will introduce you to this foe and its particular forms, beginning with Panic Disorder and its strong physical manifestations. Yet, even in these cases, where one can literally *see* the signs of distress, the root cause of that distress too often remains misunderstood by the anxious individuals themselves, their loved ones, and even their caregivers. All too often anxiety is hidden. Understanding the hidden nature of anxiety, and that self-defeating behaviors have their source in anxiety, is the first step toward positive change. To begin, consider the following brief scenarios from my clinical files, which showcase many familiar forms of underachievement.[1] Later, I will present more detailed life histories that reveal how anxiety functions as a hidden handicap to success and undermines happiness. This chapter will also introduce you to common rubrics (assessment batteries) used to gauge anxiety.

Larry, an intelligent and cultured man who looks like a stereotypical academic with wire-rimmed glasses and tweed jacket, first came to me complaining of low-grade depression and dissatisfaction. He is 55 years old and has earned two master's degrees and a doctorate. In spite of his

---

1. Throughout the book, names and some specific details have been changed to protect my clients' confidentiality.

high educational achievements, Larry still lives with his aunt and runs a small mail order business out of his childhood home. He nets an average income of $5,000 a year. Larry has never been able to obtain employment in his field of study. He is socially isolated and has never dated.

John is a 36-year-old college junior in business administration who is trying to get his life back on track after years of drug addiction. John's casual dress and unassuming manner make him appear younger than his weathered face reveals. His entire family, including his mother, sister and two brothers, are addicted to prescription medications. John is the first in his family to attempt college, although all of his siblings are bright. His five adult siblings still live with their mother. John gets mostly As in his classes, but he finds it too stressful to take more than a couple of classes each semester. It will take him a total of ten years to graduate.

Sara, a vivacious blonde with an irresistible smile, is a 19-year-old standout athlete who dreamed of playing soccer and majoring in pre-med at a prestigious university. Although she had managed to obtain a full scholarship to the university of her choice, she dropped out and returned home after a few weeks. Sara attributes her difficulties to the fact that the university was too large and too far from home. She plans to attend a small college in her hometown even though the school doesn't have a soccer team.

Helen has the looks of the quintessential college coed with streaked chestnut hair tied back in a ponytail. She was a straight A student in high school. Now that she is in college, however, she has had several semesters of highly inconsistent grades with As in some classes and Ds and Fs in others. Her parents are convinced that Helen is "partying" too much, but she insists that this is not the problem.

The list could go on and on. Alice can't concentrate on her schoolwork because she is bombarded by irrelevant and worrisome thoughts that cause her to miss a portion of what she is reading. Sally doesn't feel able to fly overseas to visit her only daughter and infant granddaughter. Susan has been unable to obtain work because she is afraid to drive and doesn't have public transportation. Patrick is a brilliant 34-year-old attorney who is addicted to marijuana. He smokes first thing in the morning and the minute that he gets home at night. At work he goes out to his car during breaks to smoke. This has led Patrick's wife to ask for a divorce and the other lawyers in the firm to confront Patrick on the quality of his work.

No one would hesitate to describe these men and women as underachievers. Their friends and family attributed their difficulties to lack of ability, low motivation, sheer laziness, or drinking too much. My patients, themselves, suspected that they were incompetent or lacking in courage. We all know people who don't appear to be doing as well as they would have been expected to do.

While many factors can contribute to underachievement and undermine happiness, these men and women shared one underlying characteristic. They all suffered from an undiagnosed Anxiety Disorder in spite of the fact that none of them, with the exception of Sally, mentioned feeling anxious on their intake forms or after I sat down with them. In Larry's case, he was so anxious that he avoided interviewing for jobs and initiating conversations with women. This left him living with his aunt in his childhood home and running a small business that was unrelated to his extensive education. Larry thought that he lacked courage. John first started taking prescription medication so that he could sleep. When he realized how much better he felt after taking the medication, he began to take it during the day as well. Sara found the unfamiliar college environment so stressful that she feared that she could have a "nervous breakdown" if she stayed in school. For Helen, anxiety prevented her from attending certain classes. If she had to miss a class due to illness, she had a great deal of difficulty going back to that particular class, so she ended up failing her classes that were small enough for the professor and the other students to notice her. One of the ironies of anxiety is that people who suffer from it are often extremely conscientious and hardworking, yet they may be perceived as lazy and unmotivated. The individuals themselves aren't always aware of the true nature of their problems. For example, John didn't realize why he had become addicted to medication since the process had been so gradual and such a part of his family culture.

These vignettes are some of the many examples of the hidden handicap that many individuals carry with them—anxiety. These stories also reveal the sometimes profound consequences of this anxiety. While some people, like Sarah, end up scaling back their dreams or allowing their anxiety to interfere with them taking steps toward their goals, others, like John, resort to drinking excessively or taking drugs to cope with circumstances that are difficult for them to face. Unfortunately, such coping mechanisms further hide the true cause of their struggles; substance abuse becomes the public face of the anxious person's struggle.

Many people drink to relax in social situations and some who suffer from more constant anxiety even sneak drinks to get through the day. Other anxiety-prone individuals may realize that smoking marijuana helps them to wind down enough to relax and to sleep. Although "self-medication" with drugs or alcohol may help in the short run, we all know that actual substance abuse ultimately leads to failure to attain goals and compromises the individual's health and happiness. By the time that people seek treatment for their addictions, they often have been self-medicating for so long that they may not remember why they originally began drinking or taking drugs. Alcoholics and people addicted to drugs are the least understood and most likely to be personally blamed for their failure to achieve a normal life. Substance abuse is often viewed as *the* primary problem with little or no recognition of a person's underlying anxiety. Family members, friends, colleagues, and even professional counselors often don't understand that there is another problem underlying the substance abuse. Alcoholism and substance abuse may be even more hidden in women than in men. They often tend to drink at home instead of at the neighborhood bar and are more likely to become addicted to prescription medications than street drugs.

Adolescents and young adults from neglectful or abusive families are likely to suffer particularly strong consequences if they abuse alcohol or drugs. They may end up dropping out of school and being labeled delinquent. If drinking leads to identification with a bad peer group, they may fall prey to a whole host of negative peer influences and end up committing crimes, sometimes to support addictions. Now these teens must cope not only with underlying anxiety but also failure, humiliation, and the criminal justice system.

In the population as a whole, alcoholism and drug abuse are far more common than we realize. Many people are functional alcoholics who drink more than is healthy but manage to do well enough in life that other people don't realize that they could have done even better or that they are often unhappy. And those who become addicted to prescription medications tend to be especially hidden.

Anxiety is so common that we have all experienced it to some degree. Almost everyone can remember feeling nervous before a performance, a difficult exam, or an important job interview. Indeed, anxiety disorders are the most common mental illness in the United States, far outstripping depression (Harvard Medical School, 2007), which we tend to hear more about.[2] The fact that there are so many words in our

---

2. Smoking and other tobacco use remains quite common. Thus, if nicotine dependence is included as a substance abuse disorder, then substance abuse disorders become somewhat more common than anxiety disorders. However, among mood disorders (e.g., depression), impulse-control disorders, anxiety disorders, and even substance abuse disorders (if nicotine is not included), anxiety disorders are the most common of those disorders.

lexicon for anxiety underscores its prevalence. As David Barlow (1988) points out in his seminal book *Anxiety and Its Disorders*, alarm, angst, anguish, apprehension, brooding, disquiet, dread, fear, fright, foreboding, nervousness, pressure, restlessness, stress, terror, tension, and unease are common synonyms. I would add feeling paralyzed, hesitant, scared, self-conscious, panicky, worried, frazzled, rattled, shaken and overwhelmed to this list. But despite the fact that anxiety is mentioned more than ever, it's not something that we hear friends and acquaintances talking about when referring to themselves unless we are very close to them. Most of the anxious suffer in silence. Unlike physical disabilities and severe forms of mental illness such as schizophrenia, anxiety is often hidden. Indeed, a surprisingly large number of highly successful, even famous, people have silently struggled with anxiety.

As early as 1976 researchers concluded that "more people in the US visit their physicians for anxiety than for coughs and colds" (Barlow, 1988; quoting Marsland, Wood, & Mayo, 1976). In 1986, one third of patients reported "severe anxiety" to their primary care doctors (Barlow, 1988). By 2007, estimates were that 36 percent of women and 25 percent of men suffered from an anxiety disorder at some point (Harvard Medical School, 2007). More recently, Andrea Petersen, writing in the *Wall Street Journal*, reported that "24 percent of a sample of 70,000 college students in one sample were diagnosed with or treated for anxiety problems in 2019." Given the reluctance of this population to seek professional help, this is undoubtedly the tip of the iceberg. Even more people are probably suffering in silence. Researchers estimate that only slightly more than a third of the people suffering from anxiety obtain treatment (Anxiety and Depression Association of America, 2020). Indeed, anxiety disorders seem to be taken less seriously than depression and other medical conditions.

The finding that a higher percentage of women report suffering from anxiety may be accounted for by several factors. Most women are smaller and not as strong as the average man, making it adaptive for them to be more vigilant and cautious. Also, men may be less likely to admit to anxiety. Indeed, they may not even be aware of how anxious they are. Historically, little boys have been raised to be tough by repressing their fear. They weren't encouraged to be attuned to fear or sadness. Consequently, some men become angry when they feel anxious. This can happen so fast that boys and men may not even be fully aware that they are afraid. Because of this, anxiety tends to be even more hidden in men.

Understanding Anxiety

Anxiety seems to be a relatively stable trait that continues to haunt a person throughout his life, since anxious adults typically remember having been anxious as children. The symptoms of anxiety, however, become more pronounced during times of stress and change. As a college counselor at a major engineering university, I saw the effects of the onset of severe anxiety as students transitioned to a huge college campus, sometimes far from their homes. Whatever an individual's underlying propensity for anxiety, life transitions, including all the stages of schooling, from preschool through college, often trigger anxiety. Now consider Miriam, who had a lifelong history of anxiety.

Miriam's Story

Her eighty-five-year-old mother still talks about what a difficult baby her only child was from the moment they brought her home from the hospital. According to her mother, Miriam fussed constantly and only seemed content when she was nursing. Her mother was surprised when her demanding infant grew into a quiet child who was extremely cautious about trying anything new or different. Miriam's parents attributed this to stubbornness. Miriam was fearful of going outside but her busy parents just thought that she preferred her many indoor activities. On her first day of kindergarten, when it was time for her mother to leave, Miriam bolted out the door of the classroom and chased her departing mother down the hall. Her mother decided that her daughter was hopelessly spoiled.

Miriam seemed to enjoy school after the first week but continued to be quiet, keeping to herself and never raising her hand. Her excellent report cards gave her parents little cause to worry. Miriam continued the same pattern in high school, and she eschewed any extracurricular activities to go straight home after school to work on her homework. Her high achieving parents considered this a very good thing. Miriam did so well that it looked like she would be valedictorian of her graduating class. However, her grades plummeted her senior year. No one suspected that Miriam wanted to make sure that she didn't have to give a speech on graduation day. She still finished in the top quarter of her class and could have gone to a number of different universities.

Miriam's parents thought that her decision to go to the small college in her hometown had to do with the strength of that school's library science program. Her aunt was excited when Miriam agreed to work in the aunt's bookstore over the summers and used what she had learned to select and order books. Miriam was content with this work and continued to live with her parents in order to save money for her own apartment. She spent all of her free time reading and didn't have any friends. Miriam preferred the company of her mother who appreciated being able to see so much of her daughter. Her mother encouraged her to find a boyfriend, but Miriam protested that she wanted to focus on her career.

This all seemed fine at first, but ten years later Miriam was still living with her parents and working at the bookstore. She no longer talked about moving to her own place. After her father died, Miriam stayed to keep her mother company. Years later, when it was time for Miriam to retire, she and her mother continued to live as two girlfriends in the family home. No longer needing to go to the bookstore, Miriam rarely left the house except to buy groceries or medicine. If relatives wondered about this, they didn't say anything. Miriam had successfully hidden her anxiety from her mother and aunt for over fifty-five years. For her part, Miriam seemed quite content and didn't fully grasp how constricted her life was. She was able to order all of the books that she wanted online.

Miriam's case was extreme. Most of my clients experienced more subtle forms of anxiety. Yet, in my forty years of working with anxious patients, I have seen firsthand what even moderate anxiety can do to a person's life. Indeed, the subtlety of anxiety in its many forms is what makes it so consequential. While Miriam recognized her own anxiety in many instances, she failed to connect some major difficulties in her life to her anxiety. Many other anxious people have no idea they are doing battle with one of happiness's most pervasive and persistent foes. Nor are they fully aware of what is standing in the way of their success in achieving their goals. As a result, they pursue strategies doomed to fail, leaving anxiety to plague them again and again. The hidden nature of anxiety is remarkable, making it far different from depression and many other psychological problems. Time after time in my career, I would learn from patients that friends and relatives had no idea of the nature and extent of their suffering. When anxiety is hidden from the rest of the world, and even the anxious person herself doesn't fully grasp its presence, there is little hope of improvement.

That Anxious Feeling

The physiology of anxiety stems from the "fight or flight" response which is evolution's way of protecting us from predators and other dangers.[3] Without the negative connotation associated with anxiety, this reaction can be looked at as a burst of energy. Barlow (1988) writes,

---

3. I use the common phrasing here, although note that this is backward: always flee before fighting!

Understanding Anxiety

"Without anxiety little would be accomplished. The performance of athletes, entertainers, artisans, and students would suffer, creativity would diminish, and crops would not be planted." In other words, the right amount of arousal can energize and motivate us, enhancing our performance in whatever we're undertaking.

The fight or flight response, which is seen in all animals, is caused by a barrage of hormones and neurochemicals flooding the person's body in response to a perceived threat to his well-being. This puts the person on high alert so that he can react quickly to the threat. We have all heard of the hormone adrenaline, the most important contributor to the fight or flight reaction. In addition to alertness and energy, this physiological reaction to danger causes increase in heart rate, perspiration, rapid shallow breathing, muscle tension, dry mouth and queasiness. These bodily responses, which aren't within our conscious control, are caused by activation of the autonomic nervous system controlled by the amygdala (our primitive brain that we share with all animals) which regulates our internal bodily functions. The primitive amygdala overpowers our rational cortex when we are reacting to a perceived danger. That we don't have conscious control over these basic reactions makes it difficult to deal with them in spite of our superior reasoning abilities.

When we're afraid, we act very much like an anxious rodent.[4] In *The Expression of the Emotions in Man and Animals* (1872), Darwin wrote, "When threatened the congenitally 'anxious' rat trembles, avoids open spaces, prefers familiar places, stops in its tracks if encountering anything potentially threatening, and emits ultrasonic distress calls." Scott Stossel, author of *My Age of Anxiety: Fear, Hope, Dread and the Search for Peace of Mind* (2013), notes that "humans don't issue ultrasonic distress calls—but when we get nervous, we do tremble, shy away from unfamiliar situations, withdraw from social contact, and prefer to stay close to home." An agoraphobic person illustrates this to the extreme. It's not surprising, then, that too much anxiety can be debilitating.

One reason that anxiety is so pervasive is that it is adaptive. From an evolutionary perspective, sensitive individuals might have been the first to notice and escape danger so they were able to stay alive and

---

4. Nevertheless, we still need this protective fear response. There is a rare genetic disorder by the name of Urbach-Wiethe disease which causes calcification of the patient's amygdala so that the person doesn't feel fear. One woman with the disorder had exposed herself to many dangerous situations which resulted in her being taken advantage of in a number of ways and almost beaten to death in one instance (Holland, 2020). There is a thin line between being an adventuresome, daring person and an adventurous person who rashly jumps into hazardous situations.

reproduce. They were the cautious men and women who hesitated to take risks. Their male peers who were less risk averse and more gregarious probably had more children with more women—if they made it to adulthood.

We can see this fight or flight reaction in all animals, from rabbits to gorillas.[5] In the presence of danger, larger animals fight, while smaller, defenseless animals run or freeze. Humans probably rely mostly on avoidance, although a portion of our population reacts with aggression. An angry explosive outburst or impulsive violent attack can be thought of as the "fight" in the fight or flight response. In modern times most people rarely need to flee or fight, yet at times we experience the same fight or flight reactions to situations or things that should be innocuous. This is anxiety.

The fight or flight response is meant to be a rare and short-lived burst of energy designed to get us out of trouble before we even have time to consciously think about the danger. People with anxiety disorders experience this reaction at the wrong times, in situations that aren't actually dangerous, at least to their physical well-being. This adverse response can be so intense that it interferes with a person's performance instead of enhancing it. In addition, overly anxious individuals often live with a chronic, low-grade feeling of apprehension and some level of "free-floating" anxiety. In describing anxiety, Barlow states, "The one robust finding is that anxious patients are chronically hyper-aroused and slow to habituate. They are continually vigilant and ready for action." Barlow cites Howard Liddell's (1949) observations that vigilant animals seem to learn faster than their easy-going peers. I would imagine that these animals would be more likely to live long enough to reproduce, so that evolution would select for high vigilance, along with high intelligence. Unfortunately, because anxiety isn't rational, high intelligence doesn't necessarily help a person to deal with it. We can imagine that the persistent fear that is anxiety can cause a person to miss out on, or be unable to fully appreciate, many of the good things in life. To borrow an idea from Ernest Hemingway, the anxious individual "dies a thousand deaths." In *Worry: Controlling It and Using It Wisely*, Edward Hallowell (1997) aptly titles his first chapter "When Life Feels More Threatening Than It Should."

---

5. Fear of the unknown is hardwired into the systems of all animals to protect them from danger. Consequently, the fear of change is one of the most problematic manifestations of anxiety in humans, since our lives are characterized by an almost constant succession of changes, both large and small.

Living in Fear

We are all born with different levels of sensitivity to life's stressors. Innate sensitivity and a tendency to overreact is apparent almost from the moment a baby is born. Nurses in maternity wards describe highly reactive infants who stand out from the other newborns in that they startle more easily and react more intensely. The anxious person feels everything more intensely. His or her anxiety extends far beyond the temporary anxiety that everyone experiences from time to time. Personality theorists include the propensity toward anxiety as part of a trait that they label "Neuroticism." Neuroticism is partially inherited but is also influenced by an individual's environment. In addition to anxiety, angry hostility (irritability), depression (not contented as opposed to clinically depressed), self-consciousness (shyness), impulsiveness (moodiness) and vulnerability (lack of self-confidence) have been found to be part of this trait.

Events and activities that are mildly stressful for most people can produce extreme, even incapacitating, anxiety symptoms in a sensitive person. Consequently, anxious people tend to overreact to minor stressors. This is exemplified when an anxious person has to perform in some way. For example, while some anxiety can energize a person who has to give a speech or run a race, it can cause an already anxious person to have difficulty remembering and organizing what she was going to say or interfere with the runner being able to pace herself properly. By hindering a person's performance in one or more areas, anxiety can have a devastating effect on a person's self-esteem. This, in turn, can cause the person to avoid taking reasonable risks necessary to excel in any area as well as to forego a number of necessary and pleasurable activities. Stossel (2013) sums it up: "Anxiety can impede your relationships, impair your performance, constrict your life, and limit your possibilities."

Ironically, the more conscientious and eager to please a person is, the more anxious she tends to be. Because she takes responsibilities so seriously, an overly conscientious individual can be overwhelmed by tasks that others find routine. Almost reflexively, she may avoid experiences that could potentially involve taking on too much. Taking calculated risks can be daunting for the anxious person. This makes it unlikely that an anxiety-prone person will take advantage of opportunities that could end up being lucky breaks.

While anxiety causes much misery, the fact that it often leads to avoidance is what makes it especially handicapping. The natural response to fear is to avoid the feared situations. But if the person allows himself to avoid these situations, he won't be able to conquer his fear of them. This means missed opportunities for success since we must take a certain number of risks to succeed in work and love. If one is unfortunate enough to be both highly ambitious and overly anxious, the frustration from unachieved aspirations and dreams may be especially acute. The avoidant person will also miss out on many pleasurable experiences large and small.

In their most severe forms anxiety disorders are difficult to miss. When a child is so anxious that he is afraid to go to school or a young teen never leaves the house, his parents are likely to insist on treatment. But family members often miss more subtle forms of anxiety in their loved ones. Lack of understanding on the part of the general public often causes family and friends to lack sympathy toward an anxious loved one. They may even fault the victim of anxiety with dismissive explanations such as "She just doesn't try"; "He's just lazy"; "She is never going to amount to anything"; or "He has no ambition." People who aren't overly anxious will say that they are able to "push through" their fear to go up a ladder or to give a speech. What these people don't understand is that the intensity of their anxiety is far lower than that of the sensitive person.

Anxious individuals themselves often don't recognize or understand the true nature of their problems, even when their symptoms are quite handicapping. They may become accustomed to high levels of anxiety and assume that everyone feels this same level of tension. I have evaluated patients who are visibly nervous but report low levels of anxiety when questioned. Other anxious people may have been able to keep their anxiety at bay by avoiding a wide variety of things. While they may not think of themselves as anxious, their constricted lives will be less than satisfying. Anxious people may perceive themselves to be lacking courage or weak. They may attribute any failures to personal flaws such as incompetence, lamenting, "I'm just not as smart as I thought I was." Later in life they may become even more self-critical, as they look back over their lives and think about the goals that they have failed to accomplish and the opportunities that they haven't taken, concluding, "I lacked initiative" or "I didn't have enough perseverance." They may become bitter and envious as they compare themselves to friends and acquaintances. This rumination puts additional stress on them, resulting in even higher anxiety. Most of their friends and acquaintances have no idea why they haven't lived up to expectations. Anxiety remains hidden even when the consequences may seem clear in retrospect.

As I've pointed out, some anxious people feel anger when they're anxious. This is particularly true of men and boys. In them, the fight or flight response may take the form of fighting rather than fleeing. Because our culture traditionally dictated that males needed to be strong, some men and boys may be more comfortable feeling anger than anxiety. This can lead to impulsive acts of violence. In addition, these individuals may start drinking and abusing substances so early in life that they are often almost completely unaware of their underlying anxiety. Our prisons are populated with some of the chronically anxious, and, in this population, anxiety tends to be even more hidden.

People who are able to function well enough to "get by" often end up fitting the profile of the underachiever. They are more likely to be underemployed than unemployed. In *Listening to Prozac* (1993), Peter Kramer describes a patient who had "applied only for jobs for which they were obviously overqualified." Like the men and women in my practice, the anxious may struggle for years, failing to function up to their potential in education and their careers as well as other aspects of their lives, including their relationships. Anxiety Disorders may be mistaken for character flaws. Furthermore, anxiety affects the overall quality of a person's life by causing the person to limit pleasurable experiences that are too challenging for her. Travel is the first thing that comes to mind since it entails a plethora of new experiences.

There are several additional reasons that anxiety isn't always recognized as a major cause of underachievement and unhappiness. As the vignettes in this book will illustrate, anxiety disorders take many different forms and can be mistaken for other medical or psychological disorders. Physical symptoms of anxiety range from ambiguous physical complaints such as fatigue to episodes of panic that are so severe that the person believes that she is having a heart attack. Individuals with an anxiety disorder, particularly Generalized Anxiety Disorder, may end up in their family physician's office complaining of vague symptoms such as lack of energy, neck and back pain, headaches, or an overactive bladder. Anxiety can cause gastrointestinal distress including Irritable Bowel Syndrome, constipation and diarrhea. It may also come into play in Fibromyalgia and Chronic Fatigue Syndrome. Because the person is likely to seek treatment for one problem at a time, the physician may not realize that anxiety is responsible for the seemingly unrelated symptoms that tend to wax and wane over the years. Our tendency to move around and change doctors, along with the limited time that doctors are able to spend with each patient, makes it difficult for a doctor to know her patients in the way that doctors did in the past. More dangerous is the fact that chronic stress weakens a person's immune system and consequently plays a role in everything from frequent colds to cancer. At the very least, stress and anxiety exacerbate existing conditions such as Crohn's Disease and Multiple Sclerosis. Anxiety hides by masquerading as other illnesses. Some anxious people don't obtain treatment until they become severely depressed, as a proportion of people with anxiety do. Others end up being diagnosed with Bipolar Disorder or Attention Deficit Hyperactivity Disorder (ADHD).

Although there has historically been a stigma around mental illness, there seems to be more shame attached to anxiety than depression or Bipolar Disorder, and, as I mentioned, anxiety doesn't appear to be taken as seriously. According to Chris Norris, PhD, a psychologist who specializes in male psychiatric problems, anxiety has a very negative connotation for many men. To be anxious is perceived as weakness. I would argue that it's also a very pejorative adjective when a woman is described as "nervous." Because of these notions, many people try to hide their anxiety problems, even from their loved ones. But hiding anxiety can end up generating more anxiety.

Anxiety can sometimes actually motivate a person to take constructive action, while depression is more likely to cause them to "shut down." According to Barlow (1988), "Anxiety implies an effort to cope with difficult situations and the physiology is there to support active attempts at coping." While depression is defined by hopelessness, anxiety may suggest hope.

The nature of anxiety makes it difficult for its sufferers to seek treatment. Remember the estimate that only a third of those who suffer from anxiety manage to obtain treatment (Anxiety and Depression Association of America, 2020). The natural response to anxiety is to avoid fear-arousing situations. Indeed, anxious individuals often attempt not to even think of anything anxiety provoking. Thinking about situations that originally elicited the anxiety or situations that remind the person of the original experience can precipitate feelings of panic. Although trying not to think about anxiety feels like the right thing to do to alleviate the immediate symptoms, it virtually guarantees that the person won't get help. Individuals who are prone to anxiety are the least likely to want to talk to others about their problems and to schedule an appointment with a mental health provider.

Understanding Anxiety

Consider the steps needed for a person to obtain treatment. The individual needs to find a psychiatrist or psychologist which often means asking someone for a referral. Next, making a call to a mental health provider and dealing with a representative of his insurance company are required. Once he has an appointment, the person usually has to drive to the provider's office or take public transportation, two things that some anxious people fear. Ultimately the anxious client needs to disclose extremely personal information to the mental health provider whom he has met for the first time. All these hurdles can delay treatment while the problem grows. The anxious clients in my practice were undoubtedly the tip of the iceberg. Sadly, for those with anxiety, trying to ignore problems only allows them to grow, thus adding more reason for the person to be anxious and thereby creating a vicious cycle.

Anxiety appears to be increasing at an unprecedented rate. Growing up in the 1950s, I can remember hearing very little about "stress" in spite of the threat of nuclear war that had us performing bomb drills in our classrooms. It is important to ask why feeling "stressed" seems to be a more common complaint today than it was for our not-so-distant ancestors. Rapid changes in the way we live, as compared to life even fifty to seventy years ago, undoubtedly account for much of this increase in anxiety. One of the major changes that has been challenging for people prone to anxiety is the increased geographical mobility in our society. As we'll see, moving is a very stressful endeavor. Major changes in the way we work and rapidly changing technology also have required huge adjustments in our lifestyles. Commuting in heavy traffic is a major source of stress these days. In addition, more people live and work in large cities which are more difficult to navigate than smaller cities and towns. Difficulty finding a place to park, needing to use public transportation, and the higher cost of living and faster pace of cities are just a few of the potential stressors that come to mind.

Consider another relatively recent social change. Since people are waiting longer to have their first child, infertility has become more common. This is extremely anxiety arousing as couples wait every month to see if they've been successful. When utilized, infertility treatments are very expensive and often not covered by insurance. This makes the whole process emotionally exhausting.

In modern-day life, there is definitely no shortage of circumstances that can elicit feelings of anxiety. At the same time, most of us don't have the physical outlets for stress that the average person had in the past. Our slightly more distant ancestors had to labor hard in order to survive and didn't have the time or leftover energy to experience much irrational anxiety. They had plenty of real dangers to contend with, and their fear was channeled into productive activities to make sure that they had food and supplies to make it through the winter. The considerably lower rates of anxiety disorders in developing countries support this possibility. Indeed, anxiety may be a disease of the elites and almost positively associated with cultural refinement (see, e.g., such early characterizations by Beard, 1869). Somewhere along the line, anxiety has lost this distinction and taken on a negative connotation. Still, our contemporary society in the United States does seem to sometimes consider being under work related stress a sign of success. Working ridiculously long hours is the norm for some groups of people, particularly in our large cities. Later in this chapter, we will see how working excessively can be one way of trying to distract ourselves from anxiety. And, as we can imagine, this can put more stress on the overworked individual. This may well be one of the Type A individual's preferred methods of distracting himself from anxiety.

In 2020, everyone in the world began grappling with the very real danger of contracting Covid-19, making fear a rational, highly adaptive response. This justified fear motivated us to wear masks and keep a safe social distance from others. Coupled with the fact that many of us were physically isolated from our loved ones and our support systems, it's not surprising that people are reporting high levels of anxiety. Along with Covid, global warming and the higher number of natural disasters have been frightening for everyone, especially those prone to anxiety. Approximately 20 percent of people in a recent survey of 8,000 adults from fifty countries said that worry and feelings of dread were severe enough to interfere with their daily activities (Flanagan, 2020). Smaller day-to-day frustrations, many stemming from fairly recent technological advances, also contribute to our stress.

While all forms of anxiety were presumed to have basically the same physiological underpinnings, the *DSM-IV*[6] divides them into different categories according to their specific symptomatology and the current assumption that each may have a slightly unique physiological basis. It identifies seven major disorders of anxiety, along with a few

---

6. The DSM is the major diagnostic manual in the mental health sciences. Although it is now updated to the DSM-5, each version contains novel content that remains useful in understanding anxiety, and in this text I frequently reference the DSM-IV.

others that we won't be dealing with.[7] We are all somewhat familiar with some of these diagnoses, at least in their extreme forms. Someone suffering from Agoraphobia, for example, is often conceptualized as being completely housebound. The reality is that Agoraphobia usually takes a more subtle form, making it harder to recognize, but still potentially quite debilitating. This is true of all seven major anxiety disorders. To the casual observer, *anxious people look and behave like everyone else.* Stossel (2013) quotes Paul Foxman, a psychologist who directs the Center for Anxiety Disorders in Burlington, Vermont: "For many, many people who have anxiety disorders—particularly agoraphobia and panic disorder—people would be surprised to find out that they have problems with anxiety because they seem so 'together' and 'in control.'" This is what makes anxiety disorders difficult to detect, let alone understand. Indeed, in an article that appeared in the July 26, 2020, edition of the *New York Times*, Andrew Solomon calls anxiety an "invisible disability," one that "is not necessarily helped by a designated parking spot." Anxiety is hidden.

As mentioned earlier, in many cases, anxiety is connected to substance abuse, another pervasive condition in today's world. While some people drink alcohol or use street drugs, others become addicted to medications prescribed by their doctors. The Opioid epidemic, which was unacknowledged for years, has become a national crisis. Barlow (1988) cites a study by Quikin, Rifkin, Kaplan, and Klein (1972). As early as 1972, these researchers speculated that many alcoholics and drug abusers might have been self-medicating an anxiety disorder. Indeed, Barlow notes that "retrospective studies indicate that severe anxiety precedes the onset of drinking or substance abuse in most cases." This idea is sometimes disputed by alcohol and drug counselors, as Barlow acknowledges in his description of the complicated relationship between anxiety and substance abuse. It has been my experience that this relationship is often causal and that alcoholics and drug addicts are seldom aware of the connection between their anxiety and substance abuse, a mistake that some of their counselors also tend to make. When combined with substance abuse, anxiety can have tragic consequences, including violence toward family members and strangers, divorce, accidental death by overdose, estrangement from family members, homelessness and suicide.

---

7. It should be noted that the authors of the DSM-5 have moved Obsessive Compulsive Disorder (OCD) to a different category, since some experts believe that it's significantly different from the other anxiety disorders. I would argue with this change and have included OCD in this book.

Anxiety and Behavioral Addictions, Including Shopping

Of course, we need to realize that substance abuse is only one of a number of addictions people develop sometimes as a way of dealing with anxiety. Workaholism, along with video game and social media addiction and watching excessive amounts of television, can be a way for people to distract themselves from their anxious thoughts and feelings. Workaholism can also be a strategy to cope with a fear of failure. Working hard is considered a good thing, making it especially difficult to know when it has become excessive. We don't think too much about pastimes like watching TV because they are so common. Although they are fairly innocuous, these activities can take up huge amounts of a person's time. Exercise is highly beneficial in health, life and anxiety reduction (see Chapter 7). But, as with many good things, it too can be carried too far. In Chapter 7, I discuss the risk of overtraining, and in Chapter 4, I discuss anorexia, which can co-occur with addictive exercise.

On the other hand, some addictions are more disturbing and purposefully hidden. Addiction to pornography is an example. Not only can this addiction greatly interfere with a person's actual relationships, it also often causes greater anxiety because of the guilt associated with it. Even more serious are love and sexual addictions that can range from promiscuity with many sexual partners to stalking, voyeuristic behaviors, and even rape, some of which may result from compulsions to act upon obsessive thoughts.

Compulsive gambling, which is sometimes a way of escaping anxious feelings, is another serious addiction that many of us have heard something about. When the gambler inevitably loses money, it can become a major source of anxiety. Not only can this addiction destroy an individual's life, but it can have devastating consequences for anyone in the person's life, particularly when it is hidden from family members, as it often is. One of my clients is a tragic example of this. Wendy's husband made a high salary as a very successful computer programmer. Since he took care of the family finances, after he died suddenly, Wendy was surprised to find that there was little money for her to live on. She had to move into low-income housing and come out of retirement and find a job that involved a long commute. She suspected that her husband likely had spent all of his earnings gambling on his golf games and sneaking off to the horse track. Her husband had suffered from anxiety for years, very possibly contributing to his gambling.

It could also be argued that shopping sometimes becomes an addictive behavior. Excessive shopping has become rampant in the Western world. That shopping is considered a form of recreation is not surprising. Hunting for bargains and unique purchases is engaging, and it can also be a social activity where one is treated with a little extra flattery by salesclerks, so shopping should only be considered an addiction if it is clearly excessive. Even then, it is not necessarily problematic if the buyer has plenty of money and a large enough house to accommodate her purchases. Certainly, shopping is a socially acceptable pastime that wealthy people have always enjoyed. Princess Diana is one of the most famous examples from our time, but the Medici family, Henry VIII, and William Randolph Hearst were also known for their extravagant spending habits. But when money is tight, what might otherwise seem innocuous can bankrupt a family and lead to conflict between spouses. At the very least, it eats up a person's time that could be put toward more worthwhile activities.

In my client population, I've found that restlessness resulting from anxiety can trigger the urge to shop. Excessive shoppers sometimes report an uncomfortable tension that is relieved by shopping. One of my clients found that when she felt anxious and restless, she could obtain relief by shopping. Shopping appeared to be an alternative to exercise for her. While some of us find going out for a run or taking an aerobics class a way of releasing tension, shoppers scurry around the mall. Young girls learn to enjoy shopping with their mothers at an early age, so it's not surprising that some of them later find it a natural outlet for anxious energy, whether they are conscious of it or not.

In other words, shopping is a necessary and normal activity that can get out of control. As my client discovered, shopping can seem like the perfect outlet for restless, nervous energy and it feels like a productive activity even when the purchases aren't necessary. However, the good feelings associated with shopping may be temporary when shopping leads to guilt and/or marital problems, subsequently increasing a person's anxiety. This can fuel a vicious cycle. Using credit cards makes the whole process easier, yet also more threatening to the shopper's financial well-being.

Even leisure travel, which is supposed to be one way of relaxing, can sometimes take on proportions that suggest a compulsive element to it. I have noticed this in my retired clients in particular. One woman described feeling anxious and restless if she wasn't either planning a trip or traveling. She tended to fight anxiety when she was home but found that she rarely felt anxious when she was on a trip. Exploring new places gave her little time to think anxious thoughts. Imagine flying from the East Coast to Egypt for two weeks, and upon returning, heading to California for another two weeks, and then less than a month later, flying back west again to Seattle. This frenzied pace could be routine for a person addicted to travel. Since traveling this extensively requires a certain income, some addicted travelers have racked up huge amounts of debt. This can threaten marriages when one partner wants to travel to this extent, especially if they go into debt to finance the trip.

In summary, anxiety is even more pervasive than we realize, although depression probably gets more press and seems to be taken more seriously. Part of this is likely because anxiety tends to be hidden. We often can't tell when a person is anxious, and few seem eager to disclose their own struggles with anxiety. Indeed, an anxious person can sometimes function very well, since anxiety doesn't necessarily cause her to completely "shut down," as depression can. In spite of how well they manage to perform, however, anxious people suffer a great deal.

Anxiety appears to continue to carry a stigma, especially when compared to depression. No one wants to be described as "nervous." For lack of understanding, loved ones aren't necessarily sympathetic or supportive of their anxious family members. They may perceive them as intellectually slow, lazy, or weak. Sometimes the anxious person himself doesn't even realize that anxiety is the root cause of his problems. He may self-medicate with alcohol or drugs and lose sight of why he started drinking excessively or smoking marijuana. Anxiety can manifest as anger and aggression. Addiction to alcohol or drugs or a tendency toward violence garner little sympathy from others. To make matters more complicated, many people who suffer from anxiety also become depressed or have other psychiatric conditions or they develop an array of physical symptoms that masquerade as medical illnesses.

It isn't difficult to see how even moderate levels of anxiety can contribute to underachievement and dissatisfaction. In an attempt to minimize the panicky feelings that characterize anxiety, sufferers naturally begin to avoid the situations that produce these feelings. This causes the anxious to shy away from many experiences and opportunities that life offers. Many anxious people fear and worry about failure more than they dream of success. Non-anxious people tend to be motivated by seeking a reward of some kind and feelings of accomplishment after they have met a goal while anxious people are often motivated by the fear of punishment or failure. The non-anxious among us actually tend to overestimate their own abilities, from intelligence to driving expertise. They tend to be overconfident in some ways which allows them to take more risks. While anxious people may be more realistic about their abilities, this doesn't always serve them well in a world that requires taking risks. Anxious people can end up giving up important goals that would require doing something that they fear, like giving frequent speeches. While they may manage to keep their anxiety at bay, their lives may end up being less successful and fulfilling than they could have been.

Those who try to hang on to their goals may still end up failing at some point along the way for fear of taking any one of the necessary steps to reach a particular goal, such as moving to a new location for a better job. In addition, failure to attain goals can lead to self-blame and low self-esteem. In turn, these problems of self-worth create even more anxiety and make it more difficult for the person to reach higher.

Anxiety impacts relationship and lifestyle goals as well as academic and career success, and friends and family who don't understand anxiety may make matters even worse by applying pressure or openly criticizing their anxious loved ones. They may offer pity rather than support. All of these responses can further undermine the anxious person's self-esteem.

We can imagine how anxiety takes its toll at every milestone in an individual's life. As would be expected, normal life transitions tend to be more difficult for those who are the most sensitive to stress. An anxious child has more difficulty adjusting to kindergarten, middle school and high school, going away to summer camp, moving, traveling overnight and, later, going off to college and looking for a job. Increased mobility in today's society makes life even more difficult for the anxious child to negotiate. In the past, most children grew up in the neighborhood in which they were born and attended much of their schooling with the same peer group. They didn't have to deal with adjusting to large middle and high schools populated by many students they didn't know.

Life can sometimes become even more challenging for an anxiety-prone young person when she reaches adulthood. The clear-cut script emphasizing the importance of performing well in school, which anxious students may have managed to master over the years, is replaced with broader expectations that require a different set of skills. Without the structure of school, it also becomes more difficult to meet people and make friends. Today's young adults are expected to accomplish these milestones away from the relative safety of their families, making these challenges even more daunting.

Barry Wolfe (2005) sums up the suffering that anxiety causes: "No one who has ever been tormented by prolonged bouts of anxiety doubts its power to paralyze action, promote flight, eviscerate pleasure, and skew thinking toward the catastrophic. None would deny how terribly painful the experience of anxiety can be. The experience of chronic or intense anxiety is above all else a profound and perplexing confrontation with pain."

When Anxiety Snowballs

The situations that anxious people struggle with tend to be highly individualized but frequently involve many necessary and/or life-enhancing activities such as public speaking, taking tests, interviewing for jobs, performing in athletic and other events, meeting new people, dating, flying, and driving. Failure to perform any of these activities not only causes problems in school and work but in life in general. Even when the anxiety is limited to one area such as test-taking, we can imagine how it could impact a person's future if their goals require academic credentials.

Any kind of change tends to be more difficult for an anxious person. Clinically anxious people are unusually sensitive to uncertainty (Stossel, 2013). Symptoms are likely to flare at times when the person is required to adjust to new situations, many of which may actually be positive changes, like moving into a higher social stratus. This makes it harder for the anxious individual to take necessary steps to achieve success such as moving to a new location to take a dream job. Unfortunately for the anxious, every developmental milestone throughout a person's lifetime involves change, from an infant's first bath to a young adult leaving for college. Anxiety can result in an overall constricted life. In later chapters we'll see how it inevitably affects relationships and limits pleasurable experiences. Anxiety is all too often the hidden cause of seemingly perplexing decisions involving foregone opportunities. For example, a parent might not realize why her daughter turned down a chance to go to Europe on a school trip.

When a person hides his or her anxiety from loved ones, things can snowball out of control. This was most evident to me during my years of working in a university counseling center. Unlike high schools, colleges don't release grades to parents of students over age 18. Since a student's grades aren't available to his parents unless he chooses to share them, an anxious student can hide any problems until they become much larger.

Mark's Story

Let us consider a bright and conscientious college student I'll call Mark. His story will serve as an example of how anxiety that is hidden becomes more problematic as time goes on. Picture Mark, who has an unassuming look about him and carries himself with hesitancy, feeling embarrassed after he has given an incorrect answer in one of his small discussion-style classes. Although he gets up and goes to this 9:00 class the following day, Mark cannot bring himself to enter the classroom for fear that his classmates and professor have remembered his mistake. The next time that he tries to attend class, Mark is even more anxious because he realizes that now the professor and students have probably noticed his absence, and he might have to explain why he missed the class. The third and fourth times that Mark gets ready for the class, he feels even more intense anxiety because now he has missed a great deal of class material. Soon getting up and getting dressed leads to so much anxiety that Mark stops attempting to get ready for this class. Within the next few weeks, Mark begins to fear and avoid other discussion classes. Consequently, he ends the semester with As and Bs in his lecture classes and Fs in his small discussion groups.

Mark might be able to turn things around and catch up in the class if he were to talk to the professor or go to the counseling center to address the problem. He is, however, even more afraid of these prospects. Like many anxious people, he has feared and avoided authority figures for as long as he can remember. When Mark fails several classes, he is terrified at the prospect of telling his parents and lies to them about his grades. Since he is so afraid of displeasing them, he may rack up a number of failing grades. His parents might not realize that Mark is having problems until he's suspended.

Since Mark's uneven transcript resembles that of a student who lacks motivation or has partied too much, his parents are likely to suspect these possibilities. They may assume that their son is immature, irresponsible and not taking school seriously. They may criticize him for not taking advantage of the opportunity they worked hard to provide him. As I mentioned earlier, it seems especially unfair that anxiety is more likely to affect highly conscientious people who push themselves to excel. When self-induced pressure adds more stress to an already sensitive physiology, anxiety can become very intense. One student who was eventually referred to me was so anxious about disappointing his parents that he had been having his father drop him off on campus every day for four years even though he had been suspended after his first year. His parents didn't find out that Justin had not been a registered student for those three years until graduation day four years later. Tragically, suicide sometimes becomes the ultimate way of trying not to disappoint parents.

One of the most tragic examples of this was a student attending East Carolina University. Although this student had not attended classes in three years, he told his family he was in school and working toward a master's degree in business administration. When his father came to attend his son's graduation ceremony, the student shot and killed his father the minute his father knocked on the student's apartment door. During his murder trial this young man stated that he could not bear to face his father's disappointment.

Although there are many reasons that people fail to live up to their potential, anxiety is one of the most common. The unfortunate thing about the lack of understanding and failure to recognize anxiety is that many anxiety disorders are highly treatable. The prognosis for most anxiety disorders is good, sometimes with relatively short-term treatment. This is especially true if the problem is caught early before it causes a person to avoid important activities leading to under-achievement and a constricted life accompanied by low self-esteem.

It is also important to realize that success shouldn't be defined narrowly as academic, career and financial success. True success encompasses much more than this. Success in relationships and leisure pursuits is at least as important to our well-being and is just as often hindered by anxiety.

The Hamilton Anxiety Rating Scale (HAM-A)

The following scale, developed in the late 1950s by Max Hamilton (1960), was designed to enable clinicians to measure the severity of a patient's level of general anxiety. While this will serve as an introduction, the reader will develop a better understanding of anxiety once its various forms are presented and explained. Also, keep in mind that mental health professionals have access to a range of more recently validated questionnaires that are used in clinical settings, yet the Hamilton scale remains useful for the purposes of this book.

Understanding Anxiety

Below is a list of phrases that describe certain feelings that people have. Rate the patients by finding the answer which best describes the extent to which he or she has these conditions. Select one of the five responses for each of the fourteen questions.

0=not present; 1=mild; 2=moderate; 3=severe; 4=very severe

1. Anxious Mood
   Worry, anticipation of the worst, fearful anticipation, irritability
2. Tension
   Feelings of tension, fatigability, startle response, moved to tears easily, trembling, feelings of restlessness, inability to relax
3. Fears
   Of dark, of strangers, of being left alone, of animals, of traffic, of crowds
4. Insomnia
   Difficulty with falling asleep, broken sleep, unsatisfying sleep and fatigue on waking, dreams, nightmares, night terrors
5. Intellectual
   Difficulty with concentration, poor memory
6. Depressed Mood
   Loss of interest, lack of pleasure in hobbies, depression, early waking, diurnal swing
7. Somatic (muscular)
   Pains and aches, twitching, stiffness, grinding of teeth, unsteady voice, increased muscle tone
8. Somatic (sensory)
   Tinnitus, blurring of vision, hot and cold flushes, feelings of weakness, prickling sensations
9. Cardiovascular Symptoms
   Tachycardia, palpitations, chest pains, choking feelings, throbbing of vessels, lightheadedness, missing beats
10. Respiratory Symptoms
    Pressure or constriction in the chest, feelings of choking, sighing, dyspnea
11. Gastrointestinal Symptoms
    Difficulty swallowing, abdominal pain, burning sensations, abdominal fullness, nausea, vomiting, looseness of bowels, loss of weight, constipation

12. Genitourinary Symptoms
     Frequency of urination, urgency of urination, amenorrhea, development of frigidity, premature ejaculation, loss of libido, impotence
13. Autonomic Symptoms
     Dry mouth, flushed skin, pallor, tendency to sweat, giddiness, tension headaches
14. Behavior at interview
     Fidgeting, restlessness or pacing, tremor of hands, furrowed brow, strained face, sighing or rapid respiration, facial pallor, swallowing, etc.

As you can now see from the Hamilton inventory, the diversity and plurality of anxiety disorders is staggering. Who hasn't experienced more than one of these symptoms? Then again, gastrointestinal problems and so on do have causes quite apart from anxiety. Let's dive deeper into anxiety in its many forms.

Panic Disorder

When assessing Panic Disorder, psychologists try to gauge the frequency, severity, and consequences of an individual's episodes of panic (Antony & Swinson, 2000). For example, clients may complete a questionnaire that asks about how often they have experienced symptoms such as a racing or pounding heart, shortness of breath, nausea or abdominal discomfort, or feeling that they are on the verge of losing control. Did several of these symptoms occur together? And did this cause the person to fear another panic attack might happen soon or to behave differently in anticipation of another attack? Let's meet Jill, who experienced an episode of panic in the first weeks of her first year in college. I'll first look at Panic Disorder followed by Agoraphobia and Post-Traumatic Stress Disorder (PTSD).

Jill's Story

Jill, a striking brunette with brilliant green eyes, first thought that she was having a heart attack. At the beginning of her first year in college she became short of breath, shaky and dizzy and her heart began to race while she was walking to a class. These symptoms were so frightening that Jill skipped this class, went back to her room and crawled into bed. Her first thought was that there must be something wrong with her heart. Later that day, her roommate took Jill to the health center where the doctor assured her that her heart was fine. Nevertheless, the symptoms continued to occur every time that she set off to walk to one of her classes. Within a few weeks, Jill was missing the majority of her classes. Although she had excelled in high school, she failed each of her first round of exams. Concluding that if there was nothing physically wrong with her, she must be mentally ill, Jill assumed that she would never be able to make it through college. She resigned herself to moving back to her tiny hometown and applied for a job at McDonald's.

As we will see with all forms of anxiety, Panic Disorder often first develops during a time of change or stress (Antony & Swinson, 2000). Jill had left home for the first time and moved to a large city three hours away from her tiny hometown. This was stressful enough, but Jill also found life in the college dormitory extremely uncomfortable, because suddenly she was living in close proximity to sixty new acquaintances on her floor alone. She was so stressed that she was unable to sleep more than a few hours a night. With this kind of sleep deprivation, Jill was barely able to drag herself to her classes and tended to fall asleep when she sat down to study. When she began to have full-blown panic attacks but was assured that her heart was fine, Jill assumed that she was truly on the verge of a "nervous breakdown."

Sudden and Severe Reactions

Descriptions of similar episodes are beginning to appear more in literature. In Sally Rooney's 2018 novel titled *Normal People*, she describes the following symptoms in one of her characters: "Hyperventilation, chest pain, pins and needles all over his body. A feeling of dissociation from his senses, an inability to think straight or interpret what he sees and hears. Things begin to look and sound different, slower, artificial, unreal. The first time it happened he thought he was losing his mind, that the whole cognitive framework by which he made sense of the world had disintegrated for good, and everything from then on would just be undifferentiated sound and color. Then within a couple of minutes it passed, and left him lying on his mattress coated in sweat."

I am discussing Panic Disorder first because it is the most basic form that anxiety takes, since it's essentially the raw embodiment of the fight or flight response. All of the anxiety disorders share this basic physiological reaction to varying degrees of intensity. However, Panic Disorder (PD) is certainly one of the most striking forms that anxiety can take considering its physiological manifestation. That panic attacks can be terrifying is illustrated by a story that Scott Stossel (2013) attributes to David Sheehan, a psychiatrist who specialized in anxiety. Sheehan treated a World War II veteran who, despite participating in many harrowing battles, maintained that "the anxiety he felt" landing in Normandy "was mild compared to the sheer terror of one of my anxiety attacks."

Panic attacks are characterized by the sudden onset of intense fear and apprehension often including a sense of impending doom. Accompanying physiological symptoms may include shortness of breath, dizziness or lightheadedness, heart palpitations, shaking, sweating and a choking sensation. Hyperventilation, which occurs when a person's breathing is so shallow that carbon dioxide levels in the blood decrease, is often part of the picture. These symptoms can last up to 45 minutes. As I've noted, the reader will recognize this pattern of physiological sensations as the fight or flight response. The physiological reaction itself is basically the same as that which susceptible people experience after drinking too much coffee. But the victim of a panic attack sometimes assumes that he is having a heart attack or "going crazy." The fact that anxiety is the cause of his symptoms is hidden in the sense that he is unlikely to understand what is happening to him and attributes the symptoms to something else. At the very least, sufferers of panic attacks may fear that they are losing control and that they could end up doing something embarrassing or losing consciousness.

Panic attacks are actually fairly common, occurring in one third of the college population in one study (Telch, Lucas, & Nelson, 1989). Because this research (1) was conducted before the surge in higher education attendance in recent decades, and (2) college life appears to be more stressful these days, the percentage could be even higher today. Usually, a person's first attack occurs in her late teens to early twenties. Women are twice as likely as men to report having had an episode of panic (Bekker, 1996).[8] We have probably all experienced at least a few fleeting symptoms of PD at some point. Some people even take the

---

8. Perhaps surprisingly, Taylor et al. (1986) reported that the highest frequency of panic attacks is between 1:30 and 3:30 a.m. One of my own clients was awakened by feelings of panic every morning at 7, even though she had never had a panic attack during the day.

symptoms of a full-blown panic attack in stride. Wilson et al. (1993) found that 27 percent of their sample of 83 college students who had had a panic attack maintained that they felt no fear, while 36 percent had reportedly experienced only mild fear. Those who develop Panic Disorder are people like Jill who become overly concerned during an anxiety attack because they believe that it signals that something is seriously wrong with them. As mentioned, a person's first panic attack often follows a period of stress or a major life transition as it did in Jill's case. The stressful event that precipitates a first episode could be anything.

Potentially stressful situations were ranked in order of perceived severity by Holmes and Rahe in the Holmes and Rahe Life Stress Inventory (1967). This inventory ranks forty-three stressors from somewhat stressful events such as minor traffic violations to tragedies such as the death of a spouse (#1). Divorce ranks #2, while moving from one house to another ranks #32. The events listed on the inventory are not necessarily all unfavorable. The reader may be wondering why a promotion (#22), which is presumably a positive life event, is included in the scale. But consider all the changes a promotion can precipitate, including greater responsibility, jealousy from peers, and longer work hours, to name a few. Indeed, many of the events on the inventory are normal life transitions, including changing to a new school (#33), marriage (#7) and pregnancy (#12).

More recently, Bruce Feiler (2020) has developed a scale he labeled Life's Deck of Disrupters. Dr. Feiler has included categories relevant to our lives today such as starting a business, being involved in a custody battle, being sexually harassed, and facing the suicide of a family member, which were not part of the Holmes and Rahe scale. He also includes public humiliation on the Internet, a thoroughly modern phenomenon that has even led to suicide. This illustrates how stressors have changed over time. Having one's identity stolen is another potential stressor that comes to mind today. I would also add losing a beloved pet.

Once a person understands that she isn't having a heart attack or "nervous breakdown," she may attribute a first panic attack to the situation she happens to be in at the time that it occurs. This can cause her to fear and attempt to avoid this particular setting and sometimes similar situations and activities. For example, if someone experiences a first panic attack the first time that she encounters the stacks at a large library, she may decide that there was something about the dark, narrow passages that brought on the episode. She might find ways of avoiding the stacks or finding someone to accompany her the next time that she needs to approach them. This fear could generalize to other areas in the library and eventually to cramped used bookstores. Another example might be a man who has his first panic attack in the basement of a dingy tavern. He might begin avoiding other taverns with similar features. Weeks later, his fear may expand to bars and restaurants of any kind. This avoidance is the real problem. Not unlike dealing with the proverbial schoolyard bully, we must face our fears in order to manage them.

People tend to be even more concerned about random panic attacks like Jill's that seemingly come out of nowhere, giving them no apparent rationale for what is happening. This may cause an individual to develop a fear of the attacks themselves and to become hypervigilant to physiological signs that may signal the onset of another panic episode. We can imagine that this would be very distracting. It would doubtless interfere with whatever a person is trying to accomplish whether at work or home as well as her ability to enjoy the moment. Monitoring subtle bodily changes only serves to exacerbate an individual's anxiety.

A typical scenario after someone experiences a first panic attack involves a trip to the emergency room. When physiological causes such as hyperthyroidism and cardiac abnormalities are ruled out, the patient is told that there is nothing medically wrong and is not always given any further explanation. The individual naturally looks for a way to explain the symptoms. They may conclude that if there is nothing physically wrong, they must be mentally ill and may begin to wonder if they are on the verge of a "nervous breakdown."[9] Panic Disorder still isn't well understood by the general public, partly because mental illness has always been shrouded in mystery and stigma. Consequently, people who have had a panic attack may picture hospitalization in a psychiatric ward as the next step for them. This thought further increases the person's level of anxiety, making future episodes of panic even more likely.

As we will see with all of the anxiety disorders, avoidance—which is the natural reaction to panic—emerges as a counterproductive coping strategy. Quite often the person who has had a panic attack is told that her symptoms are stress related. Hearing this, she naturally attempts to avoid, or at least minimize, her stress for fear of having another episode. This can lead her to make sudden and drastic changes to her life. She may resign from a stressful job or, like Jill, drop out of college. Barlow (1988) speculated that women cope with panic by avoidance while

---

9. Although the term "nervous breakdown" is familiar to everyone, it isn't an actual medical condition.

men are more likely to turn to alcohol. It could be argued that excessive drinking or substance abuse is the ultimate form of avoidance. More tragically, Panic Disorder increases a person's risk for suicide even when the person isn't clinically depressed.

It is important to note that a life-threatening cardiac condition can be brought on by sudden shock and acute anxiety. The Broken Heart Syndrome, known to doctors as Stress Induced Cardiomyopathy, can develop when physical or psychological stress or an illness triggers sudden weakness in the heart muscle. Some of the symptoms are the same as those experienced in Panic Disorder. They include chest tightness and shortness of breath. Researchers have discovered a higher incidence of anxiety disorders in these patients (Thapamagar et al., 2012). Patients can recover from this condition, although unfortunately some people die during the acute stage. While the symptoms are similar to those experienced during a panic attack, panic attacks don't cause physical damage to the heart muscle. Broken Heart Syndrome is most common in post-menopausal widowed women, particularly those whose husbands died unexpectedly.

Even if drastic measures aren't taken, people are likely to want to avoid whatever activity they were doing or situation they were in when they experienced their first panic episode. It isn't difficult to imagine how Panic Disorder can interfere with career advancement, school performance, or even day-to-day responsibilities such as grocery shopping and other necessary activities. PD can lead to frequent absences from work or class (as Jill's case illustrates). Unfortunately, the pattern of absences can resemble that of an unmotivated employee or student and consequently result in the person losing his job or failing a course. Underemployment, defined as not doing work that makes full use of one's abilities and skills, is an even more likely possibility than unemployment.

Outside of school and work, necessary day-to-day activities can become extremely challenging. If a person fears having an attack at a grocery store, the site of a previous panic attack, it can make shopping for groceries seem like a major ordeal. Panic Disorder also can greatly reduce a person's enjoyment in life by causing the individual to avoid certain events and situations such as gatherings with other people. In fact, PD can end up completely taking over a person's life. Below is a description of what can happen after someone with PD begins to increasingly restrict activities. This will lead us into the next anxiety disorder that can develop from Panic Disorder: Agoraphobia.

Agoraphobia

Nancy's Story

Nancy was a fifty-four-year-old, never-married, retired attorney who wore her hair shoulder length and dressed in a stylish way, belying her actual age. Given her impeccable dress and makeup, no one coming to her door would suspect that Nancy had not left her house for two years. She had been relying on her sister who lived nearby to bring her groceries and medication.

Nancy experienced her first panic attack while she was driving to her office one cold and rainy morning. Work had been unusually stressful for the last couple of weeks and that morning she was dreading an appointment with a difficult client. As she approached a particularly dangerous stretch of winding road, Nancy started to feel short of breath and lightheaded, and her heart began to pound. Convinced that she was having a heart attack, she drove straight to the ER. After a fairly cursory exam, Nancy was told that her heart was fine. However, she wasn't convinced that the exam had been thorough enough, especially after she had another attack while she was driving on the same stretch of road to the grocery store.

After several more episodes on her way to work and several more trips to the ER, Nancy decided that she wasn't fit to practice law. She feared that she might lose consciousness or have a full-blown heart attack while she was driving to her office. She also worried that she might faint or do something embarrassing while she was consulting with a client. She wondered if she might be having a "nervous breakdown" since none of the doctors could find anything wrong with her heart.

After retiring early, Nancy began to severely restrict her driving for fear that an episode of panic could cause her to have a serious accident. Within several months, she decided to have groceries and medicine delivered. By this time, she was becoming afraid of the panic episodes themselves. She began to look for subtle bodily signs of an impending attack even when she wasn't driving. Unfortunately, retirement afforded her more time to think about her bodily irregularities.

For a while Nancy continued going out with friends and family when they were driving, but she began to fear that she might become panicky and do something embarrassing. She started making excuses for not accepting her friends' invitations until they gave up calling her. She stopped going to singles events where she might have met someone to date and began to chat with men on Match.com. But Nancy always stopped short of going on an actual date. She couldn't drive anywhere to meet the men and also feared embarrassing herself during the date.

Understanding Anxiety

As Nancy's world narrowed, her days were spent scrolling dating sites and watching bad television. That her constricted life allowed more time for her to focus on the possibility of having a panic attack caused her to become even more anxious. She began to rely more and more on the anti-anxiety medication (Xanax) that her doctor prescribed.

Although we might expect retirement to reduce anxiety because stressors related to work are eliminated, this is not necessarily the case. Loneliness and boredom can be just as stressful as having too much to do, especially for a "Type A" person, as a lack of distractions can cause the person to focus inward. Indeed, retiring ranks #10 on the Holmes and Rahe Stress Scale. Nancy would have certainly been diagnosed with Agoraphobia had she managed to get out of the house in order to see a mental health professional.

To assess the severity of Agoraphobia, mental health professionals will ask individuals about their thoughts, feelings and behaviors in crowds and public places (e.g., when they are away from home). What did these situations evoke? Did being in the situation produce sudden terror, fear, nervousness, or physical symptoms like a racing heart (a list which includes indicators of a panic attack)? How the individual felt in *anticipation* of such situations is also important; did the individual engage in avoidance or procrastination?

Although not every person with Agoraphobia has had panic attacks, PD can lead to a person developing Agoraphobia. This disorder is even more handicapping than Panic Disorder because it usually includes avoidance. Agoraphobia is defined as "anxiety about, or avoidance of, places or situations from which escape might be difficult (or embarrassing) or in which help may not be available in the event of having a panic attack or panic-like symptoms" (*DSM-IV*). While panic attacks are uncomfortable and disturbing, if not terrifying, Agoraphobia can take over a person's life. By definition, it often includes avoiding certain settings and situations that the person associates with her panicky feelings. The number of settings connected to the individual's fear tends to grow over time (some readers will remember the process of generalization in relation to classical conditioning from Psych 101). Agoraphobia is more pervasive and farther reaching than Panic Disorder in which the panic is characterized by discrete episodes that are time limited. As the sufferer restricts increasingly more activities, the disorder gradually becomes more threatening to her happiness and success. As is the case for Panic Disorder, Agoraphobia affects more women than men (Yonkers et al., 1998).

In addition to fearing situations related to their first panic episodes, agoraphobic individuals often become anxious about going to places that might be difficult to leave if panic sets in. They may tend to avoid situations in which they would be embarrassed if they were to faint or lose control in some way. Some agoraphobic individuals fear that they might vomit or have diarrhea and not be able to find a restroom. Fearing these possibilities obviously could cause a person to avoid many different situations. Most commonly, agoraphobics fear being in crowds of people, making malls and grocery stores especially problematic. Driving or traveling by bus or train can be distressing for them because it would be dangerous to have a panic attack behind the wheel and embarrassing to lose control on a bus or train.

Some agoraphobics fear being in settings where they might have difficulty obtaining help if they were to have a panic attack. They may be fearful of going certain places by themselves or even being home alone. One of my clients, who was a homemaker, rode to her husband's office with him every morning and spent the day reading at the nearby library to avoid being home by herself. She felt panicky when she was alone in her home, although she didn't have specific fears that she could articulate.

In its extreme form, Agoraphobia can cause sufferers like Nancy to become completely housebound. Some agoraphobics even reach a point that they begin to panic at the thought of walking to their mailboxes or taking the garbage to the curb. When Agoraphobia is severe, it can lead to suicidal feelings, especially if the person has become depressed. The agoraphobic individual may feel that she is a burden to her loved ones. But as with all anxiety disorders, Agoraphobia often takes a somewhat milder and more difficult to recognize form.

Even in fairly minor manifestations, Agoraphobia can make life difficult for its sufferers. Obtaining and holding a job, socializing, and performing necessary day-to-day activities can all be very challenging. The agoraphobic employee may fear driving to work or taking public transportation. This may cause her to frequently call in sick or be late for work. Often the employee is too ashamed to tell her boss the real reason for being late or missing work, so that the boss may assume that her employee is simply unreliable. Other agoraphobic individuals may be afraid of having a panic attack and embarrassing themselves at work. This can be extremely distracting if the person is continuously monitoring her body for signs of impending panic when she should be concentrating on her work. At the same time, it heightens anxiety and actually increases the likelihood of a panic attack.

Not surprisingly, Agoraphobia often impacts a person's social life as well as her career. The agoraphobic individual may gradually lose friends after making one too many excuses for not getting together with them. The less she interacts with others, the more difficult it becomes, so that, at some point, it may even become challenging for her to pick up the phone. She may stop answering the doorbell. I had a client who had retreated to her bedroom at one point in her struggles with Agoraphobia.

Necessary chores such as grocery shopping can be extremely difficult for an agoraphobic person. Indeed, the word *Agoraphobia* originates from the Greek *agora,* which means marketplace, and *phobos,* which means fear. Additionally, the agoraphobic individual may not make doctors' appointments or may miss appointments that she had scheduled, causing her to neglect life-threatening conditions that would have been treatable at an earlier stage. Less serious than this, but certain to affect a woman's self-esteem, going to a beautician or buying makeup or new clothes may seem daunting and result in an agoraphobic woman neglecting her appearance. Not being happy with her appearance could, in turn, increase her tendency to avoid going out in public (online shopping undoubtedly has solved some of these problems for Agoraphobics). In the 2020 Covid pandemic, many of us experienced what it feels like to be agoraphobic, curtailing many of our activities to stay away from public places. Some people found returning to their past social lives anxiety arousing. The longer that we avoid a particular situation, the more difficult it becomes to go back to it.

Agoraphobia takes a completely idiosyncratic form in each person who is affected. Situations to be avoided by one agoraphobic woman are illustrated in the step-by-step hierarchy that I developed for Jane, a 60-year-old woman who feared flying to Boston to visit her children and grandchildren (shown below). Although she wasn't afraid of flying per se, Jane feared all forms of transportation that necessitated being confined in relatively small spaces with many other people because there would be no escape if she were to have a panic attack. She felt extreme apprehension at the very thought of making the trip.

Taking the Sting out of Agoraphobia: Jane's Experience with Systematic Desensitization

I will deal more extensively with anxiety treatments in Chapter Seven and management methods for parents in Chapter Eight. For now, I will briefly describe systematic desensitization therapy, which helps highlight the nature of Agoraphobia itself. Systematic desensitization is a therapy for Agoraphobia that consists of gradually exposing a person to anxiety arousing thoughts and situations, either by having her imagine being in the fearful situations or by having her actually experience each small step leading up to doing what she fears. If necessary, the therapist sometimes accompanies the patient (or enlists the person's friends or family) while she tackles the feared scenarios. In Jane's case, I taught her to imagine the steps leading up to the flight after I instructed her in progressive relaxation exercises. By visualizing each small step involved in making the trip while she was in a relaxed state, Jane was able to become desensitized to her fear of taking the trip. The hierarchy that Jane developed with my help is delineated below. Each item on the hierarchy was written on an index card so that Jane could tweak the ordering if necessary. After she was able to remain relaxed while envisioning each of these steps, her husband accompanied Jane to the airport for a series of "in vivo" sessions that very gradually became closer to flying. Jane and her husband first went to the airport to watch the planes taking off and eventually entered one of the terminals. The very last thing that they did was to approach the ticket counter and buy two tickets to Boston, Jane's "graduation" present. Sometimes anti-anxiety medications such as Xanax (because it works quickly) are used in conjunction with desensitization to accelerate the process.

Jane's Hierarchy was:

1. Seeing a picture of a Boston landmark
2. Reading about Boston
3. Thinking about the trip
4. Talking to her therapist about the trip
5. Talking to her children about the trip
6. Talking to friends about the trip
7. Hearing about someone else's trip involving a flight
8. Asking her MD for anti-anxiety medication for the trip
9. Calling to make reservations
10. Buying items for the trip
11. Packing
12. Driving to the airport
13. Checking her luggage
14. Going through security
15. Boarding the plane
16. Finding her seat and assessing who would be sitting next to her
17. Being in the air and confined to her seat

Although Agoraphobia is quite treatable, the nature of this mental illness makes it difficult for sufferers to obtain help for obvious reasons. For those who barely leave their homes, the steps to obtaining treatment must seem almost completely insurmountable. The best solution is an in-home therapist; however, this more costly service is unlikely to be covered by insurance. A person's partner or family member can play a critical role, as Jane's husband did, in whether or not their loved one is able to conquer their fear.

Post-Traumatic Stress Disorder

Let's now examine Post-Traumatic Stress Disorder (PTSD). Clinicians should note that while the *DSM-5* no longer categorizes PTSD under Anxiety Disorder, anxiety sufferers may have underlying genetic and environmental factors creating greater risk for PTSD (Lang & McTeague, 2009). PTSD has received a great deal of coverage in the popular press in the last decade, and compared to the other disorders I've discussed, it may be the least hidden. PTSD was discussed often as a condition experienced frequently by first responders during the Covid pandemic. In my own work, PTSD was relatively uncommon, but striking when present. It wasn't unusual for clients to experience several of the symptoms without meeting the full criteria for a diagnosis. Indeed, milder forms of PTSD are probably far more common than anyone realizes because people don't usually talk about their symptoms. In fact, most of us have had frightening nightmares at one time or another. Among my clients, date rape was the most common source of PTSD symptoms. This was certainly something women didn't tend to talk about, making it largely hidden. My PTSD patients who had been accident victims were much less reticent to talk about their symptoms.

The Primary Care PTSD Screener

A short screening test has been developed to identify potential PTSD. This test is made available to the public through the U.S. Department of Veterans Affairs with the understanding that anyone concerned with PTSD will seek help from a mental health professional (Prins et al., 2016).[10]

Sometimes things happen to people that are unusually or especially frightening, horrible, or traumatic. For example:

A serious accident or fire
A physical or sexual assault or abuse
An earthquake or flood
A war
Seeing someone be killed or seriously injured
Having a loved one die through homicide or suicide

Have you ever experienced this kind of event?

If yes—please answer the questions below. In the past month have you:

1. Had nightmares about the event(s) or thought about the event(s) when you did not want to?
2. Tried hard not to think about the event(s) or went out of your way to avoid situations that reminded you of the event(s)?
3. Been constantly on guard, watchful, or easily startled?
4. Felt numb or detached from people, activities or your surroundings?
5. Felt guilty or unable to stop blaming yourself or others for the event(s) or any problems the event(s) may have caused?

Sharon's Encounter with PTSD

Sharon will never forget what she was doing the day that she received the call that would change her life. Her husband had been in a horrific car accident, and by the time that Sharon got to the hospital, he was already dead. In addition to her intense grief, the enormous shock of the phone call stayed with her. Sharon began having nightmares entailing images of her husband's mangled body and his totaled car. During her waking hours, she couldn't stop seeing the image of her husband in the hospital bed. And her mind kept replaying the phone call. Indeed, Sharon jumped whenever the phone rang. She felt instant panic every time she heard a siren and avoided driving past the scene of the accident, even though this meant taking a very circuitous route every time that she had to drive to and from work. Seeing a car similar

---

10. This PTSD assessment is made available for use by the National Center for PTSD at the U.S. Department of Veterans Affairs.

to her husband's was even distressing. Sharon was unable to sleep for more than a few hours a night until her doctor prescribed an anti-anxiety medication. At times, Sharon even blamed herself for asking her husband to stop at the post office on the way to work because this might have caused him to be running late and to speed in order to make up the time.

The *DSM-IV* describes PTSD as the development of symptoms following exposure to an extreme traumatic stressor involving direct personal experience of an event that involves actual or threatened death or serious injury or other threat to one's personal integrity. Witnessing such an event or learning about unexpected or violent death, serious harm or threat of death or injury experienced by a family member or close associate can also lead to PTSD. The person's response to the stressor is characterized by intense fear, helplessness, horror, and sometimes anger and violent behavior. Some or all of the symptoms accompanying the intense fear include nightmares and flashbacks of the traumatic event, persistent symptoms of increased arousal (the fight or flight response) like startling easily and avoidance of things associated with the trauma. The sufferer naturally begins to avoid anything that could remind him of the event, thereby triggering a reaction. This avoidance of everything reminiscent of the trauma makes it extremely difficult for a person with PTSD to resume a normal life. PTSD symptoms in milder forms are fairly common. I can still remember where I was and the shock that I felt upon hearing of tragedies involving my friends. I have also had nightmares and woken up feeling panicky after remembering what happened upon awakening.

Traumatic experiences such as being abused as a child, being assaulted or kidnapped, experiencing war, being in a serious car accident or a natural disaster, or being diagnosed with a life-threatening illness can lead to the development of Post-Traumatic Stress Disorder as can witnessing these things happening to a loved one. PTSD is also found in survivors of epidemics, murder, and suicide. The excellent but very disturbing 2020 movie *Retaliation* portrays a young man with a violent streak attributable to the fact that he had been sexually abused at age twelve by a priest whom he had idealized. This character's PTSD manifested as rage, which was compounded by the fact that his mother didn't believe him when he confided in her a few days after he was raped. Sadly, this reaction from loved ones is not unusual in cases like this.

When PTSD results from witnessing something horrible happening to someone else, it is sometimes complicated by Survivor's Guilt. This syndrome is defined as a condition of persistent mental and emotional stress experienced by someone who has survived an incident in which others died. I have also seen a similar phenomenon in people who have escaped unscathed when others were seriously injured. One of my clients was in a car accident in which her sister was seriously injured, while my client received only minor scratches. Had she been the driver, she would have undoubtedly felt even more guilt. In the 1980 film *Ordinary People*, based on the 1978 book by Judith Guest, a young man struggles with the fact that he survived a sailing accident in which his brother drowned.

As I've mentioned, because we are hearing more about PTSD these days and the symptoms are anything but subtle, PTSD is not so much a hidden handicap as a widely publicized one. The symptoms are striking and not easily missed. Indeed, some sufferers react to their heightened arousal with anger and violent outbursts. It goes without saying that PTSD can be extremely disabling. The fact that so many war veterans are unemployed or underemployed is evidence of how handicapping it can be. The tragically high suicide rate among vets underscores the misery that PTSD patients endure. PTSD is truly a living nightmare. Many victims turn to illegal drugs and alcohol to get through the day and to enable them to sleep at night. Others become addicted to the prescription medications that they are given for pain and insomnia.

Importantly, as I've mentioned, less extreme manifestations of PTSD that are limited to nightmares and disturbing thoughts with mild feelings of panic are far more common than anyone realizes. Who among us hasn't had a nightmare after a disturbing event? As I have discussed, these symptoms are not something that someone is going to mention at a cocktail party or even in a small group of friends. The person will typically try to suppress any thoughts that could produce feelings of panic and fear that talking about them could make their feelings stronger. Children are especially prone to nightmares and are often reluctant to talk about them. While full-blown PTSD—especially in veterans and first responders—is finally being addressed, the less severe but still highly distressing manifestations of PTSD remain largely hidden.

Two

Social Anxiety

Panic Disorder, Agoraphobia, and PTSD are serious illnesses, "raw" in nature and closely tied to the body's fight or flight response. In this chapter, I'll discuss Social Anxiety, which is more common than the disorders in Chapter One. Although not as frequently marked by acute crises, it can be very limiting to happiness and success. In addition, much Social Anxiety is regrettably not recognized as an actual anxiety disorder but is instead misattributed to mere shyness. I will also reference Social Phobia, which is considered synonymous with Social Anxiety. Socially anxious people are exemplars of my argument in this book; they hide in plain sight. This disorder comes with shame, and friends and loved ones often don't realize why someone might avoid social situations. The quiz at the beginning of the chapter will give you an introduction to this manifestation of anxiety.

Social Anxiety Screening Tool

The Anxiety and Depression Association of America (ADAA) makes a variety of screening tools freely available to the public that individuals can complete and share with a mental health professional or use to be matched with an ADAA member professional. The following items are an extract from the ADAA's Social Anxiety Tool (Newman et al., 2002).

Are you troubled by the following?

An intense and persistent fear of a social situation in which people might judge you such as:

- Social interactions (e.g., having a conversation, meeting unfamiliar people)
- Being observed (e.g., eating or drinking in public)
- Performing in front of others (e.g., giving a speech)

• Fear that you will act in a way or show anxiety symptoms that will be negatively evaluated (i.e., will be humiliating or embarrassing; will lead to rejection or offend others)
• Fear that people will notice that you are blushing, sweating, trembling, or showing other signs of anxiety
• Perceiving that your reaction to feared situations will be greater than that of most other people

By visiting the ADAA website, interested parties can use these and other questions to provide some preliminary screening information about Social Anxiety.

Mary Ellen's Story

Mary Ellen had the look of "the girl next door" with blonde hair, blue eyes, and a shy, endearing smile. She had been a beautiful little girl, and she was growing into a lovely young lady. Mary Ellen had always been sensitive and fearful, but her shyness hadn't been much of a problem during childhood because she didn't have to meet new children once she had managed to adjust to preschool. She spent her elementary school years at a small, private school with the same group of children she knew from preschool. When she began to fall behind in second grade, Mary Ellen was diagnosed with Attention Deficit Hyperactivity Disorder (ADHD) and placed on Ritalin.

Mary Ellen seemed to be doing well enough until it was time for her to start high school. Due to her anxiety in public, Mary Ellen didn't make new friends easily, but she did meet some girls on her field hockey team. Her life took a different turn when she was invited to a party with older students who drank and smoked marijuana. Mary Ellen felt panicky upon arriving at the party and quickly accepted a drink that someone offered her. It was at this event that Mary Ellen realized that she felt much more relaxed after she had a couple of drinks. She began sneaking drinks from her parents' liquor cabinet whenever she was going out with her friends.

It wasn't too long before Mary Ellen began to do poorly academically and was suspended from the field hockey team. Shortly after this, her wild crowd started shoplifting. After Mary Ellen was caught with some merchandise, her parents managed to hire a lawyer who was able to get the charges dropped. However, Mary Ellen continued to run with the same crowd, and she had access to a sporty new convertible to drive her friends around town. These outings included drinking and driving, and Mary Ellen received more than one DUI during this time, but her lawyer was able to get these offenses expunged from her record. As you can imagine, Mary Ellen's mother and father ended up spending thousands of dollars getting her out of situations that would have landed most teens in jail. We can picture what would have been likely to happen to a teen from a less advantaged background whose family didn't have the resources to hire attorneys.

Mary Ellen's continued anxiety led her to not only sneak drinks from the liquor cabinet but now also pills from the medicine drawer. In a relatively short period of time Mary Ellen developed an addiction to these substances. She was rushed to the hospital on more than one occasion after overdosing on a combination of these prescription drugs and alcohol. By this time, Mary Ellen was being taken to a series of psychiatrists and receiving multiple diagnoses and the medications to go along with them. This shy and likeable young lady from a loving family was being treated for several serious psychiatric conditions, including Bipolar Disorder, Borderline Personality, and alcohol and drug addiction in addition to her long-standing diagnosis of ADHD. Some members of her extended family even regarded Mary Ellen as an incorrigible delinquent.

Social Anxiety is characterized by intense and persistent anxiety in social settings or situations in which the person is required to perform in some way. The symptoms are similar to but usually less intense than those experienced during a panic attack. For example, the person may blush, be shaky and sweaty, feel nauseous and have difficulty articulating his thoughts—again manifestations of the fight or flight response. Socially anxious people dislike being observed and are especially uncomfortable being the center of attention, even when the attention is positive. They don't want to do anything that might draw attention to themselves. Basically, the person is overly self-conscious and afraid of embarrassment. Consequently, people with Social Anxiety tend to avoid activities that have the potential to embarrass them, particularly situations that involve evaluation. The *DSM* states that a diagnosis of Social Anxiety is warranted only if the person's fear interferes significantly with her daily routines, occupational functioning, or social life, but milder manifestations can make a person miserable. Socially anxious people describe fearing that they will be perceived as stupid, weak, or even "crazy." Consequently, they are sensitive to criticism and fear rejection. They tend to have low self-esteem and find it difficult to be assertive. The *DSM-IV* and *DSM-5* use Social Anxiety and Social Phobia interchangeably.

From an evolutionary standpoint, our ancestors didn't have to deal with huge groups of people as we do in our large cities today. They lived in small tribes with the same groups of people. Kate Murphy (2021) sums up the writing of Robin Dunbar, an evolutionary psychologist, concluding that "human beings have the cognitive capacity to accommodate only four to six close friends." The rest of a person's social network would be considered acquaintances. Social Phobia may have been a highly adaptive trait for our ancestors, allowing them to avoid dangerous strangers. Quick social judgment probably increased their chances of survival. In fact, some evolutionary psychologists consider empathy, the ability to understand others, to be one of the keys to the survival of our species.

Mild anxiety in social situations is very common, and while it may not necessarily interfere with a person's functioning, it can certainly make life miserable. As with all forms of anxiety, we have all experienced it to some degree. Almost everyone can remember a time when they felt somewhat fearful upon entering a large group at a party or before giving a presentation. Because of this, Social Anxiety is sometimes downplayed. Back in 1985, Michael Liebowitz wrote an article titled "Social Anxiety—the Neglected Disorder," maintaining that Social Anxiety was "underdiagnosed and undertreated." In fact, people with Social Anxiety are often crippled in many aspects of life including education, employment and family relationships (Schneier et al., 1974), even when compared to those with other anxiety disorders (Bech & Angst, 1996). Indeed, the socially phobic are more likely to be single, to live alone, to be unemployed and to depend on alcohol (Norton et al., 1996). This is a highly significant problem since estimates are that Social Anxiety affects approximately 6.8 percent of the American population. Since so few people suffering from Social Anxiety present themselves for treatment and obtain diagnoses (Pollard & Corn, 1989; Marks & Gelder, 1966), the actual rate is undoubtedly higher. Like the other anxiety disorders, Social Phobia is most handicapping when a person avoids social situations rather than finding a way to push through fearfulness. And avoiding social situations isn't easy. Phillip Zimbardo (1977) has pointed out that "airplane phobics can take trains, snake phobics can live in cities and those afraid of the dark can sleep with the lights on. But what about people who are afraid of other people?"

The most common fears in Social Anxiety involve speaking, eating, or writing in public.[1] But in some cases, the socially anxious person's fear can be pervasive, occurring across a wide variety of situations. As in Panic Disorder and Agoraphobia, Social Anxiety becomes handicapping if the socially anxious person allows himself to avoid situations

---

1. People fear writing in public because they imagine that others will notice their hands shaking. This would be a particular problem for teachers writing on a chalkboard or a presenter using a laser pointer.

that are necessary to his success and happiness in life. In its severest form, Social Anxiety can be all-encompassing.

The high prevalence of Social Phobia is evidenced in our outward behavior, particularly in women. The self-consciousness that characterizes Social Anxiety can lead a person to spend several hours a day obsessing over their appearance. Some women (and men to a lesser degree) even go into debt buying clothes and makeup, getting spray tans, having their hair dyed, curled or straightened, buying multiple pairs of expensive glasses, having minor dental imperfections corrected and even undergoing unnecessary plastic surgery. On the other hand, the extremely shy may dress plainly in order not to call attention to themselves. Picture the stereotypical mousy-looking woman with short hair and no makeup.

The Shyness Connection

> "I open my mouth to say something and nothing comes out. My mind goes completely blank."—14-year-old girl during her first week in high school

Social Anxiety is sometimes considered synonymous with shyness, a trait with which we are all familiar. This is especially the case when the anxiety is more generalized (i.e., the individual is anxious in multiple social situations). While some experts make a subtle distinction between Social Anxiety and shyness, the *DSM* doesn't mention shyness. I will refer to shyness and Social Anxiety more or less interchangeably. The difference is in the intensity and chronicity. Social Anxiety can be extremely intense and even precipitate a panic attack. Shyness is thought of as a long-standing personality trait that is less intense, more generalized, and longer lasting while Social Anxiety can apply to certain very specific situations. Like most other personality traits, shyness is often conceptualized as a continuous trait with varying levels of severity. It should also be noted that shyness and introversion are different personality constructs. I will discuss the difference between the two later.

It may surprise the reader that extroverts aren't exempt from anxiety in social situations. The socially anxious extrovert has a strong interest in being with other people but experiences a great deal of anxiety in some social situations. Shy extroverts experience an ongoing push-pull between their wants and fears, which only exacerbates their anxiety. They have a more difficult time than introverts who often prefer being alone.

Social Anxiety is evident throughout the animal kingdom. Breeders know that puppies and kittens in a given litter differ from one another in terms of how outgoing they are. Years ago, our cat had a litter of four kittens, each with strikingly different personalities. One managed to get away from his mother and out of the box well before his siblings did so that he could be near the people in the household. Observations in the animal kingdom underscore the fact that there are genetic differences in the predisposition to fearlessness and sociability that are observable shortly after birth. We humans are especially social animals who have always needed to depend upon one another to survive. Indeed, a number of recent studies have concluded that loneliness can actually shorten a person's life (Bzdok, 2020).

Performance Anxiety

> "It's 2 a.m., I can't sleep, and I want to die. I'm not normally the suicidal type...."

The above quote describes Susan Cain's (*Quiet*, 2012) own feelings before an important presentation and perfectly illustrates a common manifestation that Social Anxiety takes. Performance Anxiety (sometimes referred to as stage fright) is a subtype of Social Anxiety that is limited to specific activities and not necessarily accompanied by more generalized anxiety in social situations. It can affect people who are generally outgoing and comfortable in most social situations. As you might expect, Performance Anxiety impacts athletes and entertainers who are in the spotlight, but it can strike anyone who anticipates being observed or evaluated in any way. We have probably all experienced it at one time or another before having to give a speech or interview for a job.

Performance Anxiety can be highly idiosyncratic. However, its most common form is undoubtedly public speaking. Indeed, one study reported by the National Anxiety Center found that many Americans fear public speaking more than death. There is physiological evidence for this finding. Almost everyone has a two- to three-fold increase in norepinephrine, indicating a rush of adrenaline, in their blood when they begin a lecture, but socially anxious individuals have an even stronger reaction. This causes their fear to become a self-fulfilling prophecy as self-consciousness and panicky feelings can result in an inferior performance. With public speaking important in many positions, fear and avoidance of speaking in front of groups has likely derailed countless careers. Some anxious speakers develop a stuttering disorder, although stuttering has other causes as well.

Surprisingly, a sizable number of people who were so successful they became famous had to conquer severe Performance Anxiety. Scott Stossel (2013) describes some of these well-known historical figures. William Gladstone, the British prime minister from 1868 to 1894, drank laudanum (opium) with his coffee before he had to give a speech in Parliament. William Cowper, the 18th-century British poet, tried to hang himself before he was supposed to present his qualifications for a government position. Mahatma Gandhi froze during his first case as a lawyer and ran from the courtroom. Thomas Jefferson had such a fear of public speaking that he gave only two public speeches during his presidency and was diagnosed posthumously with Social Anxiety by Duke University psychiatrists (Kendall, 2013). Henry James dropped out of law school and became a writer after he felt that he had performed poorly in a moot court competition.

It is not just public speaking, but any kind of performance—from juggling, singing and participating in athletic competitions to acting and doing stand-up comedy—that can be undermined by Performance Anxiety. Carly Simon, Barbra Streisand and Hugh Grant have described struggling with anxiety severe enough to threaten their careers. And suffering isn't confined to immediately before an event. Anticipatory anxiety can dog an anxious person for months before a dreaded occasion and even cause the person to find a way to avoid the event. Eventually, an anxious individual may give up a promising career or otherwise enjoyable hobby. It is difficult to estimate how many potential athletes and entertainers fail to follow their dreams because of anxiety. We can imagine how Social Anxiety can eventually lead to a person perceiving himself as a failure and erode his self-esteem. As with all anxiety disorders, this can sometimes even pose a suicide risk.

As briefly touched on in the first chapter, a certain amount of anxiety is energizing and may actually motivate a person enough to improve his performance in giving a speech, going on stage or running a race. Once anxiety becomes too high, however, it will have the opposite effect and interfere with the person's performance. A seminal study by Robert Yerkes and John Dodson demonstrated this more than a hundred years ago (1908). Since the act of performing is inherently stimulating, a

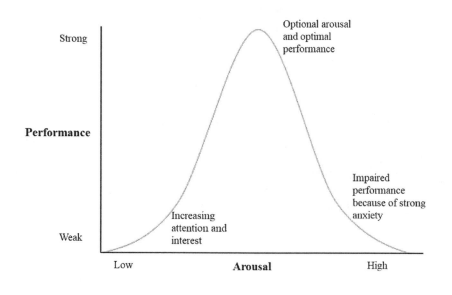

Figure 1: Yerkes-Dodson Law

person predisposed to anxiety often becomes overly aroused and doesn't perform at his best. The diagram above illustrates how this works.

Now let's turn to a common form of Performance Anxiety, test anxiety, by considering Heather's case.

Heather is a 26-year-old Argentinian with a quick wit and sense of humor to match. Her beautiful long, dark hair catches everyone's attention, and her fashionable clothing gives her an air of professionalism. She has a successful career at a major international firm but could be doing even better if she had a college degree. Heather had a straight-A average in college and more than enough credits to graduate. However, in Argentina, students have to pass oral exams in all of their senior-level classes. Several years ago, Heather passed them all with flying colors—except for one. After she failed this exam the first time, Heather became very anxious the second time and didn't perform as well. The third time her anxiety was even worse, and she didn't even attempt to answer the last question. It has been four years since this experience and Heather has not attempted a fourth exam.

Test anxiety is a form of Performance Anxiety, and like stage fright, it can occur in people who aren't necessarily anxious in most social situations. Test anxiety is characterized by dread in anticipating being tested and some level of panic during the test, which can interfere with the person's performance on the exam. Even though test anxiety is, by definition, limited to taking tests, it has impacted many lives, sometimes even causing its sufferers to drop out of high school or college. Indeed, the fact that performing well on the SAT or ACT has been a prerequisite for getting admitted to most colleges can cause some young people to forego a post-secondary education. Test anxiety may be limited to one type of testing situation such as essay, fill in the blank, multiple choice, oral exams or "hands-on" skills tests—at least initially. But the person's anxiety may begin to generalize to additional types of examinations.

We tend to think of tests primarily in relation to school, but many of us continue to be subjected to testing throughout our lives. Driving tests are something that most people have to deal with. Many professions require an exam in order for a person to obtain a license to practice. Some of these entrance exams are paper and pencil, while others have an oral component or require a "hands-on" demonstration of the person's skills. From hairstylists performing demonstrations on live subjects to prospective attorneys taking the bar exam, being tested is often a hurdle that must be navigated before obtaining licensure in a given profession.

I had a student who needed to score well on the GRE in order to get into the graduate program of his dreams. Although Henry scored in the top 5th percentile on the practice exams in the preparation book, he couldn't manage to obtain an above average score on the actual exam. He was finally able to perform well after a psychiatrist prescribed a low dose of a blood pressure medication to take the edge off Henry's anxiety.

Test anxiety can be difficult to sort out in children and teens if they don't verbalize what they're experiencing. When anxiety causes a child or adolescent to score poorly on exams, parents and teachers may come to believe that their anxious student has a learning disability or ADHD or is just not as bright as he had seemed. Students who fear tests may suffer throughout their school years, particularly now that many schools require end-of-the-year testing in certain grades for promotion to the next grade.[2]

The Many Triggers of Social Anxiety

As I mentioned earlier, Social Anxiety can be considerably more handicapping when it occurs across settings than when tied to a very specific type of performance. Socially anxious people who are afraid of

---

2. Test anxiety in children will be dealt with in greater depth in a later section of the book.

many different kinds of social situations rather than specific types of performance suffer far more. As mentioned, these individuals are often labeled shy. When we think of Social Anxiety, we usually imagine a shy person feeling awkward at parties and large group events, but there are many other seemingly more innocuous situations the socially anxious can find intimidating. Again, most of us have experienced moments when we feel anxious in a particular social situation, and most of us can recall more than one example. Indeed, most people have probably experienced some apprehension before picking up the phone to make an especially important call.

When Social Anxiety is more generalized and a person fears most social situations, it can be one of the most disabling of the anxiety disorders, particularly if it is so intense that the person can't push through his fears in order to tackle social situations. When the person avoids most social situations, it can be difficult to distinguish Social Anxiety from Agoraphobia. The person may have problems working, socializing, and relating to intimate partners along with difficulty with most day-to-day activities including interacting with salesclerks and cashiers and making necessary phone calls. Moving past the necessary chores of daily living to focus on the joys of life, it becomes clear that Social Anxiety can cause a person to miss many pleasurable life-enhancing experiences. The shy person is less likely to have a circle of friends to do things with and also less likely to get out on her own to have lunch at a nice restaurant or attend a festival. The nature of Social Anxiety makes it difficult for a socially phobic person to obtain help.

An example of extreme shyness is the girlfriend of a client's son. Jacob met Katy on Tinder when they both swiped right, and he found her funny and cute. The two seemed to click the first time that they met in person and soon began seeing each other exclusively. Katy had a wide circle of friends her own age, but when it came time to meet Jacob's family, Katy couldn't bring herself to talk and barely managed to whisper one-word answers to questions about herself. A trip to the mountains with Jacob's extended family ended with each person in the family thinking that Katy didn't like him or her. This didn't improve over the three years that they dated, although Katy showed her cute and funny personality with Jacob and his friends. She continued to seem like a different person when she needed to deal with older adults. This shows how situation-specific Social Anxiety can be. Few people would have guessed how socially anxious Katy could be.

The activities that socially phobic people fear can sometimes be highly individualized and situation specific. And because anxiety isn't rational, these situations often don't seem logical. A person might seem fine in settings that cause anxiety in most people but fear circumstances that generally seem less threatening. For example, some successful performers are extremely shy when they are off the stage. This is counterintuitive since most people would find performing in front of audiences more intimidating than interacting in day-to-day social situations. For example, Beatrice, a young lady majoring in drama who feels comfortable on stage, still avoids talking on the phone. Not only does she fear initiating a call, but she can't bring herself to answer a ringing phone. She recalls that, since around age five, she wouldn't talk to her grandparents or her cousins over the phone.

Examples of specific circumstances that can give socially anxious people pause include speaking in meetings, dealing with authority figures, arriving late to an event, using public restrooms, returning an item to a store, making a phone call, and writing or eating in front of others. While not as handicapping as more generalized Social Anxiety, fear of any of these situations can greatly limit a person, and, over time, a highly specific fear of a particular situation can generalize to similar activities. Indeed, fears of any specific social situation can sometimes have wide-ranging consequences. If we consider the ramifications of the fear of eating in front of others, it becomes apparent that it can prevent a person from taking part in many social activities. These situations range from networking lunches that are important to career success to pleasurable meals with friends and romantic dinners with intimate partners.

Let's look at an example of how fear of a very specific social situation can impact someone's life. A person who is apprehensive about speaking during a weekly meeting with his office work team may start to wonder if people have noticed that he never has anything to say. After a period of time, this individual may begin to fear attending the meetings. Eventually he may start to miss some of the weekly meetings causing co-workers to perceive him as irresponsible and making it more difficult for him to attend the next meeting for fear that someone will ask him why he missed the last one. This becomes even more complicated when generalization enters the picture. His fearfulness may expand to the point that our worker starts to look for ways to avoid all meetings. Ultimately, the person's anxiety may spread outside of the workplace, causing him to become apprehensive in any situation that involves groups of more than a few people. As time goes on, the trepidation that may have initially developed when a colleague criticized his idea in a meeting can transform into a more generalized and pervasive dread of small groups.

More General Social Anxiety

Moving toward more generalized Social Anxiety, as I've said, a person who is afraid of many different social situations will be the most handicapped. People who give in to their fear and avoid social activities will miss out on many experiences and opportunities. Shy people develop a number of strategies to avoid dealing with their fears. This can cause them to pass up many experiences large and small. For example, a party guest may spend most of her time during the event helping the host prepare food and clean up in order to avoid having to talk to the other guests. Not only does this guest miss much of the fun, but her avoidance limits her opportunity to practice and hone social skills. This makes it less likely that she will become more socially adept. Indeed, an article by Kate Murphy (2020), written during the Covid-19 pandemic, cites research suggesting that avoidance of social interaction can cause social skills to "atrophy from lack of use." Murphy goes on to point out that "people separated from society—by circumstance or choice—report feeling more socially anxious, impulsive, awkward and intolerant when they return to normal life." She describes Beth Healey, a British physician who spent a year in Antarctica, after Healey's return home: "for months, she was nervous getting on a bus and overwhelmed going to the supermarket." The social distancing that Covid necessitated may have an effect similar to this more extreme isolation.

From an evolutionary standpoint, humans have long organized in groups for safety and division of labor. If facility in interacting effectively with others was evolutionarily selected, that might help to explain the recent research finding that loneliness can actually shorten a person's life (Bzdok, 2020). After examining a large number of studies, Bzdok concluded that "having strong interpersonal relationships is critical for survival across the entire life span." His review of the research led him to conclude that "people who are socially integrated have better adjusted biomarkers for physiological function, including lower systolic blood pressure, lower body mass index and lower levels of C-reactive protein (an indicator of inflammation)." We should also include the deaths by suicide that can result from loneliness.

Understanding Anxiety

Even seemingly mundane interactions limited to one other person can be quite difficult for the socially anxious, partly because they tend to overestimate the extent to which others notice their fear. Initiating a conversation, making small talk and wrapping up a conversation can all be intimidating. It can be difficult for some socially phobic people to maintain successful dyadic conversations because they are so anxious about the impression that they're making. Instead of listening to what the other person is saying, the shy person may focus on what she should say next or ruminate about whether her previous comments have sounded foolish. This makes it difficult for the anxious person to respond appropriately in a conversation, since it reduces the likelihood that she will ask the other person questions and disrupts the natural give and take that characterizes a good interaction. The result is even greater self-consciousness and embarrassment for the socially anxious individual, particularly if the person ruminates afterward about what he said or should have said. This degree of self-consciousness would certainly take the enjoyment out of any social interaction, and it can have a disastrous effect on a person's relationships and her self-esteem, causing her even greater anxiety. Indeed, the relationship between Social Anxiety and self-esteem is a complicated one.[3] People with low self-esteem often anticipate that they will make a poor impression which can cause anticipatory anxiety and awkwardness leading to poor performance and more intense Social Anxiety. Although other people can't necessarily tell that a person is anxious, some people give themselves away by blushing, becoming shaky and sweaty, or having difficulty articulating what they want to say.

One of my clients had a daughter whose experiences illustrate the difficulty that a shy person can have in carrying on a conversation and in having meaningful give-and-take relationships. According to her mother, Amy had been an extremely shy child who could barely bring herself to say hello to anyone. Over the years, Amy became better at answering other people's questions and seemed quite poised. She, however, never asked people anything about themselves. It seemed that it took everything that she had to answer their questions so that she couldn't even think to ask them a question in return. Amy got to the point that she could talk about herself at length, but this made interactions lopsided. I thought that perhaps she was intimidated by adults

---

3. People with generally good self-esteem, however, are not invulnerable to getting anxious in some social situations.

or thought it impolite to ask adults questions, but apparently this never changed. My client's daughter grew into a charming and seemingly confident thirty-year-old woman who still didn't ask about others. Sadly, a person who is extremely self-conscious may remain self-centered and appear uninterested in other people.

Coping with Social Anxiety

With many social events difficult to avoid, people across a wide range of cultures have developed an array of social conventions to make socializing less intimidating. Costume parties are a creative way of dealing with shyness because attendees can hide behind masks. Darkened rooms at parties have a similar effect. For outdoor gatherings, wearing sunglasses can feel like having a protective shield helping a person to feel less like they are being scrutinized. This underscores the fact that some level of anxiety is extremely common in social gatherings.

Drinking is probably far and away the most common way that anxious people attempt to relax in social situations. This can be effective in the short run if the person doesn't drink too much and unintentionally embarrass themselves. As we know, however, for vulnerable people, what starts out as social drinking may evolve into binge drinking and, eventually, drinking heavily every day. Many alcoholics barely remember why they started drinking in the first place. Their family and friends often assume that their loved ones simply chose a self-defeating lifestyle (recall Mary Ellen who discovered that drinking took the edge off of her anxiety at parties and within less than a year ended up becoming addicted to alcohol and drugs).

The "tough love" approach is often suggested to family and friends of an addicted person. This concept was introduced by Bill Milliken (1968) in his book titled *Tough Love*. The philosophy is that loved ones should stop enabling an addicted person to buy alcohol and drugs and require the person to take responsibility for his behavior. This can involve no longer allowing the person to live at home, cutting off financial resources, and sometimes even withdrawing emotional support as attempts to encourage the person to go into treatment. For example, the family may refuse to bail their loved one out of jail after an arrest for driving under the influence. Tough love is probably not the best approach if the substance abuser has an underlying anxiety disorder. There can be tragic consequences when well-meaning family members attempt to apply this principle to their loved ones. It can ultimately cause their addicted family member or friend to become homeless and to resort to stealing or begging on the street. Tragically, suicide can be the end result. It is important to make sure that the person gets the right kind of treatment.

Socially anxious people may also turn to smoking to help them relax in social settings, even though nicotine is actually a stimulant that heightens arousal. Like drinking, smoking often starts out as a way of fitting in with peers, enabling an individual to feel more comfortable in social settings, but it can develop into a life-threatening addiction. Smoking gives a person something to do with his hands and an almost instant comradery with other smokers. Because people are required to step outside to smoke, it can also be a way of escaping the larger group. A friend of mine has observed that alcoholics in rehabilitation centers often substitute smoking for drinking. They tend to pick up the habit during the down time when they're sitting around the day room with other patients. Smoking marijuana may be the ultimate way to deal with Social Anxiety. It's relaxing for most people, and because it is still illicit in some places, sharing a "joint" creates an even greater sense of comradery within a select group than drinking alcohol or smoking cigarettes. Experimenting with street drugs, including nitrous oxide (i.e., whip-its) and hallucinogens, might also be included here.

Social Anxiety Early in Life

We can see potential predispositions toward anxiety around people as soon as children need to interact with the outside world beyond their families. Indeed, a whopping 40 percent of adults reported that they had been shy earlier in their lives (Carducci & Zimbardo, 1995). Manifestations of Social Anxiety can range from a child who takes ten minutes to warm up at the playground, staying on the sidelines until he is comfortable, to a rare condition labeled Selective Mutism. A child with Selective Mutism may learn to talk on time but not speak at all in certain situations. She may talk at home but not say a word at school or she may talk to children but not adults outside of her family.

Starting kindergarten is likely to be a harrowing transition for a shy child. Large classes of 25 or 30 other children are somewhat intimidating to most children, but especially to the socially anxious child. Suddenly he is no longer "Mommy's special boy" but one of many. A shy child can end up being considered a wallflower. Teachers may spend disproportionate amounts of time focusing on a few students who stand out from their classmates in one way or another. Shy children will usually do anything they can to *not* stand out. Students who are socially phobic sometimes underachieve because they're afraid to participate in class or make presentations. Approaching teachers outside of class can also be very difficult for them. Not only will this avoidance in and out of the classroom affect their day-to-day grades, but teachers may be likely to underestimate their quiet students' abilities. Some of these children may be assumed to have a learning disability or thought to not be very bright. A client of mine who was a brilliant mathematician at a major university had been considered "slow" until his fourth-grade teacher realized his potential previously masked by shyness. Teachers sometimes even regard conscientious students as unmotivated and lacking in effort. Additionally, socially anxious children may become targets for bullies, as other children can sense their lack of confidence and see them as easy marks.

Because of these issues, school can terrify shy children and they may develop an intense fear of going to school. This anxiety has been labeled School Phobia which affects from 2 to 5 percent of children and will be dealt with at greater length later in this chapter. As in all of the anxiety disorders, avoidance is the biggest problem in School Phobia. If a child is occasionally able to convince his caretakers to let him stay at home, he may fall behind and his future success in school can be jeopardized. The more days that a child misses the more difficult it will be for him to face going back to class. This can continue over the years until the school phobic teen drops out of high school or is ill-prepared to attend college.

Failure to Launch

Failure to Launch affects young people at the other end of their academic careers—young adults between the ages of 18 and 30. Failure to Launch refers to an inability to become independent and self-reliant among young adults.[4] This malady was recently described by Mark McConville in *Failure to Launch: Why Your Twenty Something Hasn't Grown Up and What to Do About It* (2020), but earlier

---

4. This syndrome has not been recognized by the American Psychiatric or Psychological Associations.

research (see below) described similar phenomena. In my years of working with this age group, I've found that although Failure to Launch has a number of underlying causes, it often has its roots in anxiety, especially Social Anxiety. Young men seem to be particularly vulnerable to Failure to Launch. It may include the reluctance to assume responsibility, a low work ethic, lack of confidence and addiction to video games and social media. I've found that an addiction to pornography can also be part of the picture in teenage boys and signal the beginning of a life-long problem. This is especially problematic because it generates guilt and increases the teen's overall anxiety. Although present across all socioeconomic strata, Failure to Launch is more likely to be diagnosed in young adults who are expected to do something significant after high school graduation. Those who have always been underachievers are behaving consistently with what had been expected of them. This syndrome will be dealt with in more detail in Chapter Six.

Some would argue that even many of the young people in college today remain immature and irresponsible. Richard Arum and Josipa Roksa, authors of *Academically Adrift, Limited Learning on College Campuses* (2011), describe the "floundering phase of the life course." Anxiety would certainly exacerbate this already difficult life stage. Back in the 1980s Susan Littwin, author of *The Postponed Generation: Why America's Grown Up Kids Are Growing Up Later* (1986), wrote that college-educated twenty-somethings are a "confused, unfocused, and dependent" cohort whose unrealistic expectations have rendered them unprepared for the 1980s. An important part of Littwin's thesis was that college graduates in less-applied, lower-demand fields were especially vulnerable to floundering. Although Littwin's book was written 35 years ago, prolonged dependency and floundering may be even more common today in the age of "helicopter" parenting. I've found that overprotective parents tend to have anxious children, presumably because they inadvertently teach the children to fear a wide variety of situations that should be part of a normal childhood.

Failure to Launch also appears to share some features with a cluster of behaviors in young adult men that Dan Kiley labeled the Peter Pan Syndrome (1983). In addition to not wanting to assume responsibility, men with this syndrome were found to have a fear of negative evaluation and a tendency toward emotional outbursts when facing stressful situations. According to Kiley, these men often abused substances as a way of escaping difficult feelings. The reader can imagine that, in many cases, anxiety—especially Social Anxiety—may be an underlying factor in young men who fit the profile of the Peter Pan Syndrome.[5]

Of course, it isn't just school success but overall life satisfaction that is impacted by Social Anxiety. The socially anxious young person's social life is typically limited in some ways, almost by definition. In the most extreme cases, she may never be close to anyone outside of her family. Socially anxious children often have few friends at school or in the neighborhood and spend much of their time at home. This can become an even bigger problem the older the child gets. By adolescence, the pathologically shy teen may still not have many friends and may not begin dating when her peers are starting to pair up. Attending dances or going to crowded bars or parties are likely to be the socially anxious adolescent's worst nightmare. This makes it far less likely that an anxious teen will find someone to date.

In today's society, life is only getting more challenging for anxious young people and dating can be especially fraught. During earlier times when young adults tended to be less mobile, socially anxious children and teens were often able to maintain the small circle of friends that they developed during their grade school years, and they frequently ended up dating and marrying someone they had known for years or a person who was introduced by a long-term friend. This didn't require having to meet strangers. Because the socially anxious have less experience in dealing with other young people, they will almost inevitably be less socially adept. They will have had fewer opportunities to learn to understand different personalities, to get along with others, or to navigate social situations, and less experience initiating and carrying on conversations. Initiating a date, which is somewhat difficult for many of us, is undoubtedly even more challenging for a shy person. That is only the first step. When a self-conscious person goes on a date, the first meeting is likely to be very difficult for her, as are the first few that may follow. For these reasons we certainly would expect shy young people to have fewer romantic relationships than their more outgoing peers. Online dating can be helpful for some young singles, but for others, it may be just as intimidating as more traditional ways of meeting and singles who have been communicating with each other online eventually have to meet. Some "matches" who mysteriously disappear may be anxious singles who don't have the courage to meet in person rather than

---

5. Like Failure to Launch, the Peter Pan Syndrome is not an official diagnosis recognized by the APA.

callous "players." Sadly, other matches may not be who they say they are. Although the steps required to meet appropriate singles and get through the first couple of encounters are particularly difficult for anxious young people, their problems relating don't necessarily stop there. Painfully shy people sometimes continue to have difficulty opening up to another person, even if they make it past the initial stages of developing a relationship. The very shy may also be extremely self-conscious when it comes time for sexual intimacy. Men may suffer from erectile dysfunction or premature ejaculation, while women may develop vaginismus, a fear of vaginal penetration and involuntary muscle spasms, that may preclude intercourse.

When Postponed Adulthood Persists

Some socially anxious people continue to live at home with their parents (remember Larry who ran a small mail order business out of his aunt's house) until their parents die, and even then, they may remain in their childhood homes. I had a thirty-year-old client (whom I'll call Alice) whose mother had been bedridden for years with multiple sclerosis. My client stayed in her childhood home in order to help hired nurses care for her mother.

Alice dressed plainly and wore her medium brown hair short as if she were trying not to draw attention to herself. She had an unassuming air about her. Alice had always been shy, and since she had few friends, her mother had been her best friend. Alice had a degree from a small girls' college in her hometown and had managed to get a position that didn't require contact with the public. She did have a long-term boyfriend who had grown up in the same neighborhood.

Alice was home with her mother so much that she became less accustomed to going out into the world and interacting with people even in superficial ways. She began to fear running into neighbors who might want to talk which made it increasingly uncomfortable for her to get out and about. She began having groceries and medications delivered. After her mother died, Alice continued to live in her childhood home even though the neighborhood had started to become dangerous. It must have taken tremendous courage for her to schedule an appointment with me. Although she wasn't actually Agoraphobic, Alice had a very restricted life. Her withdrawal from the world eventually caused her boyfriend to break off the relationship. This example shows how different anxiety disorders can appear very similar. Alice had never had a panic attack, nor did she fear leaving the house early in the morning when she didn't expect to encounter neighbors, but her life was every bit as limited as the lives of some agoraphobics. This underscores the need to fully understand the nature of each individual's anxiety before it can be dealt with. If a clinician assumes that a socially anxious patient's hesitancy to leave her house stems from a fear of having a panic attack away from home, the Social Phobia might not be addressed for some time.

In Anne Tyler's *A Patchwork Planet* (1998) one of the protagonist's shut-in clients has a story that is remarkably similar to Alice's: "I don't know why Ditty Nolan was scared to go out. She hadn't always been that way, if you believe Ray Oakley. Ray Oakley said Ditty's mother had fallen ill with some steadily downhill disease while Ditty was off in college, and Ditty came home to nurse her and never left. Even after the mother died, Ditty stayed on in the Roland Park house where she had grown up." This character probably would have been diagnosed with Agoraphobia since she didn't even leave her house to buy groceries or medication.

Even if they leave their childhood homes, people who are socially anxious are generally less likely to move from house to house, especially if it means going to a new town or state, because moving often requires surrounding oneself with strangers. And the socially phobic among us who aren't raised in a city may be less likely to move to a large city where there are more people in closer proximity to one another. This means that they may not only end up foregoing job opportunities and the chance to meet people from diverse backgrounds, but all of the other advantages, both large and small, afforded by living in a highly stimulating urban environment.

The Socially Anxious in the Workplace

Individuals with Social Anxiety are too often underachievers in work as well as school settings. Like my client Larry, who held three advanced degrees, they may not even manage to obtain work outside of the home due to a fear of interviewing, or they may settle for low-level jobs that only require filling out an application. Even when a socially anxious person does manage to interview for a position, anxiety may interfere with him making a good impression necessary to land the job. They may appear visibly anxious or fail to adequately answer questions. At least as problematic for the anxious person, many positions are never formally advertised. Because these jobs are obtained by knowing the "right" people, job seekers with a wide circle of friends have a distinct advantage. "Networking" is increasingly necessary in order to land the best jobs. This can involve talking to as many friends as possible, going to parties that afford the opportunity to meet someone who may know of a job prospect, and "working the room" at a convention, all of which can be extremely intimidating for a shy person.

Mark Granovetter is well known for developing the theory of the Strength of Weak Ties (1973) that helps to demonstrate why networking can be so important to a person's success. He considers the strength of social ties between two people to be determined by the amount of time spent together, the emotional intensity, the intimacy, and the reciprocity in offering services. The stronger the ties between two people, the higher the number of reciprocal friends they are likely to share. But Granovetter maintains that weak ties best connect one group of people to another group. These weak ties are important because they serve as bridges between the members of different groups who don't ordinarily interact with one another. Because of this, having a lot of weak ties should be especially advantageous to a person who is seeking work. It goes without saying that shy people are probably going to have fewer weak ties since they tend to have a few deep friendships rather than a large number of superficial acquaintances.

Once a shy person lands a job, the difficulties may persist. In positions that involve dealing with people, socially anxious employees will have difficulty carrying out the duties that are central to their job descriptions. Retail sales staff, bartenders, waitresses, receptionists and secretaries all have almost constant contact with the public, and doctors, nurses and teachers deal continuously with people as do professionals in the corporate world. Indeed, with few exceptions, the majority of jobs require frequent interaction with other people. Many socially anxious people probably avoid applying for these kinds of jobs in the first place, which greatly limits their prospects.

Socially anxious people who are employed in their chosen fields are likely to be underemployed because they may only apply for positions beneath their training and abilities. For example, they may obtain a position that requires a bachelor's degree even though they hold a master's or doctorate. Furthermore, whatever level of job they start in, shy workers may fail to advance in their careers due to generally poor social skills in interacting with coworkers, a reluctance to speak in groups or take the lead on a project, or failure to seek a promotion. When it might be advantageous to try to get another job entirely, they may stay with what they know instead.

Even socially anxious individuals whose fears are limited to very specific types of social interaction are likely to be less successful in their careers than they otherwise could have been. I had a client named Justin who was usually very extroverted but had a specific fear of eating in front of others. This meant that he turned down any invitation to dine with colleagues and clients in their homes or at restaurants and never invited anyone to dinner. His boss was insulted when it became obvious that Justin was making excuses not to go to lunch with him. Since he was outgoing at work, the boss and some of his coworkers assumed that Justin didn't like them. This ultimately interfered with his advancement in the company and greatly reduced Justin's own job satisfaction.

Clance's Imposter Phenomenon

Socially anxious young people are more vulnerable to developing Imposter Syndrome or Imposter Phenomenon (IP) which was the subject of several books written in the 1980s. In her 1985 book *The Imposter Phenomenon: Overcoming the Fear That Haunts Your Success*, Pauline Rose Clance describes a group of accomplished young adults who "feel that their success has been due to some mysterious fluke or luck or great effort" rather than attributable to their abilities. "Imposters" may have extensive education and training but still feel they don't know what they're doing. These young professionals experience a great deal of self-doubt and tend to worry excessively. Young adults with Imposter Phenomenon suspect that people expect more from them than they are capable of delivering. They live with the fear that someone will discover that they aren't as smart or competent as they are thought to be.

Newly vetted professionals, such as psychologists and lawyers, who meet with clients behind closed doors tend to suffer from IP more than workers in "hands-on" careers who have to perform in front of others or to produce something tangible because few people other than their clients see them in action. Even young professors who are very much "out in the open" may feel that they aren't as knowledgeable as they are thought to be. The fact that everyone is constantly being rated online makes it impossible to "hide" so that new PhDs may decide not to pursue academic positions. Artists with tangible products aren't necessarily exempt from feeling like imposters. One of my clients made beautiful silver jewelry but couldn't bring herself to market it. She reluctantly sold her creations to friends at ridiculously low prices. I would expect that the Imposter Phenomenon might be even more widespread today in our increasingly more competitive society. The added stress of such a high level of competition could certainly make young workers more anxious.

The Imposter Phenomenon can greatly interfere with a person's success if he allows his self-doubt to influence his behavior. This is when avoidance enters the picture. "Imposters" may lack the confidence even to apply for positions for which they qualify. According to Clance, these self-doubting young adults often limit their goals and tend to stay in positions that are below their capabilities (this is the very definition of underemployment) for fear of having to apply and interview for something more in line with their ability. They also typically overprepare for everything, beginning assigned projects sooner than necessary and working on these assignments for unnecessarily long periods of time. This inevitably wastes time that could have been put toward other work projects, parenting, socializing with friends and family, or simply enjoying the multitude of pleasurable activities life has to offer. Because of this, people with Imposter Syndrome sometimes appear to be workaholics since they put in so much time and effort into trying to live up to what they think people expect of them. The possibility of failure is terrifying to these young professionals. They dread evaluations that could illuminate any mistakes, even though frequent feedback from superiors is the best cure for those who have misgivings about how well they're doing their jobs.

Now let's look beyond the workplace. I discussed dating in the section on young people. Now let's see what happens when an anxious young adult begins a long-term relationship.

Social Anxiety, Cohabitation and Marriage

You might expect it would take a shy person longer to find someone to settle down with. Indeed, Elaine Aron, author of *The Highly Sensitive Person* (1996), points to a study of shy men that found that, on average, they married four years later than their non-shy peers. On the other hand, she reports that this same study found that shy women tended to marry "on time" but "were far less likely to have worked at all." This suggests that the women went directly from financially depending on their parents to depending on their partners.

As touched on earlier, inexperienced young singles may be taken advantage of in a number of ways. Once they are in a relationship, the shy partner may be less assertive, allowing the other person to make most of the decisions. They may hesitate to break off unfulfilling courtships and even stay in abusive relationships. Shyness not only makes it more difficult to enter a relationship but to exit it as well, and when it comes time to marry, a shy person may be more likely to "settle" for someone who lacks the qualities they want in a mate. Aron (1996) speculated that people with low self-esteem may make poor choices in marriage because "they consider themselves lucky if anyone wants them at all."

Cohabitation and marriage may help normalize a socially phobic person's life if the individual manages to find someone compatible despite having limited social experience and dating less than the average single person. The more outgoing partner will likely assume the role of social chairperson in the relationship and, in some cases, have most of the contact with the world outside of the home. While this arrangement may seem ideal to a socially anxious person, the shy partner may become quite dependent on her spouse, as the spouse gradually takes on more of the responsibilities that she fears. This puts the shy person in a position of less relative power, making it harder for her to assert herself in major decision-making as well as in day-to-day living. Seemingly symbiotic partnerships may not be entirely benign. The less shy partner may be controlling and purposely encourage his spouse to become more dependent on him. The socially anxious may remain in abusive marriages partly for fear of navigating the world on their own. Interestingly, Zimbardo, writing in *Shyness* (1977), observed that "men who can't manage or cope in society and break down in one way or another are often cared for by nurturing wives. When wives can't hack it, they're abandoned." The shy person's partner, on the other hand, may become tired of assuming a disproportionate share of responsibility in the relationship. I'll close this chapter with a look at a worst-case scenario for a socially anxious girl.

Irene's Story

Irene was an attractive, brown-eyed, curly-haired blonde with even features who seemed to always maintain a serious expression. Always having been shy, she had never had a best friend or a group of girlfriends. Irene began dating her future husband her first year of high school after having known Gary since kindergarten. Her parents and siblings never thought that the couple was a particularly good match. Even though Irene was a straight-A student, she didn't apply to colleges because she didn't want to live among a group of young people. Instead, she married Gary soon after high school graduation. Never having been academically successful, Gary wasn't a candidate for college. He worked in construction, and the couple remained in their small town that didn't even have a community college. Irene was too shy to interview for a job and ended up doing filing at a relative's insurance agency. But after a few months, Gary became concerned that Irene was flirting with a coworker and insisted that she resign. He began attempting to limit Irene's contact with her parents and two sisters who had been her only social contacts. Gradually Gary started controlling Irene's every move, taking over all of the shopping and insisting that she stop going to church. He resorted to physical abuse if he found out that Irene had seen her family while he was at work. But Gary's emotional mistreatment may, in some ways, have been worse than the physical abuse. He told Irene that she was fat and physically undesirable. His favorite line was that he didn't know how she got her good grades in high school because she wasn't really very smart and had no common sense. Irene was afraid to leave the marriage, not only because Gary had threatened to kill her if she left, but also because the unknown felt even more frightening than living with Gary. By this time, she was almost totally dependent on him and didn't have the confidence that she could manage without him.

Even when Social Anxiety doesn't cause problems that are striking enough for anyone to notice, it can handicap the person nonetheless. For example, no one is likely to question why an old friend married her high school boyfriend without ever having dated anyone else. Sometimes, only the young woman herself knows that she was never happy in the relationship but chose to stick with it for fear of having to negotiate the singles scene. Similarly, we may not think twice when a young acquaintance chooses a small, noncompetitive college in her hometown despite grades that would have gotten her into a prestigious university anywhere in the country. The fear of living among strangers in a dormitory setting is enough to derail the ambitions of a socially phobic young adult.

THREE

Specific Phobia

"The only thing we have to fear is fear itself"—FDR

Darren arrived home with his new girlfriend, Sally, a confident and successful corporate executive in a national company, only to find that she refused to exit the car. It was no coincidence that the family cat was ambling around the yard. Other times, Sally refused to go into a bookstore or café inhabited by a cat. She was terrified to find a rest area along the highway with feral cats. Even opening a holiday card with a picture of a cat on it could give Sally a shock.

Cat phobia is mentioned in Hippocrates's writings describing one of his patients. Much later, Scott Stossel includes a case study in *My Age of Anxiety* (2013) of Giuseppe Pardo Rogue, a leader of the Jewish community in Pisa, Italy, in the 1940s. Rogue was "impaired by crippling anxiety" from a fear of animals. According to Stossel, this fear dominated Rogue's life, leaving him barely able to leave the house for fear that he would be attacked by dogs. After his neighbors got a dog, he managed to find a way to have them evicted. Stossel quotes Rogue in describing his fear: "Its intensity matches its absurdity. I am lost. My heart beats fast. My face no doubt changes expression. I am no longer myself. The panic increases, and the fear of the fear increases the fear. A crescendo of fear engulfs me. I do die, like a coward, a thousand deaths." A young man in the community found this all very puzzling since Rogue had shown great courage in his leadership role. He seemed to be able to handle real threats to his community but was helpless in dealing with his phobias.

Specific Phobia, defined as a persistent irrational fear of specific objects or situations, is one of the most common anxiety disorders. Encountering the feared situation or object can cause feelings of panic (the fight or flight response) and even precipitate a full-blown panic attack. We are all somewhat familiar with some of the more common phobias, like snakes and spiders. There is sometimes a thin line between rational fears and phobias. Fears that don't interfere with a person's

77

functioning aren't considered serious enough to be classified as phobias. Also, realistic fear, such as that experienced when someone is told of an approaching tornado or apprehension after spotting a bear during a hike, would not be classified as a phobic reaction. On the other hand, if a person fears storms to the extent that he is afraid to venture outside if it's sprinkling, he would be diagnosed with a phobia, particularly if his fear prevents him from going to a doctor's appointment or from running a necessary errand. A person who is afraid to go to the zoo because it has a bear exhibit close to the entrance clearly suffers from a phobia. Fears of innocuous objects or situations constitute a phobia when they interfere with a person's functioning in daily activities, work, or social life. It is a matter of degree and constancy.

As is the case with all anxiety disorders, avoidance is the real problem with phobias. The natural tendency to avoid what we fear causes phobias to become handicapping. The fear itself makes for a less enjoyable life, but the avoidance can interfere with a person functioning up to their potential. As with Panic Disorder and Social Anxiety, most of us can identify with people who have phobias, at least to some extent. Many people have phobic-like reactions to certain things like snakes or spiders. And almost everyone can name a few activities that they don't like and would just as soon avoid, like climbing ladders or riding in elevators. While these particular activities can usually be fairly easily avoided without any serious consequences, some phobias can be quite handicapping. For example, people who fear driving (Vehophobia) may not be able to hold a job unless they can get to work using public transportation. While a fear of flying (Aviophobia) may not interfere much in an individual's daily life, it can definitely limit one's ability to take advantage of career opportunities, precluding certain careers altogether. Additionally, being afraid to fly can prevent traveling for pleasure and sometimes create problems in a person's relationships.

It is easy to underestimate the impact that a particular specific phobia can have on a person's life. Even fearing just one thing can prevent the person from living a normal life. Some phobias can have wide-ranging effects. For example, picture a person who fears bridges (Gephyrophobia). This person would have a very difficult time living or working in some of our most popular cities such as Pittsburgh, New York City or St. Petersburg, Florida. This could impact the person's relationships since it would be difficult to visit relatives living in these cities. The fear of bridges would preclude a number of jobs that require traveling to cities with bridges or driving on routes that include bridges.

Corporate executives who need to consult all over the world, traveling salesmen, truck drivers, and taxi drivers are just a few of the workers who need to be able to drive over bridges to perform their jobs. A fear of tunnels (one manifestation of Claustrophobia) could have the same effect. Similarly, a fear of elevators (another form of Claustrophobia) would make it difficult to work or live in a city, stay in many hotels, and even go to some doctor's appointments.

As we saw with the fight or flight response and with Social Anxiety, the tendency to develop specific phobias is an innate characteristic that we share with all animals. From an evolutionary standpoint, we can see that fear of realistic dangers, like snakes and storms, protects all animals—including us—in helping to ensure that we survive long enough to pass on our genes. Indeed, we appear to be "primed" to fear certain things. Snake phobia, for example, has been found to be almost universal among primates, typically beginning around age four in humans. And the fear of strangers is a necessary and protective fear for children and baby animals. Rather than being random, phobias often involve exaggerated adaptive responses to things and situations that are (or would have been) dangers to our lives.

Because of this, our domesticated animals sometimes develop irrational fears that are exaggerated adaptive reactions just as people do. Our cocker spaniel is extremely anxious about storms even though he isn't in any real danger. Loud noises, especially sirens, will send our cat under the nearest piece of furniture. Both storms and loud noises, which could signal the approach of a large predator, are potentially risky to an animal's well-being. But our pets continue to react even after hearing thunder and sirens for many years without experiencing negative consequences. Our primitive amygdala causes us to react in the same way that animals do, since phobias aren't governed by reason.

To date, clinicians have chronicled an exhaustive list of specific phobias. To casual onlookers, these sometimes even appear humorous, but the reality is anything but. The following list illustrates some phobias that can be grouped into three principal categories: fear of animals, illness, and natural phenomenon (along with a miscellaneous category).

Animals

Ailurophobia—cats
Apyphobia—bees
Arachnophobia—spiders
Batrachophobia—frogs

Understanding Anxiety

Cyrophobia—dogs
Entomophobia—insects
Equinophobia—horses
Helminthopia—worms
Ichthyophobia—fish
Musophobia—mice and rats
Necrophobia—dead or dying things
Ornithophobia—birds
Ophidiophobia—snakes
Tigriphobia—tigers

Illness, Injury, Blood

Algophobia—pain
Belonephobia—needles
Emetophobia—vomiting (the potential act of)
Hemophobia—Blood
Hypochondria—Illness
Mysophobia—contamination, dirt and germs
Nosocephobia—hospitals

Natural Environment

Acrophobia—heights
Agoraphobia—open spaces, crowds, or the outdoors
Aquaphobia—water
Astrophobia—storms, particularly thunder and lightning
Claustrophobia—confined spaces
Dendrophobia—trees
Nyctophobia—night or darkness
Phonophobia—a sudden loud noise
Pyrophobia—fire

Miscellaneous

Aerophobia—flying
Amoxophobia—riding in a car
Androphobia—men
Autophobia—the fear of being alone
Claustrophobia—confined spaces such as tunnels and elevators
Coprophobia—feces
Coulrophobia—clowns
Cyberphobia—computers

Dentrophobia—dentists
Didaskaleinophobia—school
Gephyrophobia—bridges
Glossophobia—public speaking
Gynophobia—women
Harpaxophobia—robbers
Iatrophobia—doctors
Metathesiophobia—fear of change
Pediophobia—dolls
Phasmophobia—ghosts
Pseudodyshagia—choking or witnessing someone choking
Somniphobia—sleep
Teraphobia—monsters
Xenophobia—strangers (note: this term originally referred to the
    fear of the unknown)

As the above list illustrates, the number of things that people fear is quite extensive. We can imagine how each of these fears may have evolved to safeguard us from all kinds of life-threatening situations. Being afraid of tigers and snakes is obviously important to our survival. Additionally, fearing dead animals and feces protects us against germs, the fear of heights helps to prevent deadly falls, and the fear of strangers is highly adaptive for young children. Fear of the dark, which is considered a normal aspect of development in children, is logical since many predators hunt at night and crimes are committed under the cover of darkness. Since these fears aren't irrational, they wouldn't be considered phobias unless they were unrealistic under the circumstances or extreme enough to interfere with a person's functioning. For example, being vigilant about snakes during a hike in the woods is normal while the fear of encountering a snake while walking to one's mailbox in the city is clearly a phobia (Ophidiophobia).

Other fears which are less common, such as the fear of clowns (Coulrophobia), fall outside of the three major categories of Specific Phobia. Some of these phobias, such as the fear of dolls (Pediophobia), don't seem as logical and are more difficult to explain. But the fear of clowns makes sense because clowns are large and intrusive strangers. My youngest son would often end up in bed with me after having had a nightmare. He didn't verbalize his fear that a clown would come through his window until several years later. It turned out that a clown had visited his nursery school and come right up to my son in a way that frightened him. Considering that clowns are very unusual strangers, it is certainly rational for children to fear them. As I described earlier, Stranger Anxiety, which is highly adaptive, emerges in babies around seven or eight months of age. Cats and dogs begin to fear strange people and animals at five weeks, while chimps start to react to strangers at around four to six months. Even adults are wise to fear a stranger who appears to be following them. Another phobia in the miscellaneous category, Autophobia, or the fear of being alone, can be particularly problematic especially when the fearful person reaches adulthood and is expected to be independent. This fear would have been adaptive when our ancestors needed to stay in groups to survive. Adults suffering from Autophobia may be reluctant to leave their parents' home or remain in unhealthy relationships to avoid being alone.

As mentioned, some things that phobic people fear, such as horses and fish, can easily be avoided without impacting their lives, but others, like birds, are everywhere. Even the fear of snakes and spiders can be more handicapping than one might think. While it is usually fairly easy to avoid snakes, a snake phobia can sometimes limit a person's life. One of my clients who loved to hike was badly startled by a venomous snake. She reluctantly gave up hiking in favor of other activities after she had a panic attack the next time that she was on the trail. When she began to fear gardening, which had been one of her favorite pastimes, my client realized that her snake phobia was interfering with her enjoyment of life to the point that she needed treatment.

Another of my clients was bitten by a spider while staying at an historic B&B. The painful bite that woke her from a sound sleep resulted in Maureen developing an intense fear of spiders (Arachnophobia). Reasoning that spiders were more attracted to old buildings, she decided to limit her vacationing to newer hotels. This was easy enough to do, although she missed the charm of historic buildings and the opportunity to meet interesting travelers that staying at B&Bs afforded. However, since Maureen's home was eighty years old, she soon started scrutinizing the area in and around her bed before turning in every night. This became increasingly more time consuming, and the anxiety started to interfere with her sleep. Her fear of spiders eventually caused Maureen to move out of her beloved house in her lovely historic neighborhood. She impulsively moved to a brand-new, generic-looking subdivision that wasn't close to her work and friends, thereby greatly reducing her quality of life. Her Arachnophobia that, at first, seemed almost inconsequential ended up having a huge impact on Maureen's life.

A third client of mine was even more handicapped by a fear of the outdoors she developed in childhood (the fear of the outdoors is categorized under Agoraphobia). She didn't remember the trigger, but her mother believed that the fear may have begun when her daughter was stung by a bee shortly after she walked out the front door one morning. Cindy remembers wanting to go out to play with the other children but being too afraid to do so. Since her family wasn't particularly oriented toward the outdoors, she didn't need to go outside, except when she ran errands with her mother or her family went on an outing. On those occasions, the family members would get into the car while it was still inside the attached garage. Cindy remembers spending many hours sitting in the window of her bedroom gazing out "like a housecat." As an adult she has continued to live the life of an "indoor cat." She leaves the house to work, shop, and go to appointments by driving in and out of her attached garage and picking a parking spot as close to an entrance as possible. Cindy's fear has curtailed many potentially pleasurable activities and left her with few friends. Fortunately, she managed to meet and marry a very supportive man who isn't an outdoorsman.

Another client of mine named Grace who was disgusted by vomit (Emetophobia) considered taking her daughter out of nursery school because she was afraid that the child would catch the stomach flu. She also worried about driving her daughter anywhere for fear that the girl could become carsick. Grace began to eliminate all outings that involved driving. This meant foregoing trips to playgrounds and museums and playdates outside of the immediate neighborhood. Grace sought treatment when she realized how much her daughter was missing.

I also have this particular phobia, although mine isn't as severe. I don't think about it unless I've been exposed to someone who comes down with the stomach flu. When this occurs, I have a sense of dread for several days or until I start throwing up. Scott Stossel (2013) and his mother also have a severe case of Emetophobia. In *My Age of Anxiety*, he gives the exact dates that he has vomited over the years. I can imagine that some people with Emetophobia may fear food poisoning, which could cause them to avoid eating out or participating in potluck meals.

Change, the Unknown, and Anxiety

More handicapping than highly specific fears, the more general fear of the unknown (originally labeled Xenophobia which is now used to refer to the fear of strangers or prejudice against people from other countries) could be considered "the mother of all phobias." Remember clinically anxious people are unusually sensitive to uncertainty (Stossel, 2013). Some researchers believe that the fear of the unknown underlies Specific Phobia as well as Panic Disorder, Social Anxiety and Generalized Anxiety Disorder, which I deal with later. Looking at it from an evolutionary perspective, we can see just how basic and important to our survival this fear is. Apprehension of the unknown causes us to exercise caution in confronting unfamiliar situations where unexpected dangers could lurk. A fearless person is more at risk of being killed and not passing on his genes. This is especially the case in the rest of the animal kingdom, particularly for animals who are lower on the food chain with a large number of predators. Stephanie Gorka, an expert on anxiety and alcohol abuse, believes that uncertain threat produces a generalized feeling of apprehension leading to hypervigilance because of its unpredictability in timing, frequency, or duration (Bergland, 2016; see also Gorka et al., 2020).

The fear of the unknown might be considered similar to the fear of change (Metathesiophobia). Both of these fears are potentially very debilitating since we need to confront change and deal with unfamiliar situations on a regular basis. Fear of change is quite natural in children, who are faced with new experiences practically on a daily basis; and it continues into adulthood in some people. The fear of change has kept many people in less-than-ideal living situations, following the same routines for years. We all know someone who has stayed in an unfulfilling career or settled into a relationship that he isn't entirely satisfied with. And many people could improve their lives if they weren't reluctant to move to a new city or state or even to a different house in a more desirable neighborhood. As with many of the phobias, we have all probably experienced some fear of an impending change or had some difficulty adjusting to a major life transition.

Phobias and Developmental Stages

All of life's passages involve dealing with the unknown so that mastering any developmental milestone requires courage for a child to venture forward. Entering day care or nursery school, elementary school, and high school all involve tackling many changes. Going into a classroom full of fifteen to thirty unfamiliar children with an adult stranger leading the group is undoubtedly intimidating for most young children. This can result in vulnerable children developing School Phobia (mentioned in relation to Social Anxiety) which is characterized by an intense and persistent fear of going to school (School Phobia will be dealt with at length in a later chapter). Going off to middle school, high school and college can sometimes be just as difficult for anxious teens.

Not knowing what to expect is an especially big factor in post-secondary education, because it often involves a young adult moving out of their childhood home and often leaving their hometown in addition to attending a new school. Navigating college is particularly difficult for students whose parents and siblings have not attended college. These first-generation students are at a distinct disadvantage in that they are far less familiar with everything about the college experience. This includes knowledge of what they need to do to prepare themselves academically, which universities are likely to accept them, ways to finance their educations, and being able to picture what to expect in day-to-day life on a college campus. Parents of first-generation students don't know how to advise and support their teens, much less how to pay for tuition and room and board.

After finishing school, the graduate is often expected to negotiate a number of major transitions. Starting a new job, leaving home, and possibly moving to a new geographic location all involve much uncertainty as the young person confronts a host of unknowns (the reader will recall that these changes all appear on the Holmes and Rahe Life Stress Inventory, 1967). Moving to a new city, especially in another state, can be particularly difficult since it involves a myriad of changes both large and small.

In addition to these major life events, smaller day-to-day changes can also be challenging for some people. For instance, some anxious people fear going to a new doctor or dentist. Even trying a different grocery store, retail shop, or beauty salon can be challenging for fearful people. They can end up becoming creatures of habit and never consider whether to try shopping at a new store much closer to home or going to a different beautician recommended by a friend with a good haircut. Friends may describe these individuals as set in their ways. These are people who vacation in the same spot every year without contemplating trying a new location for variety.

Acquired Phobias

In addition to fears that seem to be innate, or to have "arisen out of nowhere," phobias can be responses to innocuous animals, objects, and situations that develop from classical conditioning and generalization. The reader may remember John Watson's (1920) famous experiment involving Little Albert and the white rat. Young Albert was conditioned to fear the harmless lab rat that he had been playing with earlier. The experimenter interrupted Albert's play with the rat by introducing a sudden loud noise (remember that children, like most young animals, are innately afraid of loud noises, especially if they're not expected). Albert developed a fear of the rat through its association with the noise. Later studies illustrated that it was easier to condition someone to fear certain potentially dangerous things like snakes than harmless others such as the tame rat (some Musophobic people whom I know would take issue with the rat being considered innocuous).

Specific Phobia can develop outside of the laboratory by chance through this same process of classical conditioning. Persistent phobias are often triggered by an incident in a person's distant past. The person doesn't necessarily even remember the original event. For example, the woman with the severe cat phobia had been scratched by a cat when she was nine months old—too young to remember the encounter. My youngest son does remember being terrified when the clown came to his preschool when he was three years old. Sadly, this was one of his earliest memories. My oldest son has an intense dislike of horses because a horse nipped at him when he tried to pet it when he was five years old. I probably wouldn't have remembered the encounter with the horse if I hadn't happened to take a picture right before the animal snapped at him. My client who feared the outdoors thinks that there was an incident during her childhood although she herself doesn't remember it. Many children have acquired the fear of going to the doctor's office after receiving a shot, and this fear can generalize to the dentist's office or even to the barber shop. I have a number of phobias that have been with me since childhood.

As a child I had an intense dislike of dead fish. When I was growing up, we used to walk along a river in order to get to our downtown. We had to pass an area where people fished, and there were always a few dead fish lying along the riverbank. The whole area smelled of rotting flesh. I remember leaping up from a meal the first time that I saw a whole fish on my father's plate. The interesting aspect of this was my younger brothers' reactions to my disgust over the fish, as it illustrates that phobias can develop through the process of modeling (i.e., we can develop phobias by observing other people who are afraid of something). Both of my brothers developed an aversion to any kind of fish.

This example also illustrates how highly specific phobias tend to be, since I had no problem with live fish. If I happened to spot a dead fish lying at the bottom of the tank at the local Woolworths, this was another story. I also had trouble with worms and remember dreading my walk to school after a storm when worms littered the sidewalk. Surprisingly, I had no fear of snakes, dead or alive. As I have emphasized, phobias are by definition irrational. My idiosyncratic list of phobias goes on. Along with my disgust of dead fish, I have an extreme fear of any dead mammal. While some of my friends fear mice, I am perfectly comfortable handling a mouse or having one live in my house. If our cat kills a mouse, however, I need to ask my husband to handle it. Once when he was out of town, I summoned a friend's husband to deal with the mouse. The same trips past the fishing area to our downtown required us to pass a huge dam and cross a large bridge, another thing that I found terrifying. I still have nightmares of being swept over a waterfall or stuck in the middle of a bridge that has broken in half and I find it difficult to drive over long bridges.

As I have emphasized, and as is the case with all of the anxiety disorders, phobias are more handicapping when combined with the natural avoidance response. Rather than forcing oneself to confront the feared thing or situation and finding out that nothing catastrophic happens, avoiding something serves to perpetuate the fear. For example, if a child who is afraid of the dark isn't encouraged to gradually conquer his fear, he may continue to use a night light into adulthood. Far more handicapping, children who fear insects or birds may be afraid to venture outside. As was the case with my client's fear of the outdoors, this would obviously become extremely restricting if it weren't dealt with. If a child isn't encouraged to conquer this fear, he'll miss out on playing outside with the neighborhood children and may not develop an appreciation for the beauty of the natural world. And this avoidance will only become more handicapping over the years when he needs to go outside in order to function in the world. I had another young adult client who feared birds after seeing Alfred Hitchcock's *The Birds* as a child. She had organized her life in such a way that she spent very little time outside of her house.

You will recall that Maureen, who feared spiders, ended up selling her historic home, and my other client gave up her gardening hobby until she obtained treatment for her snake phobia. The woman who feared cats started making excuses so that she wouldn't have to spend time at her boyfriend's house even when he closed his cat into a spare bedroom. A client was so afraid of needles that she put off dental work until her teeth were badly decayed. Although her hair and makeup were always impeccable and she always wore the latest fashions, Emma's teeth became unsightly before she finally went to a dentist who sedated her before every procedure. While phobias can cause much discomfort, they are far more handicapping when a person gives in to the fear and begins to avoid situations in which he might encounter the feared thing.

The Ultimate Fear

Probably the ultimate fear is the fear of death (Thanatophobia), a certainty that involves a great deal of uncertainty. Thanatophobia took center stage in Don DeLillo's classic *White Noise*, where the main character Jack Gladney is plagued by a fear of death. Because many people are afraid of death, this fear is generally considered a normal part of the human condition. Philosophers and writers, along with psychiatrists (e.g., Freud, 1929; Frankl, 1959), have been grappling with this topic for centuries. From an evolutionary standpoint, this fear has the deepest roots of all, as the fear of death is our most basic survival instinct. Barry Wolfe (2005) maintains that fear of the "ontological givens"—"that we grow old, that we will die, that we will lose people we love"—underlies almost all anxiety disorders. Some who have written about the fear of death have speculated that anxious people manage to dwell on trivial fears to avoid thinking about the big ones. Historically, death was ever-present, and people of the leisure class had more time to contemplate it. Today we have more distractions and less time to think about it, but for some of us, fear of death is there.

Sarah Ward described her fear of death in "Little Stories" in the *New York Times* (2020). She wrote, "When I was little, I used to rush into my parents' room at night to ensure that they were breathing. As I grew older, I became increasingly preoccupied with death: Why do we do anything if the end is inevitable? Filled with existential dread, I'd burrow in bed for weeks." Ironically, Ward was able to conquer her fear by working for a hospice.

The fear of death can emerge as soon as children are able to grasp the concept of dying. Since his cat died six months ago, my five-year-old grandson has become aware of the fact that every living thing dies. Phillip mentioned wanting to adopt a kitten rather than a slightly older cat, which his parents would prefer—not because the kitten would be cuter, but because it should live longer. He also told me that he doesn't want to turn six because he doesn't want to get older and die. In its extreme form, death anxiety can stop people from leaving their homes for fear of life-threatening dangers or contamination. The following example illustrates the impact that severe Thanatophobia can have on a person's life.

Karen's Story

Karen is an attractive sixty-seven-year-old woman who looks considerably younger than her years. She is slim and trim, wearing her sleek light brown hair shoulder length. Her green eyes, still accented by dark lashes and brows, haven't lost their vibrancy, and her smile is wide and contagious. Karen has always been very social, active and athletic. She can remember fearing death from early childhood after she attended her grandmother's funeral. After the funeral, she had trouble falling asleep, and she experienced panicky feelings every morning when she awakened to the thought that she would eventually die. Years later, Karen again became preoccupied with death when two of her grandparents died during her middle school years. She recalls looking at her surviving grandmother and being struck by the fact that she herself would someday be old and frail. By the time that her grandparents' deaths became a more distant memory, Karen was very busy living her life as a working mother of three and was able to take comfort in the fact that her own death was probably a long way off. She didn't think much more about dying until many years later after her children had left the area and she had retired. Retirement afforded Karen more time to think, and now her own death was a mere twenty or twenty-five years away. Karen became panicky at this realization and developed a number of symptoms of Generalized Anxiety Disorder, another manifestation of anxiety which will be dealt with later. A few bouts of mild dizziness made Karen reluctant to leave the house alone for fear that she could have a fatal car accident or pass out during a walk and sustain a head injury. She also began worrying about having a terminal illness and started scrutinizing her body for signs of something amiss. Karen became fearful when her husband traveled overnight, because this meant that there would be no one to call 911 if something happened to her. What had begun as a fairly mild phobia had gradually become a severe case of Agoraphobia that had taken over her life.

This example demonstrates how persistent phobias can be; they often begin in childhood and continue throughout a person's life. This vignette also illustrates how the strength of a particular phobia waxes and wanes over the years depending upon what is going on in the person's life. As in Karen's case, phobias often become worse during times of stress or transitions like retirement. Not only was retirement a big adjustment for Karen, but it afforded her more spare time to worry. Working at a fulfilling career and raising three children had kept her busy and distracted from thoughts of death.

As in Agoraphobia, phobias can be eliminated through a process designed to reverse the avoidant behavior. After the Little Albert experiment, a researcher by the name of Mary Coven Jones was able to desensitize "Little Peter," who had been conditioned to fear rabbits. She gradually reintroduced him to a rabbit while feeding him his favorite snacks. The pairing of the rabbit with something that Peter liked enabled the boy to pet and then play with the rabbit. My third son developed a fear of dogs when he was around four years old after a large dog ran toward him when we were walking in the neighborhood. This was especially problematic because he began to fear our daily walks. After we adopted a dachshund puppy, Jeff's dog phobia seemed to evaporate almost immediately.

It is sometimes difficult to differentiate between Specific Phobia and other anxiety disorders that affect a person's behavior in the same way, even though the underlying fear in each disorder is entirely different. Specific Phobia can often look like Social Anxiety. Social activities may be limited by phobias even if a person is generally comfortable in most social settings. For example, even the fear of heights or elevators could cause a person to turn down an invitation to a rooftop party. It can also be difficult to know whether a housebound person is suffering from Specific Phobia or Agoraphobia. If a person fears dogs, for example, this could result in the same reluctance to go outside as seen in Agoraphobia. Indeed, one study found that 86 percent of a small sample of people initially diagnosed with Agoraphobia were later found to suffer from Specific Phobia (Horwath et al., 1993). In Specific Phobia the fear centers on potential harm that could be directly caused by the situation (being bitten by a neighbor's dog after going outside) while in Agoraphobia the fear centers on whether escape is possible or help available in the situation (would anyone help the person if something happened to her on a walk?).

Indeed, Specific Phobia, Social Anxiety and Agoraphobia can all have the same end result. Any one of these disorders can make it difficult for a person to hold certain jobs, to enjoy some social activities, and even to buy groceries. We will see in the next chapter that the fear of having a serious illness (Hypochondria) and scrutinizing one's body for symptoms can be difficult to differentiate from Obsessive Compulsive Disorder. Even Anorexia, in some cases, may be attributable to the fear of choking. Scott Stossel (2013) describes developing this fear as an adolescent. His chronically high level of anxiety had caused his mouth to be dry resulting in him having difficulty swallowing. This led to a fear that he would choke which in turn caused him to stop eating lunch at school. This reluctance to eat in the cafeteria continued long enough for him to become very thin.

FOUR

Obsessive Compulsive Disorder (OCD)

There is some controversy as to whether Obsessive Compulsive Disorder (OCD) is in fact an anxiety disorder. My clinical experience has convinced me that it is. Some basic questions can offer insight into OCD. You might ask yourself, "Have I been bothered by an overconcern with keeping items like clothing or tools in perfect order or arranged exactly so? Do I worry frequently about terrible things happening, like a fire or flood? Do I perform certain acts over and over again, like grooming, or checking locks or light switches? Do I repeat certain mundane acts like closing a door a certain number of times or until it feels just right?" These are just a few of many possible indicators of OCD. Online, the Anxiety and Depression Association of America as well as Psych Central offer relatively brief but comprehensive screeners that contain questions like these to determine if someone might need to see a mental health professional about OCD. Along with general strategies for reducing anxiety, I will present some specific methods for OCD management in Chapter Seven.

Obsessive Compulsive Disorder can involve obsessive thoughts alone or a combination of obsessive thoughts and the compulsions to act on them. Obsessions are defined as persistent thoughts, impulses or images that seem intrusive and inappropriate, even to the person who is experiencing them. They are intrusive in the sense that they are not the kind of thought that the person suffering from OCD wants to have. Indeed, these thoughts are often quite the opposite of what the individual would like to think. And the harder the person tries to suppress the thoughts, the more persistent they tend to be. Individuals will often avoid situations that are related to their obsessive thoughts. Quantity and quality matter, as the *DSM-IV* specifies that a diagnosis of OCD is warranted only if the thoughts or compulsions are severe enough to take up more than an hour a day or cause marked distress or significant impairment.

Obsessive Thoughts

Imagine having the thought of driving off the road into a ditch. This idea might begin when a person driving along a narrow mountain road realizes that he could accidentally drive over the edge of the mountainside. Our driver might experience a moment of panic when the thought first crosses his mind. He would naturally attempt to suppress the frightening thought for fear that, by making him more anxious, the thought might actually cause him to lose control. Focusing on the unwanted thought in an attempt to suppress it can paradoxically make it harder to ignore. The harder that the anxious driver tries not to think about it, the more persistent the thought is likely to become. We can see that this process could result in the person deciding not to take the road that he was driving on when the thoughts first occurred. This is when avoidance enters the picture and makes the obsessions far more impairing.

One of my clients who became obsessed over a dangerous curve on his route to work lost an hour a day taking a more circuitous route to avoid the bad stretch on the more direct road. This was the only thing that enabled him to stop the recurrent thought that he was going to lose control of his car at a particular spot. In Woody Allen's *Annie Hall* (1977), Allen's character is faced with receiving a ride to the airport from another character who has recently confessed that "sometimes when I'm driving ... on the road at night.... I see two headlights coming toward me. Fast. I have this sudden impulse to turn the wheel quickly, head-on into the oncoming car."

If my fearful client had been able to calm down by reassuring himself that he probably wouldn't lose control, he likely would have been able to let the obsessive thought go instead of dwelling on it and becoming more anxious. This is what most people manage to do. Just as we all have panicky feelings from time to time, and we all dislike some things that phobic people fear, we all have random thoughts, some of which are unusual or disturbing. A person who doesn't suffer from OCD doesn't become overly concerned about the thought and doesn't continue to dwell on it. According to the *DSM-IV*, the most common obsessions are fear of contamination, repeated doubts (wondering whether you have performed or forgotten some act, such as having hurt someone in traffic or failed to lock a door), or a need to have things in a particular order. These obsessive thoughts are usually not related to real-life problems.

As with all anxiety disorders, obsessive thoughts are likely to first crop up during a stressful time in a person's life. In my client's case, he was experiencing problems with a coworker. This made him anxious driving into work since he dreaded his encounter with the coworker. As with Panic Disorder, Agoraphobia, Social Anxiety and Specific Phobia, obsessive thoughts are the most problematic when they lead to avoidance. In my client's case, avoiding the stretch of road added an hour to his workday which could have been better spent.

OCD often takes a more diffuse form and manifests as a tendency to worry. There seems to be a superstitious component to obsessive worry. Worrying can feel like doing something proactive even though it has no real effect on the outcome of the worrisome situation. When a person feels helpless, worrying can feel as if they are actually doing something to address a problem. It can even seem that if they worry hard enough, they can prevent a feared result. Religious people can obtain this same relief by praying. Historically, when people had even less control over their life circumstances, many of our ancestors were more religious than the majority of people are today. Aristocratic women portrayed in films spend a lot of time praying in their private chapels when their husbands are away in battle or when their children are sick.

Some people feel uneasy when things seem to be going too well and begin to worry preemptively. For these individuals it doesn't feel normal when things are going smoothly. In her semiautobiographical book *Paula* (1994), Isabel Allende writes, "At moments of great success, I do not lose sight of the pain awaiting me down the road...." Allende's life was punctuated by tragedy, so it was understandable that she was always anticipating that something could go terribly wrong. Anxious people sometimes feel that even though everything is going well at a particular time, things could always change.

In a fascinating study Fishback et al. (2020) postulated that "those experiencing pathological worry are set apart from healthy controls by their beliefs that worry has utility and that effective worrying requires them to consider all possibilities before terminating a worry bout." He theorizes that "worriers with a good capacity for cognitive control (of their worry) may engage in prolonged worry because they believe it is adaptive to do so."

More specific obsessive thoughts may represent a person's worst fear, as was the case for one of my patients who couldn't banish the thought that he might accidently let his beloved six-month-old daughter's head slip under the water when he was bathing her.

Rick's Story

Rick was a handsome, well-dressed young businessman. A devoted father, he was horrified by the thought that he might accidentally allow his daughter's head to slip under the bathwater, and began to fear that the thought might actually be an unconscious wish. Rick remembered that he had thought that it was too soon to have a child when his wife first found out that she was pregnant. The original thought had morphed into the idea that he might unconsciously want this to happen. On one level Rick knew that these thoughts represented his worst fear and that he would never let his precious daughter drown, but the thoughts were naturally very disturbing. The sheer shock of the horrific thought made Rick extremely anxious and caused him to fixate on it. This caused the thought to recur and persist every time that he had to give his daughter a bath. The harder that he attempted to suppress it, the more persistent the thought became. Rick felt guilty for having the thought and began to wonder whether he was a bad person. This guilt naturally increased his already high level of anxiety that the abhorrent thought had generated. Rick began trying to avoid being the one to bathe his daughter which led to arguments with his wife who got home from work later than he did.

The possibility of something happening to one's child is every parent's worst nightmare. When one of my clients first held her newborn daughter, she felt overwhelmed with love. Sadly, instead of being able to bask in this feeling, her first thought was that now she was vulnerable because she could lose this beloved child.

Guilt and self-criticism often play a role in OCD. In Rick's situation, he felt guilty because of his uncertainty about being ready to have a baby when his wife found out that she was pregnant. The guilt only exacerbated his anxiety. Had it not been for his guilt, Rick might have been able to quickly dismiss the thought by thinking something along the lines of "What a silly thought. I must be reading too many bizarre news stories" or "I must be taking Freud's ideas too seriously." When Rick began to realize that he was feeling guilty for not immediately being excited about his wife's pregnancy, he was able to accept that this initial reaction didn't mean that he loved his daughter any less. He also came to understand that he and his wife had been under tremendous stress in trying to juggle their demanding full-time careers while caring for their daughter. This and their high expectations for themselves as parents caused much anxiety for Rick which took the form of obsessive thoughts. The young parents were able to take steps to reduce this level of tension. Both Rick and his wife were able to pare down their schedules at work and lower their expectations of being perfect parents.

Rick's story is one more instance of anxiety cropping up during times of transition and stress. The adjustment to bringing home a new baby is a perfect example of the fact that even a joyous event can involve considerable stress. In fact, becoming a parent ranks #14 on the Holmes and Rahe Stress Scale (1967). This anecdote also illustrates that the avoidant behavior resulting from a disturbing thought can be a bigger problem than the annoying thought itself. The unwanted thought made bathing his daughter far less enjoyable for Rick, but his attempts to avoid doing the bath began to cause arguments with his wife and put a strain on their marriage. This particular example needs to be differentiated from a person who hears voices and might actually do what the voices tell him to do as in Paranoid Schizophrenia (a severe mental illness which is not an anxiety disorder). There have been a number of tragic news stories about a parent murdering her child because she was hearing voices that instructed her to do so.

Obsessive Impulses

Obsessions that take the form of impulses to do something socially unacceptable, morally wrong or dangerous are particularly likely to result in avoidance. This can sometimes greatly limit a person's life. The following example from my cases illustrates the effect an obsessive impulse can have.

Barbara's Story

Barbara, a middle-aged homemaker who looked somewhat older than her forty-five years because of her conservative dress and hairstyle, was a very religious woman who found a great deal of comfort in going to church and enjoyed seeing her friends in the congregation. She came to see me after she began feeling an impulse to stand up in church and start shouting obscenities. Fearing that she might actually act on the impulse caused Barbara to stop attending church services which had been her main social outlet. The irony of this was that Barbara never swore, even in the privacy of her own home. As also illustrated in Rick's case, an obsessive person sometimes thinks that having these kinds of thoughts makes him a "bad" person or that he is seriously mentally ill, neither of which is the case. Barbara decided that she was sinful and grappled with a great deal of guilt for having sacrilegious impulses. This was made even worse by the additional guilt that she experienced after missing each Sunday service. The guilt in turn made her more anxious which increased the frequency of her impulses. Barbara even began to feel the impulse to scream obscenities when she was shopping for groceries.

The impulse to blurt out something inappropriate is not particularly uncommon. This form of obsession has appeared in literature from time to time. In *A Patchwork Planet* (1998), Anne Tyler's young adult protagonist describes a tense dinner with his parents. "All through supper I kept fighting off my old fear that I might burst out with some scandalous remark. It was more pronounced than usual." This passage depicts the character's longstanding impulse which was more extreme at that specific time. The character lived with guilt for not being the high achieving son that his parents had hoped for. This portrayal is consistent with the fact that obsessive impulses can persist over many years and tend to get stronger during times of stress. Ironically, the young man had just gotten out of an expensive reform school and appeared to be getting his life on track. His parents' expectations for him to turn his life around were apparently too much for him. This also illustrates that even positive expectations others have of us can be a source of anxiety if we fear we may not be able to live up to them. You will recall this aspect of the Imposter Phenomenon.

Guilt and OCD

These examples underscore the role that guilt often plays in OCD. Sometimes the person actually has a reason to feel guilty, but just as often the guilt involves a very minor transgression or simply an unwanted thought. Rick's guilt over initially thinking that it was too soon to have a baby contributed to his obsessive fear. Barbara was having sexual fantasies and accompanying guilt. She had managed to repress these thoughts but then ended up dwelling on something entirely unrelated (blurting out profanities in church) and began to suspect that she was a bad person. Had she affiliated with a religion that encourages confession, confessing her feelings might have enabled Barbara to let go of the guilt. As her therapist, I was able to assure her that many good people have similar fantasies about sexual feelings; they don't mean that someone is immoral. While we have control over our actions, we have little command over our thoughts and feelings and shouldn't hold ourselves accountable for random thoughts or impulses that cross our minds. According to the *DSM-IV* individuals with OCD have a pathological sense of responsibility. This could certainly contribute to guilt.

Guilty thoughts can be productive if they motivate a person to make amends for something harmful that she has done. And this can help to ameliorate the anxiety that the guilt generates. One of the simplest but sometimes most difficult ways of dealing with guilt is to apologize to someone we have hurt. Taking action to rectify something harmful that we have done can be especially therapeutic. This is the principle behind having delinquent teens who have wronged someone perform some type of community service or engage in another type of restorative justice process. Indeed, rational guilt, along with empathy, has enabled mankind to live together in a cooperative and just manner throughout history.

Regret, a close relative of guilt, often involves a person obsessively dwelling on something he wishes that he hadn't done or bemoaning a missed opportunity. Many of us live with the idea that life could have been much better if we had chosen a different path. Regret is defined as a feeling of sadness, repentance, or disappointment over something that has happened or been done. Woody Allen quipped, "My only regret is that I'm not someone else." Regret is also a close cousin to worry in that it involves ruminating over something that a person has done or failed to do. Like guilt, regret can be productive if it motivates a person to turn his life around. But when it doesn't lead to a constructive change, regret only serves to increase a person's anxiety.

I've found that a high number of my patients with OCD also have features of Obsessive-Compulsive Personality Disorder. According to the *DSM-IV,* the central characteristic of this disorder is "a preoccupation with orderliness, perfectionism, and mental and interpersonal control at the expense of flexibility, openness, and efficiency." One of the most striking features of Obsessive Compulsive Personality Disorder is difficulty in making decisions both large and small. A person with a tendency toward obsessing is painfully aware of the fact that every time he makes a decision, he is choosing one fork in the road and by doing so eliminating other paths. This is why obsessive-compulsive individuals are often indecisive to the point that they fail to take necessary action to improve their lives. They often end up staying in less-than-ideal jobs or relationships and may maintain lifestyles that don't suit them.

Andrew Miller has written a thought-provoking book on the nature of choice, aptly titled *On Not Being Someone Else: Tales of Our Unled Lives* (2020). The thesis of his book is basically that every decision we make precludes another choice. One of the characters in Emma Straub's 2020 book *All Adults Here* describes this reality but puts a positive spin on it when she muses: "'You know what I've been thinking about?' Rachel asked. 'All the people I could have married. The good news is that I think you have to stop when you have children, because you know, whoever you give birth to wouldn't be there if you'd made different choices.'"

It's not just the large, important decisions but small, day-to-day decisions that are difficult for a person with Obsessive Compulsive Personality Disorder. This can slow a person down as they go about their day. In my work at the university, students who came in complaining of procrastination often had features of this personality disorder. Often the procrastination resulted from their underlying perfectionistic tendencies.

An obsessive person who is acutely aware of the fact that taking one path eliminates other possibilities may be virtually immobilized and consumed with angst. Angst is defined as a pervasive feeling of deep anxiety or dread that tends to be unfocused. The anxious person often experiences a feeling of vague apprehension which, along with the fear of the unknown, could be partially attributable to the person's failure to make decisions necessary to move on with life.

Images and Flashbacks

Sometimes obsessions take the form of images that keep popping into a person's head. A student of mine who had never even had a minor fender bender couldn't suppress the visual image of his car crushed in a horrific accident. He traced this thought back to a frightening video that he had seen in his high school driver's training class. At first this thought mostly interfered with his concentration while he was driving, but as time went on, the thought began cropping up while he was trying to study. This distraction made it necessary for Ben to study for longer periods of time and greatly reduced the effectiveness of his study sessions. This example illustrates how obsessive thoughts, images and impulses which initially occur in particular situations can generalize to similar situations and start emerging at other times. In Barbara's case, she began to worry that she might yell obscenities at the grocery store if she was forced to wait in a long line. She began trying to get her already overworked husband to do more of the shopping. Barbara's worry even creeped into pleasurable activities such as shopping for clothes that had always been a distraction from her worries. She started to obsess about blurting out something to the effect that "this f-ing dress is the ugliest thing I have ever seen."

Even though a person with OCD realizes at some level that his thoughts, impulses or images are out of character, and that he won't act on them, the thoughts themselves often disrupt his day-to-day activities. At the very least, obsessive thoughts are distracting and can interfere with any activity such as studying that requires concentration. But once again, the bigger problem is the avoidant behavior that is the logical result of the thoughts. Avoiding situations associated with the thoughts like driving to work, parental duties, and necessary day-to-day chores causes a person to be far more handicapped. The fact that it took our driver an extra hour to get to and from work every day extended his already long workday. And Rick's avoidance of giving his daughter baths was beginning to affect his marriage. In addition, in both Rick's and Barbara's cases, avoiding enjoyable activities reduced day-to-day pleasure. Rick had thoroughly enjoyed watching his daughter splash in the water during her bath and had prided himself in sharing parental responsibilities with his wife. Barbara had always looked forward to seeing acquaintances at church and had found singing the hymns uplifting. She had especially enjoyed shopping for clothes, since shopping had actually distracted her from her worries and was a good outlet for her nervous energy.

Less dramatic thoughts than those in the previous cases involve the fear of contamination or doubts about remembering to do something such as locking a door. People are more inclined to act on these mundane thoughts, since they aren't irrational, the action can often easily be completed, and the person feels that they're addressing the problem. Doing something in response to a thought can temporarily lessen the anxiety that the thought has generated. This is when compulsions enter the picture.

Compulsions

Compulsions are defined as repetitive behaviors (e.g., handwashing, ordering or checking) or mental acts (praying, counting, repeating words silently) a person feels driven to perform in response to an obsessive thought or according to rules that must be applied rigidly

Four. Obsessive Compulsive Disorder (OCD)

(*DSM-IV*). The behaviors or mental acts are aimed at preventing or reducing distress or preventing some dreaded event or situation. However, these behaviors or mental acts either are not connected in a realistic way with what they are designed to neutralize or prevent or are clearly excessive (*DSM-IV*). Extreme compulsions can eventually take over a person's life, resulting in relationship and social problems as well as difficulty holding a job. Consider a perfectly rational thought that most of us have had at one time or another: "Did I lock the front door when I left?" It is easy enough to check the door again if you have only walked as far as the car. But what if your thoughts return throughout the day, disrupting work and making you want to run home to check yet again that the door is locked?

Some compulsive behaviors result from superstitious ideas that have been incorporated into societal folklore such as "step on a crack, you break your mother's back" that or bad luck follows a person who has seen a black cat.[1] The person usually realizes that these beliefs are totally irrational but feels compelled to adhere to the magical thinking. However, many compulsive behaviors are highly idiosyncratic. Compulsive behaviors may be futile attempts to exert some control even though we have no control over a particular situation. Taking an action feels like we're doing something productive. According to the *DSM-IV*, the most common compulsions are washing and cleaning, counting, checking, requesting or demanding reassurances, repeating actions, and placing objects or engaging in actions in a particular ordering.

As with the other anxiety disorders, OCD, particularly the fear of contamination, probably has its roots in our evolutionary history. That is, some compulsive behaviors would be adaptive if they weren't excessive. For example, our ancestors who liked to keep things clean may have survived in greater numbers than their less fastidious peers. Discussing evolutionary advantages and cleanliness during the Covid pandemic, Elias Aboujaoude (2020) makes this analogy: "Giraffes with long necks could reach high up food sources and thereby survived to reproduce at higher rates than short necked giraffes. In a similar process of natural selection, humans with a psychological horror of germs survived the evolutionary competition with germ-neutral ancestors. OCD may represent the extreme end of an adaptive trait that protected our progenitors from diseases potentially far worse than Covid-19."

---

1. The superstition surrounding black cats is thought to have started as far back as the Middle Ages (Nikolajeva, 2009).

This probably explains why a tendency toward compulsive cleaning is extremely common.

Although a tendency toward compulsions is usually chronic, compulsive behaviors are most likely to first emerge when a person is under stress or dealing with a major change. The compulsions tend to wax and wane depending upon the amount of stress that the person is experiencing. Also, the tendency toward compulsions can take different shapes depending upon what is happening in a person's life. It's not surprising that excessive cleaning became the compulsion "du jour" during the Covid pandemic. Many people reported spending more hours cleaning than ever before. The stress of dealing with the risk of getting seriously ill along with the increased time spent at home makes cleaning the perfect outlet for anxiety. Given how contagious the virus was, the cleaning was logical and constructive, if at times excessive. Indeed, cleaning can be a good way to channel stress since a clean and organized home can be calming. Cleaning can even be considered therapeutic. Not only is it goal directed and productive, but it can also distract a person from worry and allow her to work off anxiety. It is certainly a better way to cope with stress than drinking or smoking. However, excessive cleaning can eat up many hours in a person's day that could be spent in better ways. A client's husband hired a bi-weekly cleaning service in hopes that this would reduce the time that she spent cleaning. He stopped the service when he realized that his wife was not only cleaning before the cleaners arrived but also cleaning immediately after they left.

There are many examples of compulsive behavior. One of my clients, who worried that she could develop cancer, spent up to an hour a day scrutinizing her body for lumps and signs of skin cancer. This was a sizable portion of her already busy day and tended to be even more extreme when she was under stress and could least afford to be wasting additional time. Kleinknecht (1986) describes Compulsive Slowness, a rare disorder that leads individuals to spend hours completing simple tasks such as getting dressed and doing household chores. This would seemingly make it impossible for the person to hold a full-time job.

Another of my clients was a graduate student who had received incompletes in all of his classes one semester because he felt the need to spend hours a day cleaning his apartment and organizing his desk before he tackled his schoolwork. Of course, this behavior would be labeled procrastination, which has a number of underlying causes including OCD. Greg found graduate school extremely stressful. His anxiety led to the compulsive cleaning which was so time consuming that it caused him to miss deadlines on papers. The more worried Greg was about a particularly important assignment, the more he cleaned and the more poorly he performed academically. Receiving a low grade on a given project naturally increased Greg's anxiety, causing him to ramp up his cleaning efforts, ultimately becoming a vicious cycle. By the time that he came in to see me, Greg was spending an average of three or four hours a day cleaning and organizing. If he could have channeled some of this anxious energy into studying, it would have been adaptive, but being too anxious to concentrate, Greg put his nervous energy into excessive cleaning. Of course, this couldn't have been more counterproductive, since it used up the time that he needed to spend studying. His poor performance in his graduate program eroded Greg's self-esteem and even brought about thoughts of suicide.

OCD has been the subject of a number of films, my favorite being *As Good as It Gets* starring Jack Nicholson. In addition to compulsive checking and handwashing, Nicholson's character has a number of more unusual compulsions. He avoids stepping on cracks and intermittently blurts out insulting remarks to whomever happens to be nearby.

Compulsions can crop up at any age. One of my clients who had a mild case of OCD herself noticed that her extremely precocious two-year-old granddaughter was already showing signs of compulsive behavior. One of Maddie's first words was "messy," and she was already keeping her toys and books in order. She also spent some time flipping through her picture books and smoothing out each page.

Some years ago, I had a nine-year-old client named Jason who, when doing his homework, felt the need to dot all of his "i's" in a particular way for fear that something would happen to his mother if he missed an "i." Even at nine years of age, Jason realized that this was irrational and that his efforts couldn't protect his mother. But he couldn't let go of the behavior. Compulsively checking every "i" to make sure that each of his dots were perfect circles caused him to spend hours doing homework that should have taken twenty minutes. It turned out that Jason was under a great deal of stress because his overly critical fourth grade teacher tended to focus on him. Jason's resulting anxiety manifested itself in this seemingly unrelated compulsive behavior. Once the source of the stress was recognized and dealt with, Jason's compulsions seemed to almost magically disappear.

Making differential diagnoses between OCD and some of the other anxiety disorders isn't always easy. Sometimes obsessions and compulsions involve the fear of acting out behaviors that would be so embarrassing to a person that the compulsive individual becomes afraid to go out in public. When this happens, it is difficult to discriminate between OCD and Social Anxiety or Agoraphobia. Remember that my client who first worried that she might shout obscenities in church began to fear that she might do this at the supermarket or in a dress shop. Barbara had progressively curtailed a number of necessary and pleasurable activities by the time she came to see me.

Hoarding in Life and Literature

Hoarding behavior, which is often associated with OCD, deserves special attention in this section. Hoarding disorder, new to the *DSM-5*, is defined as "a persistent difficulty in discarding possessions, regardless of their actual value, to the point where the person's accumulated goods congest living areas and impede their intended use." Hoarded items may include items that just about anyone except the hoarder would consider worthless. Joan Acocella, writing in *The New Yorker* (2014), describes the hoarder as follows: "they tend to go in for energetic collecting, often at inexpensive emporia, thrift shops, yard sales and the like." Hoarding is related to other anxiety disorders beyond OCD. In fact, 25 percent of hoarders suffer from Social Anxiety and some agoraphobics' houses appear to be hoarders' havens.

Hoarding is a particularly good example of an adaptive behavior gone awry. In our past, people who socked away enough food to get through a severe winter or a period of drought undoubtedly survived in larger numbers than their less prepared neighbors. Costco and other wholesale clubs probably owe their popularity to our tendency to try to keep our homes well stocked. Hoarding becomes handicapping when the sheer number of belongings that the person accumulates starts to make life more difficult. The most common materials hoarded are newspapers, magazines, old clothes, bags, books, mail and paperwork, but cash and checks are sometimes mixed in with the junk. The end result of hoarding can be a house crammed with newspapers and magazines stacked floor to ceiling, necessitating walking through "tunnels" in order to navigate the clutter. Hoarding can even be dangerous when excessive "stuff" blocks doorways, when flammable materials are stored too close to heat sources, or when a firearm is lost amidst the mess. In one reported case, a hoarder's situation became so deplorable his granddaughter was not allowed to visit (Kilbride, 2010).

Four. Obsessive Compulsive Disorder (OCD)

Claire had a severe case of Hoarding Disorder and had filled her home in part with purchases from television home shopping. Anyone meeting this fashionably dressed and carefully groomed woman would never have guessed the chaos that she returned to when she went home. She admitted that visitors could barely make it through the door of her apartment and told me her family was afraid of what might happen if there was a fire. Claire's situation was similar to that of a pair of brothers from a wealthy and prominent New York City family who have become almost famous. Homer and Langley Collyer, both educated at Columbia, lived as recluses in a large Manhattan brownstone they had inherited. They were found dead amidst tunnels of debris, including thousands of books, fourteen grand pianos and passbooks to bank accounts with what would be worth about $30,000 today.

There are several houses in our neighborhood that have boxes stacked floor to ceiling in every inch of their front porches, suggesting that the owners have run out of space inside. In one case, newspapers and magazines fill an old car that hasn't moved from the curb in front of the house. Again, hoarding is more common than you might think. Many people whose yards and houses look perfect can't get their cars into their garages because the garages are so full of junk that no longer fits into the house. Those with smaller houses who don't have garages are forced to rent storage spaces to accommodate the overflow. Indeed, the storage industry is booming in a way that wouldn't have been predicted fifty years ago. One of my retired clients, who had struggled with anxiety for years, decided that she needed to go back to work to cover the expenses incurred on her frequent shopping trips. This also gave her less time to shop, meaning she wouldn't need to rent additional storage space. Wealthy hoarders sometimes have multiple houses crammed with their collections of furniture, accessories, and souvenirs.

As with the other anxiety disorders, we can all identify with not being able to part with certain sentimental objects. This has even spawned a new profession that we started to hear about around the turn of this century. Many women are hiring organizers to come into their homes, with a special focus on their closets, to help them to decide what to part with. In fact, Marie Kondo's concise book *The Life Changing Magic of Tidying Up* (2010) was on the bestseller list for some time. There have also been a number of books on downsizing and simplifying our lives. A monthly magazine titled *Real Simple* was introduced in the 1990s. The magazine is dedicated to making our lives easier through simplification and organization.

Hoarding has been the subject of several films and books. The 2009 film *Grey Gardens* is based on a true story of a mother and daughter who filled a dilapidated twenty-eight-room mansion with junk and garbage along with a large number of cats and kittens. The two were Obsessive Compulsive, Agoraphobic, and likely delusional. They had their food delivered and rarely left the house but still managed to accumulate an astonishing amount of stuff. Discarded carry-out containers and empty cat food cans littered the floors in every room. The film was especially interesting as the daughter had a flair for drama which presented itself as dressing up in outrageous costumes and twirling around the four rooms of the mansion that were still inhabitable. She aspired to perform onstage, and her mother encouraged her despite the daughter having no talent. Although these women—who were close relatives of Jacqueline Kennedy Onassis—are portrayed in a way that suggests that they were able to keep up their spirits in spite of living in squalor, other hoarders become depressed and even suicidal.

Hoarding has been featured in literary fiction as far back as Charles Dickens's *Bleak House*. Dickens described a character's shop where "everything seemed to be bought and nothing to be sold." Sherlock Holmes, in Arthur Conan Doyle's detective series, was described as having a "horror of destroying documents" to the point that "every corner of the room was stacked with bundles of manuscripts." More recently, Lisa Jewell's *The House We Grew Up In* (2013) describes a family affected by their matriarch's hoarding. A nonfiction book aptly titled *Stuff: Compulsive Hoarding and the Meaning of Things* by Randy O. Frost and Gail Steketee (2010) provides a look into actual hoarders' lives.

Tourette's, Kleptomania, and Related Syndromes

Tourette's Syndrome is a lesser-known disorder that also appears to be related to OCD. Indeed, 50 percent of patients diagnosed with Tourette's have symptoms consistent with OCD. Although Tourette's is often chronic, it becomes worse when the person is under stress. You may have heard of Tourette's because it has been featured in several films, most recently *Motherless Brooklyn*, loosely based on the 1999 novel by Jonathan Lethem, as well as the Jack Nicholson film *As Good as It Gets*, referred to earlier. This condition is characterized by a person making inappropriate comments or having loud outbursts for no discernible reason. It often starts with a tic, such as excessive eye blinking, and progresses to the point that the person is unable to stop himself from saying or shouting nonsensical phrases. In *Motherless Brooklyn*, the character interjects his speech with wildly irrelevant phrases such as "Consensual reality is both fragile and elastic" and "It heals like the skin of a bubble." Jack Nicholson's character blurts out mostly insults to innocuous people he happens to encounter. That Tourette's can be extremely handicapping goes without saying. Nicholson's character lived alone and was portrayed as not having any close friends, a not-uncommon scenario for a person with severe OCD and Tourette's. The protagonist in *Motherless Brooklyn* could barely carry on a conversation because he kept interjecting nonsensical phrases. In the latter film, this character with Tourette's was a brilliant detective who wouldn't have been able to hold a job without his partner who helped deal with the public for him. While these are fictional characters, they are portrayed in fairly realistic ways.

Trichotillomania, a rare psychiatric condition that was originally classified under Impulse Control Disorders in the *DSM-IV*, has been reclassified as an obsessive-compulsive related disorder in the latest version of the *DSM*. In fact, Trichotillomania is sometimes referred to as compulsive hair pulling. It is characterized by a person pulling out hair from any part of her body, but especially the scalp, eyebrows, and eyelashes. This disorder is clearly related to anxiety and becomes worse during times of stress. A related disorder which is somewhat more common is Dermatillomania. It manifests as persistent picking at the skin on one's face, chest, arms, legs, or fingers. The compulsive picking can result in permanent scarring. Like Trichotillomania and other anxiety disorders, Dermatillomania becomes worse during periods of stress and when a person is especially anxious. Once again, this type of behavior may be far more common than we realize. Nail biting, which shares some similarities to picking at the skin, affects a sizable proportion of children between the ages of ten and eighteen and continues into adulthood for some people. When extreme, nail biting can lead to infections and scarring.

Dermatillomania could be considered related to excessive grooming that is sometimes observed in other animals. Our closest relatives engage in grooming behavior to remove ticks and other parasites. Grooming in apes and monkeys is a highly social behavior that has been observed to reduce tension in the groomer as well as the recipient of the grooming. Excessive grooming, or Psychogenic Alopecia, is sometimes a form of stress relief for cats. If medical reasons for the grooming, such as fleas, ticks, and allergies, are ruled out, excessive licking is probably a cat's response to stress. This would seem to be similar to picking at the skin in humans. We humans, especially women, often find it relaxing to have facials and manicures.

Another rare disorder which is now classified in the same section as Obsessive Compulsive Disorder (*DSM-5*) but was classified in the *DSM-IV* under Somatization Disorder is Body Dysmorphic Disorder (BDD). Body Dysmorphic Disorder involves obsessively focusing on a perceived flaw in one's appearance. The flaw is either very minor or even completely imagined. One of my clients called me because he feared that a large lesion covering half of his face was a sign that he had AIDS. I was relieved when he came to the office with no lesion. This was at the height of the AIDS epidemic before life-saving medicines were available. My client, who was prone to anxiety, had been under stress at work and had recently found out that a friend had AIDS. The focus in Body Dysmorphic Disorder can be on the person's face or body. When the face is involved, the person may spend hours a day studying themselves in the mirror and attempting to fix the problem. This might involve inordinate time applying makeup to hide imperfections and even obtaining plastic surgery. When the focus is on the body, BDD can lead to Anorexia, Bulimia, or excessive exercising. One of my clients who was of normal weight became convinced that she was overweight and spent hours a day exercising despite having three young children and a full-time job that kept her quite busy.

Kleptomania, which is classified under Impulse Control Disorders in the *DSM-5*, can have underlying obsessive-compulsive features. Most people are familiar with this disorder. Every now and then, we hear about a high-profile person being caught leaving a store with some item that he could have easily afforded. Some people who suffer from Kleptomania describe having an urge to steal an object (worthless to them) and becoming increasingly more anxious until they have managed to take it. The urge to steal (the obsessive impulse) is temporarily satisfied when the compulsive action (sneaking the object out of the store) is completed.

My client Edith, described below, sought treatment for Kleptomania, which made even routine trips to the grocery or drugstore a cause for anxiety and guilt.

An extremely religious and ordinarily very honest forty-year-old professional woman who sought treatment with me described experiencing the urge to steal items that she noticed in stores but had no personal use for.

Four. Obsessive Compulsive Disorder (OCD)

Edith's anxiety would build until she had taken the object and made it out of the store. At this point tremendous guilt would set in. Edith started becoming fearful when she had to shop for groceries or go to a drug store because she anticipated not being able to suppress the urge to steal. This fear heightened her anxiety, thereby increasing her urge to take something. Kleptomania appears to be exacerbated by stress, and like all of the anxiety disorders, tends to wax and wane depending upon what is going on in the person's life. My client was grappling with guilt over not conforming to some of the strict principles of her conservative religious background. Kleptomania sometimes results in a person's house being crammed full of the objects he has stolen. This would earn him a secondary diagnosis of Hoarding Disorder.

Some patients with Borderline Personality Disorder (BPD) share some features with people with OCD. The thoughts and feelings underlying the cutting and self-harm that are the most striking features of BPD are sometimes similar to those in OCD. Some Borderline patients describe having an impulse to cut or otherwise harm themselves along with a build-up of anxiety that is released after the cutting. Individuals with BPD often have a history of having been physically, emotionally, or sexually abused as children. Many carry a great deal of anxiety, unwarranted guilt, and anger that they sometimes direct toward themselves. Indeed, some cutters are engaging in compulsive self-mutilation. It could also be argued that one of the eating disorders shares some features with OCD. Some of my patients with Bulimia reported feeling anxious before they purged and relief afterward.

While readers may not recognize some of the more unusual forms of compulsion, I believe these rare disorders have similar underlying features in anxiety as compulsions to shop or hoard—much more common tendencies. Now we will move on to another common anxiety disorder which presents in a more subtle way but can greatly affect a person's quality of life often without the person recognizing the extent of her underlying anxiety.

FIVE

Generalized Anxiety Disorder (GAD)

I began the book with Panic Disorder because I think of it as the most basic form that anxiety takes. Panic, caused by the fight or flight response, seems to be the very essence of anxiety. While the symptoms of Panic Disorder are striking, the attacks themselves are delimited. In contrast, Generalized Anxiety Disorder (GAD) is subtle but persistent. Of all of the anxiety disorders, it can be the most difficult to recognize because it's often poorly understood by the person suffering as well as by her friends and family. It is well hidden. Shortly, I will introduce you to Susan, who, while shy as a child, would later develop full-blown GAD. First, consider two screening assessments for Generalized Anxiety Disorder that will give you an idea of the day-to-day struggles that a person with GAD experiences.

GAD Screening Batteries

The Anxiety and Depression Association of America offers a screener that can be completed and shared with a health care provider. The screener begins by asking about excessive worry and about whether an individual is troubled by worrying uncontrollably about *minor things*. The respondent is then asked to list the topics that cause the most worry. Next, the respondent is asked to think about the past six months and how often the person has been bothered by feeling keyed up or on edge, being easily fatigued, experiencing muscle tension, having difficulty falling asleep and experiencing other physical problems related to GAD. Finally, the individual is asked how much he or she is bothered by worry overall and how much the physical symptoms interfere with work, social activities, etc.

Likewise, in *Worry*, Hallowell (1997) offers a self-assessment screener. Hallowell's screener takes an even simpler form, where the individual answers "yes" or "no" to questions like "Do you find something to worry about even when you know everything is OK?" "Do others comment on how much you worry?" "Do you lose perspective easily, worrying over some relatively minor matter as if it were a major concern?" "Do you tarnish good times with worry?" "Do you worry about health in a way that you know or others have told you is excessive or irrational?" "Do you develop physical symptoms in response to stress?" Hallowell poses an extensive list of questions, fifty in all. Collectively, responses indicate whether an individual is not an excessive worrier, is in the potential danger zone with some tendency to worry, or solidly in the danger zone and should consider consulting a professional. I recommend sitting down and taking the time to complete the online GAD screener by the Anxiety and Depression Association of America as a way of becoming familiar with the symptoms of GAD.

Susan's Experience with GAD

Susan, a natural beauty with smooth, flawless skin and golden-brown hair, has the looks of a young woman who could have broken many hearts. From a middle-class family with educated parents, she was expected to go off to college after her high school graduation. Instead, she has continued to live with her mother in the small apartment that her mother rented after she and Susan's father divorced.

Susan worries almost constantly about anything and everything. She has a number of minor health problems and fears that each new symptom could signal a life-threatening illness. Susan worries about her future, especially in regard to whether she will ever have a boyfriend and marry, but she is even more preoccupied with fears of potential day-to-day calamities. She worries that she may get food poisoning or that someone could break into the apartment while she and her mother are sleeping. Susan also scrutinizes her cat's behavior for fear that the cat might be sick.

Susan has always been considered exceedingly shy. She has no friends and has never had a boyfriend. In high school she was a loner who attended classes without interacting with the other students and went straight home after school. Susan's grades suffered somewhat because she missed quite a lot of school due to different illnesses, however, she would have been able to get admitted to a number of universities. But the idea of college seemed too intimidating for her to even consider. For a while, after graduating from high school, Susan was employed in the bookstore where her mother worked because she was able to get the job without interviewing. Although the job sorting books in the back room was perfect for a shy person, she began to miss

*work because of an array of physical symptoms such as dizziness, nausea
and headaches and lost the job after two months. Her mother regards Susan
as an unmotivated underachiever and has given up trying to encourage her
to do more. She now wonders if she had always overestimated her daughter's
abilities.*

As is so often the case, Susan's anxiety symptoms came to a head when
she was confronted with a major transition during an already stressful
time in her life. Her parents' divorce shortly before Susan's high school
graduation created the perfect combination of stressors to precipitate
an anxiety disorder—a distressing event and a major life passage. While
Susan had always found attending school highly stressful, she had
become used to the structure and didn't have difficulty getting reasonably good grades. Upon graduating, she was expected to do something
entirely different. The idea of going off to college or getting a job caused
her so much anxiety that Susan became overwhelmed and immobilized.
In addition to her long-standing Social Anxiety Disorder, she now had a
full-blown case of Generalized Anxiety Disorder (GAD).

As mentioned, I began the book with Panic Disorder because the
fight or flight response is the basic anxiety response. All of the anxiety disorders involve this response, usually to a lesser intensity. I close
this section of the book with GAD because, in my opinion, it is the most
all-encompassing form of anxiety. The physiological symptoms of GAD
are due to a sustained low-level fight or flight reaction. Although this
is the basic physiological component of fear that we share with all animals, GAD includes a cognitive component (i.e., worry) that is unique to
humans.[1] Like panic, it's ubiquitous in humans all over the world.

According to the *DSM-IV*, GAD's characteristic features are anxiety, which is manifested by a constellation of physiological symptoms,
and excessive worry. We can think of the physiological symptoms as
similar to but considerably less intense than those experienced during a
panic attack. Unlike the extreme but short-lived reactions in Panic Disorder, this lower grade physiological agitation is more or less constant.

---

1. The intolerance of uncertainty (introduced in relation to Specific Phobia) may also
be an especially central feature of GAD (Dugas et al., 2004). These authors believe that
people with GAD find ambiguity stressful and upsetting and that they have difficulty
functioning in uncertain situations. They go on to point out that since everyday life is
filled with uncertainty, a person who is intolerant of uncertainty can easily find numerous "reasons" to worry. According to this line of reasoning, we might expect some
patients with GAD would agree with the statement "When everything is going well now,
I worry that things could change." Dugas et al. (2004) have developed a scale of 27 items,
including "uncertainty keeps me from sleeping soundly."

In other words, a person with GAD is in a perpetual state of mild fight or flight arousal.

Bandelow et al. (2013) describe GAD as a "common and disabling disease." They write that it is characterized by worry about "extant dangers whose likelihood is overestimated and whose negative consequences are viewed as catastrophic." These authors conclude that "worries can rapidly generalize to multiple areas of every day experience including health, family relationships and their occupational or financial situations."

GAD patients are undoubtedly born with systems characterized by high reactivity which shows up as an exaggerated startle reaction that continues throughout their lives. They may begin to develop symptoms of GAD in childhood or adolescence (50 percent) or young adulthood (50 percent) (*DSM-IV*). Feelings of low-grade panic and free-floating anxiety tend to wax and wane depending upon what is happening in the person's life. As Susan's case exemplified, they are more pronounced during times of change and when the person is under stress, but in the end, GAD is the most prevalent anxiety disorder in the elderly (Mantella et al., 2008).

The worry in GAD is by definition either unrealistic or excessive. According to Craske et al. (1987) and Ruscio et al. (2005), it often concerns minor matters. I think of this worry as fairly realistic but blown out of proportion to the person's actual life circumstances as Kessler and Wittchen (2002) maintain. In almost all cases I've encountered, GAD sufferers find their worry difficult or impossible to control. Most important to my thesis, Ruscio et al. (2005) found that 70 to 80 percent of worriers reported functional impairment in household, occupational, interpersonal or social functioning. This illustrates that worry isn't just annoying but often quite handicapping.

Although GAD is one of the most common anxiety disorders, it is also one of the most hidden and can be easy to miss. We all probably worry about some things from time to time, and many of us have some physiological symptoms that are related to stress. Because of the array of physical symptoms, a sufferer may be more likely to consult her family doctor than a mental health practitioner.

Even if the anxious individual goes to a psychiatrist or psychologist, her low-grade generalized anxiety is often overshadowed by a less subtle anxiety disorder, such as Panic Disorder, since one or more of the other anxiety disorders frequently accompany GAD (*DSM-IV*). In Susan's case she would have been diagnosed with Social Anxiety in addition to GAD. GAD may also be mistaken for other psychiatric conditions. The restlessness and difficulties falling asleep that are often part of GAD have sometimes led to anxious people receiving diagnoses of Attention Deficit Hyperactivity Disorder (ADHD) and Bipolar Disorder (formerly Manic Depression) that aren't warranted. Bipolar Disorder has been the diagnosis "du jour" for some time. I believe that countless people have been incorrectly diagnosed with this serious mental illness and placed on psychotropic medications that muddy the picture and don't improve their conditions. This isn't to say that GAD doesn't sometimes co-occur with ADHD or Bipolar Disorder.

The struggles of one of my clients illustrate the confusion in diagnosing underlying GAD. This 38-year-old college graduate I'll call Doug had not worked in years due to profound depression. The last four of those years had been spent lying on his father's couch because he was unable to care for himself. When Doug came to me, he was carrying a diagnosis of Bipolar Disorder and was on a cocktail of different medications, including two mood stabilizers, several antidepressants and heavy doses of tranquilizers. In years past, when someone presented with a diagnosis of Bipolar Disorder, I knew exactly what I was getting. The client had typically been hospitalized after a manic episode, administered Lithium until he was stabilized, and released under a psychiatrist's care. With Bipolar Disorder a go-to diagnosis for some years, it's often difficult to sort out exactly what's wrong with a patient when he's been given this diagnosis (Bipolar Disorder is actually quite rare, affecting approximately 2.8 percent of the U.S. population). After many sessions, I came to realize that Doug most likely had a long history of Generalized Anxiety Disorder, along with ADHD, before he had become depressed. Some of his symptoms of GAD, including panic attacks, restlessness, and sleep difficulty, were mistaken for mania. When a psychiatrist started gradually reducing and eliminating some of his medications, Doug was able to function much better and began to talk about finding a job. This bright young man had lost years of his life thanks to a misdiagnosis.

As with the other forms of anxiety, there may be an evolutionary explanation for high reactivity and worry. We were all primed toward focusing on potential danger to survive long enough to procreate and raise our offspring. Just as the fight or flight response was crucial to survival, a continuous state of low-grade arousal could have ensured that a person would remain vigilant and react quickly to a sudden threat. It was adaptive to worry about being able to make it through the winter or being attacked by a tiger if this meant storing enough food and taking precautions to avoid getting eaten.

While we might expect people who have had difficult lives to experience more physiological symptoms of anxiety and to worry more, this isn't necessarily the case. Those of us who have had fairly stable and secure lives aren't exempt from excessive worry. The propensity to worry is undoubtedly something that some of us are born with.[2] Others develop generalized anxiety from trauma, particularly in childhood.

It can be tricky to determine whether the physiological manifestations of GAD stem from the worry or if the worry is an outgrowth of the bodily reactions. One theory is that the constant anxiety and low-grade dread that characterize GAD cause the patient to search for explanations for her feelings. In other words, the person with GAD may actually look for something to worry about. Worrying, in turn, can feed physiological arousal, making the person feel more anxious and perpetuating a vicious cycle. This is a likely explanation since many GAD patients seem to have been born with a tendency toward high arousal. I will focus on the worry component of GAD first.

The Designated Worrier

The worry in GAD is, by definition, excessive and difficult to control so that it can interfere with the sufferer's ability to concentrate on other things, but in contrast to the illogical fears that characterize Phobic Disorder and OCD, the focus of the worry in GAD is usually not completely unreasonable or entirely irrational. Those with generalized anxiety tend to worry about day-to-day problems involving themselves or their loved ones just as we all do from time to time. Most of us have experienced a few mild symptoms of Social Anxiety, Specific Phobia, OCD and even PTSD and this may be especially true in regard to GAD. In fact, the worry characteristic of GAD wouldn't be abnormal if it weren't excessive and long-lasting. Because of this, it is not surprising that people suffering from GAD often assume everyone worries like they do, particularly since they have been living with these symptoms for so long. Several of my clients responded incredulously, stating something to the effect of "You're telling me that everyone doesn't worry like this?" As with Social Anxiety and OCD, the worry in GAD sometimes takes the form of self-critical thoughts.

---

2. Worriers can take comfort in the fact that their anxiety has taken a higher form than the pure panic of PD involving the primitive brain that we share with all animals. Worry involves the more evolved prefrontal cortex which can channel free-floating anxiety into something more tangible that could lead to productive action.

Understanding Anxiety

Although people suffering from GAD tend to be perpetually worried, the worry is often shaped by what is happening in a person's life. As with all forms of anxiety, worry is exacerbated during stressful times and major life transitions. Anything can become the focus of worry. As I theorized earlier, it's almost as if a person with a propensity to worry looks for a target for the worry. Fishback et al. (2020) predicted and found that high GAD symptoms were related to the belief that worry has utility. Some people with GAD actually seemed to value their worry. Several of my own patients felt that their worries were part of their identity although, as Fishback et al. (2020) point out, this seems incongruent with the fact that these same GAD patients described their worry as excessive and uncontrollable.

As mentioned, we all worry to some degree. Consider Janet, a fairly "normal" worrier who wouldn't necessarily be given a psychiatric diagnosis because her symptoms lasted less than six months. Janet was a student who spent considerable time agonizing about her upcoming dissertation defense. This is not too surprising given the stressful nature of completing the hurdles in a doctoral program which culminate with the oral dissertation defense. The defense involves a group of four to six professors asking questions about the student's research, sometimes in a room full of other students and professors. But after Janet passed her oral defense, she still couldn't stop worrying. The worry had seemingly taken on a life of its own. With the original focus of her worry removed, Janet began to fear that things were going too smoothly at work and to wonder if she was performing well enough. She also had a vague feeling that something terrible could happen to someone in her family. Even though Janet knew that these worries were irrational, she had difficulty putting them out of her mind. Janet began to have trouble not dwelling on newspaper articles that described misfortunes and tragedies, fearing that similar mishaps could befall one of her loved ones. Her worry wasn't completely irrational. Although they were statistically very unlikely, the worry was focused on events that could conceivably happen. Janet wasn't able to relax and let go of these worries until several months later. Considering her anticipatory anxiety leading up to her defense, Janet had been miserable for four or five months around something that lasted less than two hours.

The worry in GAD is distinguished from the worry in OCD and Specific Phobia by the fact that it is usually more rational and less intense and tends to be focused on more varied situations depending upon what is happening in a person's life at the time. Typical worries in GAD may include fears about health problems, worrying about family members and worrying excessively about the future as well as a general fear of dying. These are all things that normal people sometimes think about from time to time. Health problems are at the top of the list because, as we will see, many of the physiological symptoms of GAD mimic serious medical conditions including heart problems. A different but common type of worry in GAD involves replaying social mistakes as the Social Phobic does. The person with GAD may live with chronic guilt that is entirely unwarranted.

The worry that characterizes GAD can actually be productive if it inspires action. For example, worrying about the future can be constructive if it leads to planning. Worrying about failing an exam could motivate a student to study, while worrying about a house fire might prompt a homeowner to install smoke detectors. Remember, from an evolutionary standpoint, worry helped us survive. Here again, we can see that an adaptive trait can become problematic and handicapping at its extreme. Much of the worry associated with GAD is, by definition, nonproductive. The worry often takes the form of a vague feeling of apprehension that can cause a person to shy away from taking risks necessary for success.

Worriers might take comfort in the finding that worry may be correlated with high IQ, at least in GAD patients. According to the results of one study in *Frontiers of Evolutionary Neuroscience* (Coplan et al., 2012), high IQ scores were directly related to higher levels of worry in GAD patients. In other words, the higher the person's IQ, the more inclined they were to worry rather than to just report a host of physiological symptoms. Along this line, Wolfe (2005) wrote that his smarter patients tended to be the most anxious.

When Worry Is Maladaptive

Chronic worry can be quite handicapping to a person's success and can certainly interfere with his enjoyment of life. In *Worry*, Hallowell (1997) states that "the final common pathway for underachievement is often excessive worry. A person can hold himself back by pouring over the dangers of a new idea." Hallowell goes on to describe a patient of his who had all kinds of creative business ideas but always ended up second guessing each new scheme, thereby managing to talk himself out of following through on his ideas.

As I've pointed out, because we all worry once in a while, worriers often assume that everyone agonizes like they do, even though their worry is clearly excessive. This makes it less likely it will occur to them to consider treatment. As I mentioned, more than a few of my clients who had come to me about another problem were quite surprised to realize that most people didn't worry as much as they did. But worry is not innocuous. It significantly interferes with an individual's ability to concentrate, particularly during activities that require intense and sustained focus. And worry can certainly suck much of the joy out of a person's life. Recall one of the items on Hallowell's quiz: "Do you tarnish good times with worry?"

Once again, avoidance is an even larger problem. Worrying is even more encumbering when it causes a person to avoid necessary activities and potentially fulfilling experiences. It's natural for a person to attempt to avoid situations and experiences that generate worry. Indeed, it's adaptive to do so when worry is rational. For example, a person who isn't worried about a hurricane threatening his home on the coast may fail to evacuate to a safer area. People not worrying about a pandemic may become quite sick or even die. On the other hand, if worry causes a person not to take a job that could involve infrequent flying, it can derail the person's success. If someone is so worried about catching the flu that she curtails all social activities during flu season, this will limit her pleasure in life, at least during the winter months, and she may lose friends by repeatedly turning down their invitations to get together.

As with the obsessive worry seen in OCD, there is often a superstitious component to the worry characteristic of GAD. At some level, a person feels that if he worries hard enough, he can prevent the thing he fears from happening. Rationally he knows that worrying can't control the outcome of whatever he is brooding about but worrying feels proactive. One of Hallowell's items reflects this: "Do you feel compelled to worry that a certain bad thing might happen, such as a business deal falling through, or your child not getting picked for the team, or your financial situation collapsing, out of an almost superstitious feeling that if you don't worry the bad thing will happen, while if you do worry about it, your worrying might actually prevent the negative outcome?" Irrational worrying can be an individual's attempt to exert control over something that is completely out of the person's control. The dedicated worrier feels that they are taking preventative action even though they're likely to be immobilized by the worry and often don't actually do anything.[3]

---

3. This is reflected in two items on Hallowell's quiz: "Do you tend to brood over possible danger rather than doing something about it?" and "Do you become immobilized by worry?"

Five. Generalized Anxiety Disorder (GAD)

The worry that characterizes GAD isn't directed toward one or two things or situations as it is with Specific Phobia. This worry tends to be more general and all encompassing, although, as I have pointed out, the specific content of the worry will fluctuate over the course of time depending upon what is happening in the person's life. And when everything is going well, the person with GAD will often still manage to find something to worry about. Hallowell (1997) describes one of his patients who admitted that he "worried constantly, but especially when things were going well." Some GAD patients acknowledge that everything is going reasonably well for them but couch this with the disclaimer that things could change quickly.

A tendency toward feeling guilt, which is often completely unwarranted, is sometimes part of the picture in GAD. Worriers sometimes feel that they don't deserve good things or that there is a balance between good and bad that evens out over a person's life. The example of Isabel Allende (1994) cited earlier illustrates the feeling that one doesn't deserve too much joy or success when others are suffering. Allende's grandfather's philosophy that life is "strife and hard work" had a lasting influence on her. She felt she didn't deserve any good fortune that came too easily to her, and she was sometimes uncomfortable when things seemed to be going especially well. Again, these examples illustrate the superstitious nature of worry.

The epitome of this phenomenon is Survivor's Guilt, a syndrome characterized by a person feeling that they should not have survived a trauma which others didn't. Survivor's guilt is sometimes a symptom in PTSD. A close cousin of this condition might be a phenomenon characterized by an individual's realization that he had advantages and luck that a sibling did not. This is especially likely to occur when a sibling has a serious disability. Consider the book *I Know This Much Is True* by Wally Lamb (1998). The main characters in the book and its film adaptation are identical twins. One suffers from severe mental illness. At times, the healthy twin's life is overshadowed by his brother's problems. The normal twin seems to live with the feeling that he doesn't deserve to enjoy a better life than his brother has. This underlying guilt, which he doesn't seem to necessarily be conscious of, may shed some light on his propensity for self-destructive behavior.

The excessive worry characteristic of GAD is especially troublesome for students who need to be able to concentrate for long stretches of time, but it also interferes with a person's work, social activities, and overall enjoyment of life. For example, a person who worries about her health may spend a great deal of time and money visiting doctors. Additionally, she may miss work or perform poorly because she is distracted by worry. She may not enjoy spending time with family and friends because her worries are always in the back of her mind. And she will have difficulty enjoying the moment if she is distracted by worry. That worriers sometimes turn to alcohol and drugs (both prescription and illegal) to quiet their minds is especially problematic and can even lead to an accidental overdose or suicide.

The Body's Response to GAD

The second component of GAD, and its most characteristic aspect since it distinguishes it from the other anxiety disorders, is the array of physiological symptoms that accompany the worry that I've described. As noted earlier, these physical symptoms indicate that the person with GAD is often in a perpetual state of low-grade "fight or flight" arousal. The reader will recall that Susan's physiological symptoms were the most handicapping aspect of her condition because they resulted in her missing school and work. Most people with GAD manage to function better than Susan, whose symptoms were extreme and complicated by her Social Anxiety, and Doug, whose underlying anxiety was masked by side effects of his drug cocktail. The source of their problems is typically far less obvious. The following case study illustrates how GAD can impact a life even when the person appears to be functioning quite well and exemplifies how worry and physiological symptoms go hand in hand. It also illustrates generalized anxiety's hidden nature. Our focus will now turn toward the physical manifestations of GAD, but worry is incorporated into the vignette, since it was part of this patient's profile and is usually part of the picture in GAD, almost by definition.

Joanne's Story

Joanne is a 71-year-old, well-educated and fun-loving retired professor of sociology. She has a bounce to her step and appears to be full of energy. With her sleek hairdo and stylish wardrobe, along with her contagious laugh, Joanne lights up a room. She travels extensively and enjoys a large group of friends who would be surprised if they knew the extent of her anxiety.

Joanne's childhood was fairly unremarkable in regard to stressful events. She had loving parents, grew up in a small Midwestern town and lived in the same house until she went away to college. Joanne did describe always having been restless for as long as she could remember and having been told that she had a lot of nervous energy. Additionally, she remembers worrying about her parents from a young age. Her mother remembers Joanne being a colicky, hard-to-soothe baby.

Joanne's physiological symptoms of GAD began early. She recalls waking up one morning at age nine feeling short of breath and a little weak. She stayed home from school that morning but felt better within a short period of time. Joanne didn't miss any more school, and after about a month, these symptoms gradually dissipated and didn't recur. The only other indication of anxiety in her childhood that she could remember was difficulty falling asleep. This began after she went to her great-grandmother's wake. Joanne couldn't stop picturing her great-grandmother lying in the open casket and had a recurring nightmare that the casket was at the foot of her own bed. The reader may recognize this as characteristic of PTSD.

Around age fourteen, and possibly precipitated by hormonal changes and the transition to high school, Joanne started waking up frequently to urinate. This became worse five years later when she went to college and lived in a dorm. This was quite problematic since the frequent trips down a long hall to the bathroom interfered with Joanne getting sufficient sleep. Throughout college and into her twenties and thirties, Joanne continued to have difficulty falling asleep, and she awakened frequently throughout the night. She never felt refreshed in the morning and was tired and lacking in energy throughout the day.

Joanne didn't have any additional symptoms until she was in her mid-thirties and developed a weakness in her legs that would come and go. This mysterious symptom didn't last more than a couple of months, probably because she was too busy raising three young boys to dwell on it. Many years later, after she retired, Joanne began to feel dizzy from time to time and worried that she might faint. This was about the same time that she started experiencing a host of gastrointestinal problems.[4]

Over the years, Joanne visited doctors for her sleep problems, urinary frequency, weakness in her legs and dizziness, along with headaches, back and neck pain, and general fatigue. With each new symptom, Joanne imagined the worst possible explanation for it. The Merck Manual *became her Bible, and the Seven Signs of Cancer publicized by the American Cancer Society were always in the back of her mind. Joanne was diagnosed with Irritable Bowel Syndrome by one doctor, but most of the doctors could find nothing wrong.*

From time to time, Joanne wondered if she had a "light" case of Chronic Fatigue Syndrome. And according to the aforementioned Merck Manual, *her aches and pains were consistent with the pattern characteristic of mild Fibromyalgia. Although some people with GAD take to their beds, Joanne*

---

4. It would seem logical to assume that anxiety would lessen in retirement when people are out from under the pressures of the work world. In fact, the lack of distractions can make symptoms more difficult to ignore and the extra time can be filled with worry.

remained vibrant and active during the day. However, she felt drained by around four o'clock in the afternoon, and she slept ten hours a night. Joanne noticed that she often woke up with clenched fists. Additionally, her dentist suspected that she was grinding or clenching her teeth. These observations suggested that she wasn't even completely relaxed while she slept.

Over the course of her life, worry was Joanne's constant companion, particularly during stressful times and major transitions. During her childhood, she worried that something would happen to her parents or her younger brothers. Throughout her years in school, much of Joanne's worry was focused on having to speak up in class or give a presentation. In elementary school, she worried that her teacher would call on her or assign a speech. During high school, she agonized for days before having to give a talk. In college, Joanne felt tremendous stress during her entire semester of rhetoric. She had much difficulty sleeping and spent many hours writing and practicing every speech.

When Joanne started graduate school, her assistantship required teaching some classes. She experienced tremendous anxiety before each class, feeling low-grade panic and a sense of doom as she was walking to the university. She overprepared for each class, writing out every word that she planned to say. Her husband joked that, by the time that her excessive preparation was taken into account, Joanne was probably earning around twenty-five cents an hour.

When she entered the work world, the focus of Joanne's worry turned to the fear that she wasn't competent to do her job. She felt as if she were an "imposter" in spite of her many years of education. Driving to her office, she fantasized that getting into a minor car accident would save her from work for a few weeks. During the early years of her marriage, Joanne worried that her husband would have a fatal car accident, and after she became pregnant, she worried that the baby would have disabilities. She worried about Sudden Infant Death Syndrome (SIDS) for the first year after her boys were born, and when they got sick, she worried that they had something serious. When each of her children was ready to eat solid food, Joanne worried that he might choke to death. Years later, when her boys were in high school, Joanne obsessed about car accidents and was unable to sleep until they were safely in the house.

When her children seemingly miraculously made it to adulthood, Joanne was surprised to find that her worries weren't over. In fact, things seemed even worse in some ways because she no longer had any control over what her adult children were doing. When she became a grandparent, Joanne worried about something happening to her precious grandchildren. Her anxiety concerning her grandchildren was even stronger than what she experienced when her own children were young because she had no control over their safety.

Although they were not as focused as we see in Specific Phobia, Joanne's worries were fairly specific in that there were many things that she *didn't* worry about. She didn't worry about her own flying or driving and didn't hesitate to drive long distances by herself. She enjoyed sports like rollerblading that are sometimes considered somewhat dangerous. Although she initially felt panicky and imagined the worst whenever she or one of her children had a worrisome symptom, she didn't continue to dwell on it after a doctor assured her that there was nothing seriously wrong. And when she had symptoms of a full-blown panic attack, Joanne was able to shrug them off and continue whatever she was doing at the time. She managed to conquer her fear of public speaking and taught many lecture classes over the course of her career. This illustrates how individualized worry tends to be since many of us have some anxiety about flying or driving cross country, and unlike Joanne, many people find panic attacks terrifying.

As Joanne's story illustrates, GAD includes a number of physiological manifestations of stress, along with the almost continuous worry and free-floating anxiety. Indeed, according to Brown and Tung (2018), the physiological symptoms alone are sometimes enough to warrant a diagnosis of GAD. As in Joanne's case, the physical symptoms don't necessarily all occur at the same time. Each symptom tends to wax and wane over the years depending upon the level of stress that the person is experiencing. But the individual with GAD doesn't necessarily connect her symptoms to the stress in her life. It can feel as if each symptom has "just come out of the blue."

The physical manifestations of GAD can include shortness of breath, tightness in the chest, dry mouth, trouble swallowing or the feeling of a lump in the throat, heart palpitations, trembling, twitching, feeling shaky, dizziness, and sweating. These are the same sensations that characterize a panic attack, but they are much less extreme than those experienced in Panic Disorder. Additional symptoms that are common in GAD are fatigue, restlessness, weakness, tingling sensations, insomnia, GI problems (nausea, heartburn and diarrhea), frequent urination, and a tendency to startle easily (think of vigilance in the animal kingdom). Dry eye, which is a more serious condition than it sounds like it would be, can even be caused by chronic anxiety. During times of stress, cortisol slows the production of beneficial oils so that people with chronic anxiety may have less of the oils to lubricate their eyes. Sustained anxiety can also contribute to skin conditions such as acne, eczema, psoriasis and rosacea. People with GAD usually have ongoing physiological tension which often leads to neck, back and jaw pain, muscle aches and soreness, and frequent headaches. They may be more sensitive to pain. Some of my clients reported waking up with extreme stiffness all over their bodies and noticing that their hands were clenched and their fingers were sore. This would seem to indicate that some GAD patients aren't even relaxed while they sleep and may at least partially account for the fact that they often don't feel rested in the morning. Even tinnitus, which one might not expect to have anything to do with anxiety, appears to be related. According to Hou et al. (2020), there was a significant increase in the lifetime incidence of tinnitus in anxiety disordered patients. We can imagine that GAD patients may account for a sizable number of the primary care patients who visit their doctors.

In addition to these symptoms and the general heightened arousal in GAD, some patients tend to be irritable and subject to angry outbursts. This makes sense given that people with GAD seem to be especially sensitive to stress. This can make an otherwise agreeable person impatient and difficult to be around and cause her to carry guilt about things that she has said and done.

Joanne's symptoms weren't unusual in the patient population that I saw. Another client of mine came in one day with a page-long list of everything that was wrong with her from head to toe. She planned to present this list to her primary care doctor. Katherine's scalp itched, her head ached, her eyes were dry, and she had nasal congestion, clogged ears and jaw pain. At the bottom of the page, she had noted tingly feelings in her toes and pain on the top of her right foot. In between her head and foot problems, Katherine had neck pain, joint pain in her knees and hips, indigestion, acid reflux, and vaginal dryness.

Individuals with GAD are frequently given one or more of several diagnoses. Irritable Bowel Syndrome (IBS) is not an uncommon diagnosis in this population. Sometimes people with GAD report that they ache all over (possibly from their chronic muscle tension) and are diagnosed with Fibromyalgia. This disease is characterized by widespread muscle pain and tenderness. The symptoms of Fibromyalgia tend to wax and wane and often seem to be exacerbated by stress. People with generalized anxiety may also be diagnosed with Chronic Fatigue Syndrome (CFS). CFS is a disease involving extreme fatigue that is made worse by exertion but doesn't improve with rest. There has been some controversy as to whether Fibromyalgia and Chronic Fatigue are bona fide medical disorders.

Although it seems counterintuitive, both Fibromyalgia and Chronic Fatigue can be more handicapping if the patient doesn't push herself to get out of bed and gradually start moving. When someone feels exhausted, it's natural to assume that the person should rest. However, staying in bed all day only makes her weaker. Furthermore, not moving doesn't ameliorate muscle aches and pains and often makes them worse. Additionally, the less active a person is, the more time there is to notice aches and pains and to become anxious about them. That most people don't have the luxury of lying around all day actually may save them from becoming more disabled. Ironically, wealthy women and men, and those supported by spouses, may become the most incapacitated.

There are undoubtedly even more people who have only a few milder symptoms of GAD. They may still be somewhat handicapped and not enjoy life as much as they could. GAD patients may have less stamina for exercise and may require more sleep than the average person, partly because anxiety and tension are energy depleting. There is also some evidence that people with generalized anxiety don't obtain quality sleep. Sleep studies have revealed that their sleep cycles may be abnormal. Some individuals with GAD tend to "run on high" until they more or less collapse at the end of the day. They often run out of energy by late afternoon and describe feeling "drained." These people may even appear to be high in energy because they are restless and tend to be constantly busy until they "burn out" each day because they can't sustain this level of energy expenditure. Unfortunately, when they drag themselves off to bed, GAD patients often have difficulty falling and staying asleep (some people with GAD tend to have even more difficulty with sleep maintenance than with sleep onset insomnia).

As I explained, the physiological symptoms of GAD can be likened to a sustained fight or flight reaction, which we've seen is meant to be a short-lived occasional occurrence. This constant physical tension puts a great deal of ongoing strain on a person's body. It can weaken her immune system and result in frequent illnesses such as colds and other viral infections. Consequently, the person with GAD is likely to spend much time and money going to different doctors for medical problems that seem unrelated to her anxiety symptoms. Sometimes people with generalized anxiety will ask a physician if there is something wrong with their immune systems.

Although as with other anxiety disorders, everyone has experienced some of these symptoms from time to time, as Joanne's case illustrates, innate sensitivity to stress seems to predispose a person to developing Generalized Anxiety Disorder. GAD patients tend to be the same people who have always responded poorly to stress and to change. People with GAD tend to feel high levels of tension in situations when other people might experience only mild stress. As we saw with the other anxiety disorders and the GAD vignettes, the symptoms of GAD are likely to flare during stressful times and when a person is navigating major life transitions. Unfortunately, addictive behaviors such as drinking, taking prescription drugs and smoking may become preferred methods of coping, exacerbating the other physiological effects and making the person's overall health even worse in the long run.

When symptoms flare, GAD may cause a person to miss school or work (resulting in unemployment as in Susan's case), but more typically, people with GAD drag through each day with low energy, sometimes doing a less than adequate job of everything that they attempt but managing to hang onto their jobs. All of this can make it difficult for the person to hold a full-time job or to finish a degree program, let alone maintain a high-powered career that can require putting in sixty or more hours a week. Women with GAD often find it especially difficult to juggle childrearing with careers. Some ambitious people, particularly those with a lot of "nervous energy," manage to excel at their work but have little energy left over for anything else. Their relationships may suffer, and they may derive less pleasure from life.

As I have emphasized, Generalized Anxiety Disorder can be one of the most difficult forms of anxiety to diagnose. Although they experience a myriad of somatic symptoms, individuals with GAD often present with one or two problems at a time when they visit a doctor, depending upon which symptoms are most uncomfortable for them at the moment. Because of this, along with their tendency to go to different doctors for different ailments, none of their doctors may recognize the underlying pattern of their symptoms in order to diagnose GAD. One of my patients, describing her encounters with doctors, explained: "I went to a neurologist for my migraines, a GI doctor for my stomach pain, a chiropractor for neck pain, a urologist for urinary frequency and a cardiologist for my racing heart." My client's primary care physician didn't have the time to hear all of her complaints. By going to different doctors, she was able to get twenty minutes of attention for each issue, but none of the physicians understood the full picture in order to identify her pattern of symptoms suggestive of GAD. Patients with undiagnosed GAD are likely to be given a number of medical tests to rule out such diseases as Multiple Sclerosis and Lupus. The time and money expenditures for these patients can be quite large.

Five. Generalized Anxiety Disorder (GAD)

The fact that their symptoms aren't life threatening contributes to a doctor's inclination to get their patients with generalized anxiety out the door. One of the most common complaints that GAD patients bring to their doctors is being tired all of the time but also sleeping poorly. A patient who is not medically savvy may present with vague statements like "I feel bad" and not be able to articulate what she is experiencing. Also, people with GAD may fail to realize that they are extremely tense because they are so accustomed to high levels of "nervous energy" and muscular rigidity.

Psychiatrists characterize GAD patients as having "high somatization vulnerability." This is defined as the tendency to experience emotional distress as physiological symptoms and to be especially aware of mild changes in their bodies which they often fear could be indicative of a major illness. They may be quick to jump to the "worst case scenario" to explain their symptoms. This can lead to obsessive scrutinizing of one's body as some OCD patients do. And if the person looks hard enough, she is likely to find something amiss. This is a similar construct to Anxiety Sensitivity as measured by the Anxiety Sensitivity Index (ASI). Patients scoring high on this test are high on the trait of interoceptive awareness. In other words, they are highly attuned to their bodies. This means they may notice things that other people don't think much about. The GAD patient may or may not be a full-blown Hypochondriac (now labeled Illness Anxiety Disorder in the *DSM-5*). A visit to the doctor can reassure some GAD patients that there is nothing seriously wrong—at least until another symptom emerges. According to the *DSM*, Illness Anxiety Disorder involves a preoccupation with having or acquiring a serious illness and repeatedly checking for signs of illness or frequently visiting the doctor and having diagnostic tests or "exhibiting maladaptive avoidance 'of doctors or hospitals.'"[5]

Some patients with GAD happen to be afraid of going to doctors. This isn't surprising given that a doctor's visit can be stressful, particularly if an anxious patient is convinced that the doctor will deliver bad news. The person's tendency to avoid the doctor's office complicates the picture and makes the person's condition even more handicapping, as avoidance tends to do in all anxiety related disorders. This tendency to shun doctors means that the patient may worry that each symptom is indicative of something serious but not obtain the reassurance that she has nothing to be concerned about. These patients will be less likely to

---

5. This is reminiscent of compulsive checking in OCD.

be able to stop worrying about a given symptom. They may continue to be preoccupied with it and live with a higher level of anxiety because of it. This can perpetuate their high level of anxiety, making their symptom even worse.

GAD in Times of Transition

As I have mentioned, since change can be stressful for anyone, individuals with generalized anxiety are likely to have more difficulty negotiating any new adjustment and to develop more acute symptoms during times of transition. Consequently, coping with major life passages can be especially difficult for GAD patients. Young adults with GAD will tend to experience more symptoms when it is time to move away from their parents and when they are expected to assume any new responsibility. They may have more physiological symptoms when they think about changing jobs or leaving troubled relationships. To manage stress, some people with GAD almost completely avoid any new challenges. They may feel overwhelmed and be hesitant to make changes such as moving to a more adequate dwelling in the same area, let alone moving to a new city or state. Over the course of their lives, GAD patients fearing change may remain in less-than-ideal situations and consequently end up living with chronic dissatisfaction. Ironically, older patients with GAD may have more symptoms in retirement when they are supposed to be relaxing, because they have more time on their hands to notice bodily sensations and to worry and fewer distractions to take their mind off their symptoms and worries.

During times of transition, when GAD patients develop more acute symptoms, they are likely to receive additional psychiatric diagnoses. Concurrent diagnoses of Specific Phobia, Social Anxiety, Agoraphobia, Panic Disorder or OCD are not uncommon. In addition, people with generalized anxiety are more likely to develop PTSD after a traumatic experience. GAD patients are also prone to developing depression with some estimates as high as in 50 percent of cases, sometimes years after developing their first symptoms of anxiety.

It may be that people over 65 with GAD experience more feelings of regret than others in their cohort. With younger GAD patients worrying about the future, older patients with fewer decisions left to make in life might focus their worrying on ruminating about the past.

Six

Anxiety and Underachievement Across the Life Span

The major anxiety disorders discussed in prior chapters occur throughout the life course. This chapter discusses more specifically how anxiety affects people across the life course from infants to young adults and individuals in different stages of adulthood. Along with introducing new material, it will serve as a summary of the foregoing chapters. One theme is that although anxiety may take somewhat different forms at different stages, there is often continuity in the presence of anxiety over the life span. Many anxious adults remember feeling afraid of certain things or being socially anxious as children. Relatedly, and as shown throughout previous chapters, anxiety often follows a cumulative disadvantage process in which early problems of anxiety snowball into further anxiety and other mental health and life problems.

A second theme is that stages of development do entail somewhat different risks and sources of anxiety. This is true later in childhood, for example, when peers and social comparison processes become increasingly important to pre-teens and teens, but also later in life when older adults may become preoccupied with reflection and regret. I will discuss specific conditions that arise along the life course such as School Phobia and Empty Nest Syndrome. As an important preface to Chapter Eight (Parenting), I'll stress that anxiety disorders tend to be even more hidden in children. Children have less understanding of what they're experiencing and more difficulty articulating symptoms and experiences. In fact, many anxiety disorders begin in childhood whether parents realize it or not. A third theme concerning anxiety over the life course is that social and life *transitions* themselves present risks of precipitating anxiety. That is, beginning school, work, or a marriage entail major changes in social structure and relationships that can present new problems with anxiety.

Infants and Young Children

When their infants and children have problems of any kind, parents tend to blame themselves when, in fact, the issues often have nothing to do with anything that the parents have done or failed to do. Indeed, a predisposition toward anxiety often runs in families. This section on infants and children will hopefully enable parents who are reading it to be easier on themselves.

Because we don't usually think about infants as anxious or label them as such, and because babies can't describe their feelings, anxiety may be especially hidden at this stage. Back when I was working with very young children, parents would bring their three- to five-year-old offspring in to address their fears of the dark, the doctor's office, or dogs. The parents usually were unaware that their children had any problems with anxiety prior to this. In actuality, a predisposition toward anxiety can be apparent very early.

This predisposition to be overly sensitive to stress of any kind can be observed in newborns who appear to be "wired" to react too quickly and too intensely. Nurses have reported that they can spot these overly reactive infants in the nursery. These babies startle easily, are quick to cry, and cry frequently. Some researchers have speculated that the strength of a newborn's startle response may predict the likelihood that the child will develop an anxiety disorder at some point (Stossel, 2013). The stronger startle reaction remains throughout the person's life as evidenced by an anxious adult jumping at an unexpected noise. This reactivity is labeled behavioral inhibition and over the course of a child's development presents as caution, withdrawal, and hyperarousal to new situations. Kagan (1994) labels these infants highly reactive, while Aron (1996) classifies them as highly sensitive. In *Your Child Is a Person* (1965) Chess, Thomas and Birch label this behavioral attribute Level of Sensory Threshold. According to Kagan (1994) one in five healthy infants reacts to stimuli with vigorous motor activity and distress, and two-thirds of these infants become inhibited children (see also Kagan & Snidman, 2004). Consistent with this, Kagan (1994) and other researchers testing his theories have found that 15 to 20 percent of infants who react the most strongly to changes or novel situations are considerably more likely to develop anxiety disorders in adulthood than are their less reactive peers.

It may be obvious to seasoned parents that they have an unusually sensitive baby from the moment that they leave the hospital. Diaper changes, dressing and bathing are all likely to be met with screams from their newborn. A sensitive baby may be unusually uncomfortable in a slightly wet or dirty diaper and react intensely to noises and abrupt changes in temperature. Even small changes in routine will often be difficult for a highly reactive infant.

Studies suggest that most animals, including but not restricted to humans, have an inborn fear of the unknown. This makes new situations inherently challenging. This tendency to be cautious and slow to jump into new situations can be observed across the animal kingdom. Scientists have estimated that 20 percent of animals, from dogs and cats to birds and fruit flies, can be characterized as slow to warm up (Cain, 2012). Kagan (1994) found that different breeds of dogs varied dramatically in their degree of timidity; for example, beagles and cocker spaniels were generally more outgoing than terriers or shelties.

The overly reactive infant may become the toddler who is prone to throwing tantrums which we can think of as a manifestation of the fight or flight response. The physiology of a tantrum involves the amygdala and hypothalamus, the same areas of the brain that are activated during the fight or flight response (Fields, 2015). During a tantrum a child will have a faster heartbeat and tense muscles just as a teen or adult experiences during a panic attack.

Anxiety in infants and toddlers shows up so frequently that two syndromes are considered to be normal at certain stages of development (i.e., separation anxiety and stranger anxiety). Most normal infants begin to develop Separation Anxiety around four to six months of age. Separation Anxiety is characterized by a child becoming excessively anxious when separated from a parent, usually the mother. The child may cling to his mother and scream when the mother puts him down or tries to leave the room for a minute. Distress over separation may be worse if the child is already stressed by hunger, fatigue, or illness. This reaction to being separated from one's mother is an adaptive behavior that is common in normal four- to eighteen-month-old babies because it is important for children of this age to be close to their primary caretakers in order to survive. It typically peaks between ten and eighteen months and then fades, but Separation Anxiety can continue for years in vulnerable children.

In overly anxious children, Separation Anxiety may continue into early childhood. A preschooler may refuse to visit friends, especially if it involves staying overnight. The school-aged child with Separation Anxiety may be afraid to go to school or camp. One anxious client of mine remembered wanting to go outside to play but being so afraid to leave her mother that she opted to stay indoors most of the time, even during her elementary school years. Separation Anxiety is more common in girls, and children prone to Separation Anxiety are likely to be the same children who end up being labeled shy during their childhood years. When Separation Anxiety appears to be particularly strong in an infant, it may predict high levels of anxiety in the baby's adulthood. Like all anxiety disorders, Separation Anxiety tends to get worse during times of change.

John Bowlby and Mary Ainsworth have studied attachment and Separation Anxiety extensively. In his book *Attachment* (1969), Bowlby reported that children react in characteristic ways when separated from their mothers. He hypothesized that a strong attachment to the mother is a survival instinct that helps to ensure a child is protected from dangers of all kinds. Bowlby believed that caregivers who are responsive to their infant's needs help them to maintain feelings of security. Somewhat paradoxically, this enables babies to feel secure enough to explore their worlds. In 1978, Mary Ainsworth took Bowlby's theory a step further in her book *Patterns of Attachment: A Psychological Study of the Strange Situation*. In her laboratory study described in the book, mothers of children from 12 to 18 months left the room in which they had been playing with their children. During the short time that their mothers weren't with them, some of the infants happily continued playing while others showed much distress. When the mothers returned, some of the children crawled or toddled toward their mothers while others remained where they were as if they could have cared less about their mothers' return. Based on these observations, Ainsworth labeled the infants Securely Attached, Insecure/Ambivalent, and Insecure/ Avoidant. Studies have replicated these findings and have found that these attachment styles predict how children with each attachment style may continue to be affected by their early relationships with their mothers. Those children who were not securely attached may be more anxious later in life.

Stranger Anxiety is also a normal and highly adaptive reaction that usually appears around eight to nine months of age in most infants but can begin as early as six months. Stranger Anxiety is defined as the distress that young children experience when they encounter people with whom they aren't familiar. Babies who react strongly to being separated from their mothers also tend to be especially fearful of anyone they don't see frequently. This is protective in that it may prevent a child from being harmed. Indeed, young children are more likely to be afraid of men than women and tend to fear adults more than other children. We can see this reaction when babies and toddlers look terrified sitting on Santa Claus' lap. This shouldn't be too surprising given that Santa is a large and very unusual looking stranger. Likewise, very young children may prefer to play in the backyard instead of the front yard, if their house is on a busy sidewalk where strangers may walk by. If Stranger Anxiety persists into middle childhood and causes an older child to be afraid to walk a few blocks to a friend's house or to fear being outside in his own yard, the anxiety has become more problematic.

Preschool and Elementary School

Along with Social Anxiety, phobias often crop up first in childhood, sometimes as early as age three. Fear of dogs is one of the most common, probably because dogs are everywhere and some of them are big, loud, fast moving, and unpredictable. As mentioned in the chapter on Specific Phobia, one of my sons became afraid of dogs when he was around the age of five. This fear was almost magically cured after we got him a puppy. Remember the Little Peter study in which a child was deconditioned not to fear rabbits. Some children fear insects, bees, birds and other animals they may encounter in their yards or playgrounds. Many sensitive children fear the dark and have trouble falling asleep. They may fear shadows, monsters or "bad guys" they imagine are lurking in their dark bedrooms. Other children have a fear of water which makes bathing them a struggle. In fact, depending upon their experiences, children can develop almost any of the phobias described in Chapter Three.

The development of a phobia in early childhood can portend the development of other forms of anxiety later. Children who experience specific phobias are almost five times more likely to develop Social Anxiety during their teenage years. In *My Age of Anxiety* (2013), Scott Stossel tracks his own progression of anxiety from Specific Phobia when he was six to Social Anxiety beginning around age eleven to Panic Disorder in his late teens and finally Agoraphobia in his young adulthood.

A sensitive child may worry about many things in his young life. However, it is difficult to know exactly how much a young child worries because many children can't or won't articulate their concerns. Children with a tendency to obsess may worry about something bad happening to a loved one. Some children begin showing a tendency toward obsessive behavior such as needing to have their toys arranged in a certain way like my client who felt the need to dot his i's in a particular way for fear that something would happen to his mother if he failed to do this. GAD can begin at a surprisingly early age. One of my clients described her child as a "four-year-old hypochondriac." This young girl had developed several symptoms suggestive of Generalized Anxiety Disorder. For months after she had an ear infection, the little girl insisted that her mother take her temperature and check her ears, sometimes several times a day.

Remember that the fear of uncertainty and change is hardwired into us. Children encounter change frequently because many seemingly small things are new to them. As sensitive children grow, they will typically be slow to warm up to new situations, particularly those involving other people. As toddlers, they may be afraid to go to the playground, wade into the water at the beach, jump into a pool or attend story hour at the library. Even more problematic, anxious preschoolers will likely have considerable difficulty starting day care or nursery school. In addition to being an entirely new experience involving many unfamiliar children, attending preschool requires being separated from one's caregiver.

Due to this low tolerance for stress and a difficulty warming up to new situations, an overly anxious child can be thwarted at any step of development, particularly during times of change. Going off to kindergarten can be terrifying. Even children who have gone to nursery school can be overwhelmed by the much larger elementary school. The first few weeks of school can involve a morning struggle to get the child ready and into the classroom.

Once they are more acclimated to elementary school, anxious students may still be too shy to speak up in class or to make friends. The fearful child may even be too anxious to concentrate on schoolwork. These children are sometimes mistakenly thought to be slow. They may end up being labeled Developmentally Delayed or Learning Disabled. Anxious children who are visibly restless are also frequently given a diagnosis of Attention Deficit Hyperactivity Disorder (ADHD). While anxiety and ADHD can co-occur this is not necessarily the case, so that too many anxious children carry a diagnosis of ADHD and are being medicated for it. Test anxiety and the fear of giving oral reports are common, even in children who are not generally anxious.

School Phobia. Some children end up developing full-blown cases of School Phobia. As defined in an earlier chapter, this syndrome is an irrational and persistent fear of going to school. It's sometimes difficult to differentiate School Phobia from Separation Anxiety, since the child's underlying worry may be that something could happen to her mother or father while she is away from them. Some children suffer in silence, while others put up a fight every morning when it's time to get ready for school. Children with School Phobia may have difficulty falling asleep as they lay in bed worrying about the next school day. This can be a particular problem on Sunday nights as they anticipate having to start a new school week after having a brief respite.

Children suffering from School Phobia may develop actual physical symptoms such as nausea or attempts to fabricate an illness. In many cases, the anticipation of going to school ends up being more distressing to them than the actual experience once they get into the classroom. If caregivers don't deal with School Phobia promptly, children can end up missing quite a bit of school, and as is the case with all avoidance behaviors, the more school they miss, the more difficult it is for school-phobic children to go back. Although Monday mornings are usually the hardest days, beginning school after a holiday break is likely to be even more difficult. Many child psychologists warned it would be especially challenging for children to return to school after having been kept home for months during the Covid pandemic. If parents inadvertently reinforce the child's resistance by sometimes giving in, it makes the child's behavior—whether it's throwing a tantrum or feigning an illness—even more persistent. Missing school often affects the child's learning and grades, sometimes causing the child to fail a grade. After being held back once or twice, the school-phobic teen may end up dropping out of school or being expelled for truancy. The following vignette describes how School Phobia impacted a child who was referred to me.

Travis's Story

Travis was a precocious but somewhat awkward twelve-year-old who began to fear going to school after he was bullied for being overweight. Prior to this, he had enjoyed the schoolwork and had excelled. His parents, who were both overworked professionals, didn't have time to deal with Travis' refusal to go to school and allowed him to stay home with his nanny several times a week. Because he missed so many days of school, Travis was eventually placed in a special school for truant preteens. As one might expect, most of the other students at the school were tough kids with severe discipline problems who saw Travis as a perfect target for serious bullying. This compounded his fear of going to school, and Travis' grades plummeted. It wasn't long before every-one seemed to forget how bright he was. In addition, he was perceived as hav-ing an attitude problem. Travis ended up missing so many classes during his first two years of high school that it looked as though he wouldn't be able to accumulate enough credits to graduate. He finally began to do much better after he passed the GED exam and enrolled in the community college where he excelled in all of his subjects, especially the sciences.

The Middle School Years

Navigating middle or junior high school is often particularly diffi-cult for sensitive children. It usually means leaving a small elementary school to attend a larger school with many unfamiliar classmates. Expo-sure to this many new children is an adjustment for any twelve-year-old. Compounding this, children hit middle school or junior high when, due to rapidly changing hormones, they are at a particularly vulnera-ble stage in their development. In addition, their peers are becoming more important to them, and neurological changes make adolescents more aware of their impact on others. This can make anxious young adolescents extremely self-conscious, particularly if there is anything that might be construed as different about them. As they enter middle school or junior high, students may be required to move through dif-ferent classes with different teachers and different groups of children in each of their classes. Needing to deal with a different set of classmates each hour could exacerbate anxiety. As was the case for Travis, starting middle school is a time when sensitive children often become a target for bullies who are able to sense their fear. Socially anxious children tend to avoid eye contact, look downward, and walk with slumped shoulders, all behaviors which project an air of submissiveness and lack of confidence that screams, "You can pick on me!" Children who look or act differ-ently from the others are, unfortunately, especially likely to be targeted. Today, social media is enabling bullies to operate 24/7 with hundreds of people looking on. Tragically, this can end in the victim dying by suicide.

Adolescents may continue to have these same issues when transi-tioning to high school. This is compounded by the fact that most high schools are larger than most middle schools. In addition, high school students have the added pressure of needing to maintain a certain grade point average if they hope to go to college. For those with test anxi-ety, the SAT and ACT loom large. Additionally, dealing with potential romantic partners assumes greater importance and can be particularly fraught. Parents may be of less help in offering support, especially because students are struggling to be independent and may value their peers' opinions more than those of their parents.

I address parenting practices that can help anxious children further in Chapter Eight. For now, a critical insight is that middle school and high school are socially difficult for almost all students. Robert Crosnoe (2011) has studied problems of not fitting in during the high school years and finds that the *average* teenager reports one or more problems of fitting in, such as feeling rejected, unwanted, or not part of things at school. These problems are especially common among students with traditionally stigmatized traits such as obesity. In the worst-case scenario, stigmatization leads to what sociologists call a Spoiled Identity, where the person comes to believe that one stigmatized trait encapsulates his or her whole self. When students internalize social stigma in this way, and/or engage in self-defeating coping mechanisms like alcohol or drug abuse, the effects on school achievement and their futures can be profound. Other students simply disengage to preserve a positive sense of self-worth; if the student can convince *themselves* they don't care about school, then not fitting in is less of a problem. But disengagement from school will reduce the student's options for going to college.

If even the average teenager is susceptible to feelings of not fitting in, anxious and shy teenagers may be especially susceptible, as their self-esteem may be lower to begin with. For example, shy boys rate themselves as less attractive and shy girls describe themselves as being less intelligent (Zimbardo, 1977).

In Crosnoe's research, the social challenges of high school included bullying but were much more pervasive and subtle than that on the whole. His respondents described "the look" they got from others in the school (or the corollary of this, being explicitly avoided and overlooked). Children with any visible differences (e.g., physical traits or clothing) may be targets for this kind of stigma. Effeminate boys may have an especially hard time. A sensitive child's anxiety is likely to compound the effects of these widespread social processes affecting a great many high school students.

Young Adulthood

Reaching adulthood is supposed to mean having the freedom to choose one's environment—at least to the extent that economic reality allows. Because of this, we might expect that an anxious person would fare better at this stage, since he should be able to adapt his environment to suit his own needs. However, this is the time when the young person is expected to negotiate the daunting life hurdles of leaving home, pursuing further education or training, and finding work. In all these realms they will need to draw not only on academic skills but also on social skills to succeed. The young adult must make one of the most important decisions that he will ever have to make—selecting a career. In his 2020 book *On Not Being Someone Else: Tales of Our Unled Lives*, Andrew Miller quotes Nietzsche: "A man chooses his career at an age when he is not fit to choose. He doesn't know the various professions; he doesn't know himself; and then he wastes his most active years in this career, giving his whole mind to it, acquiring experience."

As introduced in Chapter Two, the Failure to Launch syndrome may be becoming more common (McConville, 2020). This disorder, which is more prevalent in boys, includes the failure to assume responsibility, lack of confidence, and a low work ethic. This inability to become independent and self-reliant is epitomized by the young high school graduate who spends hours in his room, emerging only to eat. Today's version of Failure to Launch almost always involves video game addiction, which partially replaces the addiction to television which was so common in the sixties, seventies, and eighties. In the first half of the 20th century, young boys often had the option to work for a family member and girls frequently married right after high school. Today, if these graduates don't go on to college or join the military, expectations for them are less defined. Failure to Launch can affect students who were highly successful and expected to go away to a competitive college as well as those who did poorly in school. Interestingly, teens and young adults are more likely to receive this diagnosis if they had been expected to achieve.

If the young adult decides to attend college, this marks a big transition. In *On Not Being Someone Else* (2020), Miller writes, "For young people, the choice of college—if there is one—marks the first time that they'll have made a big decision with insufficient information." For first-generation students whose parents didn't go beyond high school, this decision is even more fraught because their parents can't help them as much with the process. Young people can become so anxious during the transition to college that they drop out after a few weeks. This phenomenon is so common that it has been dubbed the "Freshman Freak

Out." Students arrive on campus and are faced with so many changes that they can quickly become overwhelmed.

Many aspects of the first-year college student's life will be different. In addition to being away from home, these students will find themselves in a mini community, usually considerably larger than their high schools, surrounded by many unfamiliar faces. At a university, many of their introductory classes will be taught in large lecture halls, and they will typically be living in a dormitory with shared bathrooms and communal meals. As earlier vignettes demonstrated, the resulting stress can precipitate a first panic attack or cause the worry and low-grade physiological arousal of GAD to develop. Some first-year students drop out in the first couple of weeks of college, while others manage to stay in school until they find out that they have done poorly on the midterm exams or after they have gone home for Thanksgiving break and get a taste of the security of home.

Some anxious students excel academically all the way through college because they are so bright that school has always come easily to them. These academically oriented students may actually fear graduation because this milestone means having to deal with entirely different sets of expectations. Some of these inveterate students may end up with several majors and degrees. Consider Larry, described in the introduction, who held two master's degrees and a PhD but never held a job in either field.

For young people who continue their education beyond a bachelor's degree, graduate school tends to be especially stressful. It requires navigating a number of hurdles, any one of which can present problems for an anxious student and cause her to leave the program. Some students make it all the way to their dissertation defenses only to become so anxious that they either don't go through with the defense or perform so badly that they barely pass. Although this phenomenon isn't necessarily attributable to anxiety, a sizable number of graduate students never actually finish their doctoral programs. These individuals who are dubbed ABD or All But Dissertation live in a sort of limbo until they complete all of the requirements, if they ever do. With a ten-year time limit for finishing in many programs, many of these students have the unfinished thesis hanging over their heads for years. This certainly contributes to much anxiety. Many people eventually give up without actually making an active decision to let the dissertation go. In some cases, this results in guilt and regret.

Entering the Workforce

Once it's time to enter the work world, an entirely different set of skills is required. Social skills may be more important than ability or knowledge. Those with Social Anxiety will undoubtedly find the world of work intimidating. Most careers demand far more interaction with other people than is required in high school or college, where a shy person can slip in and out of lectures without being noticed. A reluctance to deal with people unfortunately precludes retail and service positions as well as teaching and most careers in medicine and law. The social challenges of starting work begin with the job interview itself. Some anxious people may not be confident enough to apply for a job, particularly one that would require anything beyond filling out a short application followed by an informal interview. They may end up working for a relative or friend of the family in a field or setting they don't particularly enjoy. One study found that, on average, socially anxious men began a stable career three years later than other men (Aron, 2002).

As I have described, once they have started a job, socially anxious employees may avoid certain "optional" activities that are important for advancement in their careers, such as entertaining clients or participating in public speaking engagements. Additionally, these anxious workers may be reluctant to accept promotions that would require moving to a new location or they may stay with one employer when it might be advantageous to apply somewhere else. All of these factors contribute to the anxious person's likelihood of being underemployed—working in a position that doesn't fully utilize his or her abilities and skills. Anxiety may greatly limit a person's chances of making a significant contribution to the world, at least through his career.

The other major life task that historically has been expected of a person in their twenties and early thirties is finding a lifelong mate. As we saw in the second chapter, this can be especially challenging for the person suffering from Social Anxiety. It is difficult for a shy person to meet potential mates because it often requires going to parties or bars, mingling with groups of people, and approaching strangers. Less intimidating small-group settings, such as small classes or hiking groups, provide a more natural alternative but joining these activities can seem daunting for a socially anxious single person. Today, Internet sites for matching singles do make it considerably easier for some shy young people. Those young adults who might have met potential partners through small church groups now have an online alternative for finding someone to settle down with. This enables them to develop a connection very gradually before having an in-person meeting. Meeting each other in person is only the beginning, though. At some point, one of the potential partners has to suggest spending more time together. Getting to know another person requires increasingly more self-disclosure and eventually sexual intimacy, both of which are likely to be especially difficult for a self-conscious person.

Parenthood and the Middle Years

Once a young person has found a partner, there are still hurdles ahead. Young couples are often expected to marry and may not get away with slipping off to the Justice of the Peace. Expectations for weddings have gotten more grandiose over the years. For a shy person, anticipating being the center of attention for a day can seem like the ultimate nightmare.

Becoming a parent is a major life transition that used to occur in the early twenties but is now more likely not to happen until a person's late twenties or early thirties, if at all. More young adults are choosing not to have children, but those who do become parents have plenty to worry about at every stage of their children's development. Parenthood is rife with reasons to be anxious. Having children is among the greatest of life's joys but can become a source of intense anxiety. The moment a person has a baby, there is a possibility of losing that precious child. John Irving captures the anxiety of parenthood in his 1976 book *The World According to Garp.* Irving's main character worries about everything, but especially the safety of his family. Garp epitomizes the anxious parent as he grapples with all of the potential dangers to his family. His family even had a special code for anxiety named after his son's fear of the giant toad that he thinks resides in the ocean. Mistaking "Watch out for the undertow" as "Watch out for the 'undertoad,'" the child conjured up a fearsome sea monster resembling a giant toad.

Historically there have been even more dangers to very young children than there are today. Childbirth is much safer, a number of childhood diseases have been eradicated, and many illnesses are far more treatable. In addition, it's easier to baby-proof a child's environment. Cribs, car seats and toys all have to meet safety standards that didn't exist in the past. Nonetheless, there are still a great deal of things for a parent to worry about. The 24-hour news cycle often focuses on parenting gone wrong or blames parents for things that happen to children.

An individual's thirties and forties may be less challenging since the person may have settled into a stable career and relationship by this time. Although much has been made of the "midlife crisis," some experts contend this concern is overblown (Reid & Willis, 1999). But these decades are certainly not without stress. Based upon my experiences in dealing with this age group in private practice, I do believe that the decade of a person's forties may be the first time that he or she realizes that he has been in the wrong career or marriage. It goes without saying that this can be a major source of anxiety even if the person doesn't act on his feelings. For the people who leave their long-term relationships or are left by their partners, separation and divorce are two of the most stressful experiences they have to endure. Remember getting a divorce is highly ranked on the Holmes and Rahe Stress Scale. Facing workplace challenges, getting along with one's partner, and rearing children can all test a person. If anxious people have anxious children, this can exacerbate parenting issues.

Late Adulthood

The anxious person's fifties may seem like relatively smooth sailing. Children often have moved out of the home and things may seem peaceful. This is not the case, however, for a person who suffers from Empty Nest Syndrome. Defined as a parent experiencing feelings of sadness and loss when the last child leaves the home, this phenomenon affects almost every parent to some extent and isn't a clinical diagnosis. But for anxious parents, it can be particularly acute. On the other hand, a large proportion of parents have children who never leave or come back to live at home. This is so common that these young people have been dubbed the boomerang generation. Again, divorce is an extremely disruptive possibility at this stage, but many anxious people will opt to remain in less than satisfying, or even abusive, marriages in order to avoid the unknown. Your fifties can also be a time when you begin to look back over life and begin to have regrets about earlier decisions. Regrets can produce anxiety as an individual ruminates about what they "could have" or "should have" done differently. By the fifties it may be too late to undo something that has been set in motion earlier because any one decision has triggered a lengthy trajectory of consequences. A friend's mother started to wish that she had finished college in her fifties, but she was too anxious to return to it.

Retirement

By their sixties, some anxious adults may be able to retire. Retirement would seem to be the perfect stage for the anxious since it has traditionally meant less is expected of a person. The retired were supposed to be free to do absolutely nothing. This is changing, however. Endless days of playing golf or focusing on other hobbies are no longer necessarily considered the ideal. Now we're hearing about second acts, suggesting there is an expectation for us to "reinvent" ourselves. This can mean embarking on a second or third career or starting a business. Today, a person on the verge of retirement with adequate financial resources is faced with an almost endless number of choices. Realizing they are no longer bound to a particular geographical area, some retirees realize that they could move almost anywhere in the world. While this could seem liberating, it requires making life-altering decisions from an overwhelming number of possibilities. Today's recent retiree wonders, "Should I move to a smaller house or stay put?" "Should I move across town or out of state?" "Should I move closer to the children or near my elderly mother?" "Should I consider an over fifties retirement community, or is it the time to build that dream house or renovate an old mansion?" Then there is the question of how to spend one's time. Should a person try a career long dreamt of? Is it time to get a real estate license or open the gift shop or bookstore that was fantasized about many years earlier? To make matters even more complicated, our partner may have completely different ideas of what they want from retirement. Trying to convince a partner to support relocating or starting a business can create a tremendous amount of anxiety for both people.

People thrive when they feel that they have purpose. Therefore, the realization that they might not be contributing to the world in the same way can be anxiety arousing to a recent retiree. Sometimes guilt plays a role because the person feels that she should be doing something "worthwhile." Boredom is also a source of anxiety, particularly for retirees who had spent long hours on their careers. Some people who had always looked forward to retirement as a time when they expected to be especially happy are shocked when this turns out not to be the case.

Understanding Anxiety

One of my clients described waking up every morning to a panicky feeling as she pictured the day ahead and wondered how she was going to fill it. She hadn't felt this way on workdays and still didn't feel anxious when she had plans for the day or was traveling. Long stretches of time can be particularly unsettling for a Type A person.

In addition, the recent retiree can feel that he or she has endured some major losses. She may feel a loss of identity as a professional, employee or parent. Some sixty-somethings have even lost their spouses. Not only will grief cause depression and anxiety, but the widow or widower's entire worlds will have undergone massive change. They may no longer be able to afford to stay in their homes and may need to move to a completely new locale, sometimes far away from their support networks.

In today's mobile society, seniors are less likely to be geographically close to their adult children and their families. This can contribute to loneliness, especially for those who had pictured having their extended families nearby. It can also contribute to the feeling that they aren't needed and lack purpose, as they may not be able to help with grandchildren as grandparents have traditionally done. The loneliness and the feeling that they are no longer making a contribution to the world, which might have been ameliorated by playing a more active role in their grandchildren's lives, can contribute to anxiety and depression. However, with people having fewer children these days, aging parents can't necessarily count on having grandchildren. This can be a source of great anxiety as the person waits and wonders if they will ever experience the joys of being a grandparent. This wait can be years now that young couples, if they choose to have children, are waiting longer and making infertility problems more likely. Volunteer work could fill the void, but an anxious person may have as much difficulty applying for a volunteer position and working in a volunteer setting as they had in earlier years when they needed to navigate the world of work.

To sum everything up, at each developmental stage and transition point we need to confront change and make major decisions. Many of life's opportunities involve making large changes.[1] While normal people often anticipate new situations with excitement, anxious individuals may feel dread. Because anxious people find change so stressful, they may stick with what they know but be inclined to wonder if they

1. In addition to passing up major academic, career and relationship opportunities, an anxious person may miss out on many interesting and pleasurable experiences, both large and small, that would require trying new things.

should have done something else. Failure to make a decision inevitably becomes the decision. This is how a person ends up staying in situations that aren't ideal for that person such as an abhorred job or, far worse, an abusive marriage. The anxious person can end up with a lifetime of regret over the opportunities they have passed up. He may receive a gold watch and a fortieth anniversary party yet look back over his life and wonder what he missed.

Rolling with the Changes ... or Not

During each stage of life, and especially at each transition point that requires a major adjustment, the overly sensitive person is more likely to develop any one or more of the anxiety disorders described in this book. As we have seen, the way in which anxiety manifests is quite individualized and can change over time as an individual is required to negotiate each stage in life. Typically, anxious people do tend to experience some free-floating or generalized anxiety much of the time. This will be exacerbated during times of change or stress. Particular anxiety disorders may be more likely to appear at certain stages in a sensitive person's life. Social Anxiety is particularly common during adolescence and young adulthood. During early adolescence, teens become increasingly aware of how others perceive them and often become more self-conscious. At the same time peers become increasingly important in their lives so being shy becomes more problematic. Social Anxiety continues to be especially handicapping when the person reaches his twenties and is expected to find a job because interviews are intimidating, and most work settings involve contact with groups of people. Also, the young adult is expected to become involved in an intimate relationship, another challenging hurdle for any socially anxious person.

As we have seen, a person may have a first panic attack after a major change like going away to college, moving to a new city, or taking a new job. During times of stress, the tendency to worry excessively can progress into full-blown OCD. The individual with GAD will inevitably experience more symptoms when she is under stress and during times of change. GAD symptoms may grow in number and intensity as the person ages. Indeed, GAD is the most prevalent anxiety disorder in the elderly (Mantella et al., 2008).

In thinking about my own life, I have pondered the relationship between anxiety and my choices in education and career. A curious and adventuresome person at heart, I have often experienced a push-pull between what I want to do and the steps necessary to carry out a goal or plan. After graduating from high school, while I might have considered going to a university on the East or West coasts, I chose one two hours away from my Midwestern home. And instead of selecting the huge University of Illinois in the state I grew up in, I chose the smaller University of Iowa which was closer to home although in a different state. In this case, I probably would have been happy at any number of colleges, and Iowa turned out to be an excellent fit for me. After I graduated from college, I applied to and was accepted at a top graduate program, but because it was 1,000 miles from home, I never matriculated.

Later, when I had an opportunity to take a challenging position in a major corporation, I stayed in the low-paying State of Illinois position that I found incredibly boring. Fortunately, my desire to do something more saved me from remaining in this position for life. Ironically, my seventy-two-year-old supervisor served as a sort of reverse role model for me because I was inspired not to end up like her. Several years later I did pursue graduate school, moving my family three states east to State College, Pennsylvania. Truth be told, I may not have applied to a PhD program had I known what I was getting into. Yet, I did persevere, and it was one of the best experiences of my life. Anxiety influenced many of these decisions but fortunately was not ultimately deterministic.

SEVEN

Managing Your Anxiety

In this chapter I speak directly to the reader struggling with anxiety. Family, friends, and significant others of those with anxiety will find the topics and approaches discussed here helpful, so this chapter is written for them too. Health professionals may also find a fresh perspective on stressors and ideas that can serve as adjuncts to traditional therapies. With that said, if you recognize yourself in these pages, then your anxiety is a little less hidden than it was before. That recognition is the first step to living your life to the fullest. Chances are you didn't fully understand exactly what was holding you back. Now that you do, be patient with yourself. Step back a minute and look at yourself as you would a loved one or your best friend. Now treat *you* as you would treat your best friend. Stop judging and criticizing yourself. You are not weak and cowardly. Think about your anxiety as you would any physiological condition whether Type 1 diabetes or asthma. You aren't to blame if you perhaps have been born with a greater reactivity to stress, and there is much you can do right now to start dealing with your heightened sensitivity. Don't feel guilty about spending time on yourself.

I'll start by introducing (1) the importance of taking care of your overall health and (2) ways that you can reduce the stressors in your life. In order to mitigate anxiety, you will need to deal directly with stressors in your immediate environment, in your relationships, at your workplace, and in other aspects of your day-to-day life. To be clear, by stressors I am talking here about the real things that affect you, not your reaction to them. Only then will I address how to cope with stressful aspects of your life that you can't change, but this comes *after* dealing with the stressors themselves. Finally, I will consider strategies for managing each of the major anxiety disorders.

Importantly, *if you are feeling suicidal or if you're suffering from PTSD, you need professional help immediately.* In this case it is vital you do not try to go it alone. Tell your family physician, a trusted family member or a friend so that they can help you to find someone who specializes in anxiety disorders. In general, anxiety sufferers can benefit greatly by consulting a mental health professional, but if you aren't ready for this yet, there are a number of things that you can do on your own to start taking care of yourself.

Before proceeding, here is a further cautionary note: Some of my clients have inadvertently made taking care of themselves stressful! One was a graduate student in a demanding program that required 70 to 80 hours a week of studying. She had read a self-help book that recommended that to reduce stress she spend twenty minutes a day doing something that she enjoyed, get a massage once a week, fix herself a healthy milkshake every day and meditate thirty minutes a day. Being a high achiever by nature, my client immediately incorporated all of the suggestions into her routine. It wasn't long before all of these new habits put even more stress on her as she tried to fit them in between her studying. And her twenty minutes of "relaxation" always gave her time to think about everything that she needed to do for her graduate program.

Promoting Overall Health to Reduce Anxiety

No matter what form your anxiety takes, there are some things that you can do that are good for everyone. Poor health is itself a stressor. As a starting point, get a thorough physical to identify health concerns and areas for improvement. A physical can also help rule out medical causes of anxiety such as hyperthyroidism. A doctor can also make sure that your medications aren't causing heightened anxiety.

For many people, one easy change that may give you quick results in lowering your anxiety level is to gradually reduce the amount of caffeine you're consuming to see whether this makes a difference. One of my clients was "cured" in one session after she indicated on her intake form that she was drinking eight cups of coffee a day. Be sure not to underestimate the amount of caffeine that's in soft drinks and energy drinks and, to a lesser degree, some teas. On the other hand, there are foods, as well as certain herbs and teas, that can be calming. It is also important to drink enough water. Paul Foxman (2007) emphasizes that the symptoms of dehydration are the same as those of anxiety (I would imagine that he is referring to *mild* dehydration). In addition, mainstream medicine is starting to recognize that certain supplements can be useful in controlling anxiety (see the appendix for books on foods and supplements that may reduce anxiety). Diet and nutrition are a cornerstone of taking care of your overall health. We are what we eat. You have some control over your diet, and making healthy choices is empowering. Even when healthy options for a meal are limited, ask yourself what's the *most* healthy option available.

Next, incorporating exercise into your day may be one of the best ways to start addressing your anxiety. A number of studies have found that exercise reduces anxiety (Stonerock et al., 2015). Researchers at Duke University reviewed studies on exercise in patients with high levels of anxiety and concluded that regular exercise *did seem* to reduce anxiety but that more rigorous studies were needed to reach a definitive conclusion. My feeling is that moderate exercise is extremely beneficial. Anecdotal reports from my own clients suggest that exercise can make a big difference in a person's level of anxiety. I've found that many of my clients who were too restless to meditate or enjoy a massage benefited from aerobic exercise, especially if it was outdoors. Indeed, some people who were regulars at the gym realized that they much preferred running or biking around their neighborhoods or hiking in the woods. Even twenty minutes of aerobic exercise can often reduce anxiety symptoms and improve a person's sleep. Moving also decreases muscle tension. In addition, the activity itself can distract you from anxious thoughts. It is important to start these types of activities gradually and find something that you actually enjoy. Forcing yourself to do something that you hate will be difficult to sustain. This can contribute to guilt when you don't follow through, resulting in increases in anxiety. My own particular preferences in my later years are biking, hiking, tennis and pickleball. The latter is a sport that almost anyone can learn in a very short time.

In contrast, competitive athletes should beware of overtraining. A number of scientific studies on overtraining have been conducted on collegiate swimmers. During some periods, collegiate swimmers may train for hours each day, swimming 10,000 yards or more. These high workout loads make them vulnerable to overtraining (Morgan et al., 1987; Tobar, 2012). Overtraining not only decreases athletic performance but also has a host of negative effects on an athlete's mood and psychological well-being, including increased tension. This phenomenon is so common at elite levels that college coaches in many sports would be well advised to post "signs of overtraining" on the locker room door along with the workout schedule.

Alongside exercising, sleep is extremely important. You should make this a priority and don't fault yourself if you need more sleep than the average person. High levels of anxiety throughout the day are exhausting. Many people with anxiety have difficulty falling or staying asleep. There are a number of ways to make it easier to fall asleep and many good articles and books on improving your sleep quality (see the appendix for books on sleep hygiene and learning progressive relaxation, guided imagery, mindfulness, meditation and breathing exercises, all of which can help you to fall asleep more easily and improve the quality of your sleep).

Reducing Stress

Now let's turn to the specifics of your situation. How can you eliminate as much stress from your life as possible? First, you'll want to look for signs of stress within yourself. One of the main reasons people visit their primary care doctors is fatigue. If you are chronically tired, this can be the first sign that you may be under too much stress overall. Now focus on your feelings throughout the day and figure out what you're doing or thinking about when you catch yourself feeling more anxious or tense. You can set the timer on your phone to buzz every hour and then when the alarm goes off, ask yourself how you're feeling. Self-awareness is the first step to addressing any problem and making changes. You can keep a diary of what you did hour by hour and how you felt during that time. Do this on two separate days—one, a typical day, and the second, a day that you had anticipated enjoying. You may be surprised at how much seemingly small things throughout your day are affecting your mood. Do you wake up feeling anxious or does something cause your day to start badly? Does listening to the news or looking at social media have an adverse effect on your mood? Are there things on your "to do" list that you dread? Are you scrambling to get ready for work every morning?

Be mindful of the Holmes and Rahe Stress Scale and don't take on too many life changes at once. For example, don't attempt a voluntary move if you've just started a new job. First, examine your environment. Is there anything about your immediate living space that is making life more stressful for you? If you are living alone, do you prefer this, or would it help to have a roommate or a pet? Loneliness can put a great deal of stress on social animals like ourselves. According to Amy Sullivan (2018), when someone feels lonely, levels of the stress hormone cortisol go up. On the other hand, if you have one or more roommates and find living with these people to be stressful, can you afford a place of your own or change roommates? Overcrowding is invariably stressful. Laboratory experiments have determined that mice living in overcrowded conditions show more "anxiety-like" behaviors than mice with more spacious habitats (Lin et al., 2015).

Pets. If you're living alone and don't want to have a roommate, you may consider getting a pet. Might pets help reduce stress, anxiety, depression and feelings of loneliness? The effect of pets on psychological well-being and other outcomes is often studied, but unfortunately, epidemiological evidence of a beneficial pet effect is tenuous at best (Herzog, 2011).[1] Nevertheless, I would argue that dogs, in particular, may have value for the anxious person. Dogs do double duty since they are terrific companions and also require you to get out and walk them. Some dogs can be excellent exercise buddies, motivating you to run with them. For some, though, man's best friend can be high maintenance and actually increase your level of stress. If you live in an apartment or close quarters, the dog's barking might lead to increased stress. This is not a decision to be taken lightly. If you do decide to get a dog, it will be important for you to research the different breeds in order to get a dog that matches your lifestyle. A good cat can also be an excellent companion and can have a calming effect on the household. For me, there is nothing as soothing as a purring cat on my lap. After a frustrating day of running unpleasant errands, my oldest son once remarked, "I have to get home and get under a cat." Stroking a purring cat can rapidly calm me down when I'm feeling stressed. Yet, similar to dogs, it can be tricky to find a good cat whose habits don't actually contribute to your stress. It may be best to adopt a cat several years old rather than a kitten so that you know what you're getting. If you need a pet that's lower maintenance than a cat or dog, you might find that even watching fish swimming in a tank is relaxing. There may be a reason computers and televisions now have fish tank screen savers.

Beyond animal companionship, plants may have a calming effect for you. Get out in nature frequently, whether deep in the woods or to your local park. If you are looking for a calm, verdant atmosphere, a nearby college campus is worth a visit. Indeed, many colleges consider the entire campus to be an arboretum rather than setting aside a

1. Scientifically, it is difficult to study the effects of pet ownership because the decision to own a pet may be confounded with other personal factors or life circumstances. At the same time, our common knowledge of the effects of pets may be biased. In both the media and personal information channels, "pet regret" doesn't make a good story.

specific parcel of land. Closer to home, consider outdoor or indoor gardening and houseplants. There is an entire subdiscipline of the psychological sciences dedicated to Horticultural Therapy, with positive effects on mood and stress well documented (e.g., Rodiek, 2002; Van Den Berg & Clusters, 2011).[2] Finally, consider this: You may have a personal appreciation for particular kinds of trees, flowers, and plants that may or may not be present where you live today. For example, if you grew up in New England and now live in the South, you may experience some kind of arboreal dissonance when you go out in nature—expecting birch trees and you get southern pines! Do what you can to learn about and appreciate your new environment, and perhaps you can grow a "piece of home" indoors or out.

Marital and Family Life

Living with other people can sometimes be comforting or sometimes contribute to your stress, often both at different times. If your partner or spouse seems to make your stress worse, consider counseling or read one of the excellent self-help books that I've included in the appendix. As Michelle Weiner-Davis advocates in *Divorce Busting* (1992), there are a number of things that you can do to improve your relationship just by making changes yourself. This is important to remember if your partner doesn't see the need for counseling or self-help exercises. Some small things that you can start doing tomorrow to improve your relationship are to (1) let your partner know when you appreciate something that they've done, (2) tell your partner that you love them whenever you're thinking it, (3) do little things to make your partner's day a little easier, and (4) be generous with your compliments. Each of these small things can make a big difference in your relationship. They certainly make for a more pleasant and less stressful environment. Your immediate family should be your safe base where you can always feel comfortable. Here I need to include the importance of hugging. If you have a partner, hug them often. I find that snuggling with my husband every morning is comforting and starts the day off right. Frequently holding hands with your partner can also be comforting and relaxing. But don't stop with your partner. Hug everyone who is open to it and smile at everyone else. A smiling face is an antidote to a

---

2. Yet, it is probably also true that even more rigorous, randomized control trials are needed in this field too.

stressful day. You can limit the time that you spend on social media so that you have more time for your loved ones. But you may feel the need to have some alone time each day, apart from your family.

In terms of your day-to-day routine, limit your exposure to social media. Everyone's life sounds easier and more exciting than your own. The effects of social media can be insidious. You may end up comparing yourself unfavorably to others without being fully aware that this is impacting your self-esteem. Try to avoid stressful phone trees to the extent possible and don't overdose on the news. The media has to repeat the latest bad news over and over; it's their job. But you don't have to listen to it or listen more than once. You may find it best to get your news from a newspaper, rather than television, which tends to be more graphic, and to put your television in an out-of-the-way room in the house.

Around the House

Now let's look at your physical living space itself. Are there things that bother you about your house that you've put off addressing? Take a few minutes to write down all of the negative aspects of your house in one column and things that you can do to address the problems in a second column. For example, do you get enough natural light? Sunshine and light are positively related to mood (Kampfer & Mutz, 2013). Get rid of dark, heavy draperies. I'm surprised at how many homes are closed up and dark. Next, ask yourself if your home is more cluttered than it needs to be. Clutter causes much more stress than people realize. Can you simplify your life by parting with the things that don't give you joy (Kondo, 2010)? There are now many creative storage solutions that can minimize clutter. If you recognized yourself in the section on hoarding in Chapter Four, you may need professional help in order to deal with your possessions. In addition to finding a good therapist, keep in mind that there are now plenty of consultants ready to help you simplify and organize—if you can afford it. If you have children, chances are that they have too many toys. My mother-in-law used to tell me to rotate the toys to minimize the clutter that they created. I now realize that this was one piece of advice that I should have considered. Some of my clients have found that it is important for them to have one room in the house that is set apart in order for them to have a place to retreat to.

Neighborhood Environments, Commutes, and Moving

Consider the world outside the sanctuary of your home. Is your neighborhood conducive to healthy living? Again, being outdoors, among trees, enjoying greenspace, it's all beneficial to your mental health. Do you feel safe? Living in a high crime area is stressful because the need for constant vigilance makes it impossible to relax. Are there sidewalks for walking and running?

Is your street noisy? Noise can wear you down even if you don't feel that it bothers you. In an article addressing noise pollution, Deepak Prasher (2000) states that "it is clear that noise is a stressor," and "if you think that you're getting used to that highway noise, think again." Soothing music inside your home might help to lessen the deleterious effects of outside noise, but you'll want to be able to sit on your balcony or in your yard without being bombarded by noise from traffic or planes. Research has shown that people who live near highways and airports have higher levels of anxiety and other psychological disorders than those who live in quieter settings (Floud et al., 2011; Orban et al., 2016).

Is your neighborhood a "bedroom" community in which neighbors don't know one another? One of my favorite neighborhoods in our city has porches that should be conducive to socializing with neighbors. Unfortunately, I seldom see anyone actually sitting on these porches because the occupants of the houses have to work long hours to be able to afford them. I've been in that situation myself; before my husband and I downsized, our cat had our 3500 square foot house all to himself most days. Spending time with neighbors is good for your mental health, especially if you don't work outside of the home, since this can ameliorate loneliness. As I pointed out, perceived loneliness contributes to a person's stress (Sullivan, 2018). After I retired, I realized that I lacked a sense of community until we moved to a neighborhood in which people tended to be more social.

Do you live in a big city? Large cities are inherently more stressful than smaller cities or towns. Noise, crowding, problems parking, public transportation, and elevators are just a few of the things that can be frustrating. The greater opportunities in a city may certainly make some sacrifices in convenience worth the trouble, but there may come a time when you feel ready to try a less populated, slower paced area. Woody Allen once joked, "Authentic being can only be achieved on the weekend, and even then it requires the borrowing of a car."

If you have identified major concerns with your home or your neighborhood, you may want to move. Unfortunately, remember that moving is high on the stress scale so you want to consider this option very carefully. If you do decide to look for another home, be careful to view places on weekdays so that you can get a feel for whether the neighborhood has a lot of traffic and noise. Buyers tend to see prospective houses and apartments on weekends which are likely to be quieter.

When moving, pay special attention to how you will get to and from work, school, and other important destinations. If you look at a home on the weekends, you are unlikely to get a true feel for what the commute to work will be on a weekday. Long commutes reduce emotional well-being and induce stress (Kahneman et al., 2004; Novaco & Gonzales, 2009). Although you might believe that it "all balances out" and that other features of a home make up for a stressful commute, research shows this is not true. Economists refer to the negative effect of commuting as a behavioral paradox; the effects are negative and demonstrably not balanced by other benefits (Stutzer & Frey, 2008).

Working with Census data, Burd, Burrows, and McKenzie (2021) estimate that in 2019, "the duration of the average one-way commute in the United States increased to a new high of 27.6 minutes, and a record 9.8 percent of commuters reported daily one-way commutes of at least 1 hour." For your own well-being, you don't want to contribute to those statistics if you can avoid it. Spending more than twenty minutes commuting each way is probably too much. Twenty minutes is about the amount of time that it takes to gear up for work in the morning or wind down at the end of the day. It's also not only the commute itself, but the time taken away from other activities that contributes to unnecessary stress. These other activities include healthy habits such as exercising, relaxing and getting enough sleep as well as leisure pursuits that bring you joy, such as hobbies or spending time with your family and friends.

You should also pay attention to the nature of the commute. "Silent" modes of travel like walking and biking don't have the same negative effects as commuting by car, bus, or train, even when they are long (Olsson et al., 2013). Backaches, headaches, digestive problems, high blood pressure, fatigue and difficulty sleeping can all be related to driving in traffic. I, personally, would gladly add five or ten minutes to a drive to avoid a major highway in favor of a picturesque two-lane road. You may feel the same. Although it can be a major stressor of city living, in certain situations, public transportation can be less stressful than dealing with traffic and parking. This is especially true if it's not too crowded and you can read a book or listen to music or a podcast.

Overall, travel to work is such a huge consideration that it might be worth trading your larger home that is farther from your workplace for a smaller, similarly priced one that is closer. Also, because unnecessarily large homes require more upkeep, they can be much more time consuming and expensive to maintain and increase your stress. The move toward downsizing is testimony to this. (However, remember, as noted earlier, that living spaces that are too small for your family, and all of your possessions, can add to daily frustration.)

Beyond the commute itself, when considering buying a house, scrutinize the neighborhood as carefully as you do the house. You often have to make a trade-off in the size of the house and its cost versus the overall desirability of the neighborhood. You will almost invariably get less house for your money in the more desirable neighborhoods, but I believe that you are better off making a good neighborhood your priority. It is easy to fall in love with a particular house because it has that dream kitchen you always wanted while overlooking features of the neighborhood that can undermine your life satisfaction. If you've been able to choose a particular city or town, you'll be defeating your purpose if you move too far away from what drew you there in the first place. If you're living in an outlying suburb, you may quickly realize it feels like you could be living anywhere.

Stress at Work, at Leisure, and Your Personality

The workplace is a common and well-known source of stress. What people appreciate less often is that leisure activities can also be stressful. That is, many supposedly recreational and leisure activities today are far too much *like work*. Consider the lawyer who competes in the courtroom all week long only to spend all weekend playing in a golf tournament or the emergency room doctor who travels to vintage car races every weekend. For these individuals, life is one nonstop effort to be the best, constantly cultivating oneself and constantly in competition mode. Some people are naturally competitive. Most of us have been socialized to be competitive because school and work require it. Sociologists like Annette Lareau (2011) have found that the parallel cultivation of the self in work and leisure is a defining feature of middle-class life and parenting. But a constant pressure to perform can create anxiety.

Certainly, jobs and careers are a source of major stress and anxiety. Almost every industry and profession has documented "burnout" among some proportion of its workers. A crucial aspect of workplace stress is that some of the sources of stress are more "intrinsic" to the occupation and career, while others are specific to the organization or your role in the organization (Cooper & Marshall, 1976). For example, sociologists have long argued that teachers' work is inherently uncertain and that this uncertainty can lead to stress and even burnout (Lortie, 1975; Dworkin, 1987). On the other hand, the work in one's field may be very clear cut, but a lack of job security, limited opportunities for promotion, or conflict with management can still create workplace stress.

As a place to start, focus on the aspects of your work and career that might be creating *unnecessary* stress and ask yourself if there are some things that you might be able to do to alleviate it. Addressing workplace stress might involve talking to your boss about the nature of the work, asking for a change in office seating to get closer to a window, learning to be more assertive with coworkers, making yourself unavailable after hours, not taking work home with you or working from home more. Many of these suggestions involve not over-committing yourself to doing more than you can handle.

If your dissatisfaction is more intrinsic—if you don't enjoy the actual work and find it difficult to make it through the day—it might be time to think about a different career. Changing jobs or careers is a life change that can be stressful and costly but sometimes worth it. After all, we spend a huge chunk of our lives on our jobs. Whatever your career, try not to get involved in the culture of overworking. I realize that this is easier said than done because the entire culture of some occupations is competitive. In our culture as a whole, it seems to have actually become fashionable in some areas of the United States for professionals to work long hours and complain about how little sleep they're getting. Here, I need to make special mention of shift work that changes from week to week and working at night, neither of which is natural for people. We definitely aren't meant to be nocturnal. Studies have found more health problems in night shift workers, including depression and sleep disturbance (Beltagy et al., 2018).

If you are working full time *and* have children, please realize what a full set of responsibility this entails. You may want to try to cut back on your work hours or get more help with the children. The lack of support for working parents in the United States makes combining work and childrearing quite challenging. There is no such thing as the

Superwoman who effortlessly juggles work and parenting even though "other" women may appear to be doing everything. The urge to be an involved father, particularly when gender expectations still encourage you to devote yourself to work and you are unlikely to have had a father who himself was as involved in his family as his work, is also challenging. Don't hesitate to lower your expectations for yourself.

To return to insights on competition in work and leisure, given the ubiquity of stress and anxiety that is often unavoidable on the job, take a careful look at the activities you are engaged in during your leisure hours. Are these activities just more competition? Consider pursuing the more "free and open" version of the activities you enjoy and try to compete against yourself rather than others. More generally, it is important to realize that what you do in your leisure time contributes to the total demands and stress you place on yourself. Is the vacation travel that is supposed to help you relax and refresh actually stressing you out? Are you over-extended because you have taken on too much possibly because you find it hard to say no? Do you have a huge number of interests and projects that are starting to make you feel overwhelmed?

But consider how your individual personality interacts with meeting your obligations. Are you a perfectionistic? Do you expect to do everything and to do it all perfectly? I'll deal with perfectionism later in this chapter. On the other hand, some people find a stress-free environment—if there is such a thing—deadly boring. These "Type A" individuals may actually be more anxious in a quiet, slow-paced setting because they thrive on activity. I was recently rereading Edith Wharton's *The Custom of the Country* (1913). A doctor in the book explains that "nothing was so wearing to a high-strung nature as monotony." Some people feel the need to keep busy and feel that they are less anxious when they are actually doing more. For example, if you're Type A, you may prefer exercise over meditation. In a life-long learning class on healthy living that I took, the instructor asked for a show of hands to indicate how many people would like to meditate. Everyone in the class raised their hands, but when he asked how many actually meditated regularly, only two or three people indicated that they did. Even still, the Type A person should strive for a vibrant, stimulating environment rather than a frenetic one. I suspect it is the rare individual who doesn't need some break from competition.

Debt and Anxiety. A final note before turning to more specific issues. Whatever you do, don't let any of the recommendations in this book be a reason to go into debt. Accumulated debt can be a constant source of anxiety and aggravation that you are reminded of at least once a month when the bills are due. Alina Comoreanu (2021) reports that Americans collectively owe nearly $1 trillion to credit card companies, with an average household debt of $8,089. If you are in debt, develop a plan to address this. There are some excellent free community counseling services, but you should probably avoid private services that charge a fee, as this actually adds more debt. The personal finance website WalletHub.com can get you started on debt recovery.

Managing Anxiety and Its Specific Forms

Once you've done everything that you can do to reduce the stress in your life, you will need to deal with the things that you cannot change by learning to react to them differently and teaching your body to relax. Basically, you will want to counteract the fight or flight response. Herbert Benson (1975) coined the term *the Relaxation Response* as a technique for "turning off" the fight or flight reaction. I'll describe how he recommends doing this in an upcoming section on techniques for dealing with panic. Although I deal with nonmedical approaches that you can implement yourself, ideally you will involve your primary care doctor or a mental health professional in addressing your anxiety. When indicated, a low dose of an antidepressant medication can sometimes seem to have an almost miraculous effect in reducing anxiety in all of its forms.[3]

First, since quality sleep is so important, one of the most helpful practices I have found for people suffering from any of the anxiety disorders that involve worrying is to spend ten minutes before bed writing down all of their worrisome thoughts. Paradoxically, this often enables the worrier to let these thoughts go because they will have the thoughts down on paper so they can be dealt with later if necessary. Scarlett O'Hara in *Gone with the Wind* was onto something when she stated, "I'll think about it tomorrow." If this has the opposite effect and makes it harder for you to fall asleep, try writing down a couple of things for which you are grateful. This can have a calming effect, as it tends to increase your sense of well-being. Journaling every night takes

---

3. In the last few years, we have heard a great deal about CBD products for anxiety. And in the last couple of months, there have been articles about the possibility of using "magic mushrooms" containing psilocybin for treating anxiety and depression. While this sounds promising, more research needs to be done on these approaches.

a bit longer but can be very therapeutic. You can either write about stressful encounters or negative feelings or about activities you especially enjoyed and pleasant thoughts you had during the day. Even just writing whatever comes into your mind can have benefits, as it may end up revealing lurking worries you can now confront. The writing process is also an inherently analytical process; composing a personal narrative may lead to insights about how your values or priorities are changing or to some other new realization. Writing Therapy, a form of Expressive Therapy, has been widely used by mental health practitioners in individual and group settings and is associated with positive changes in mood and self-esteem (Donnelly & Murray, 1991). The therapist may assign different topics for a client to address such as "write about your earliest memory" or "write about a traumatic memory from your middle school years." You might experiment with different topics for your writing to see what puts you in a positive frame of mind.

Now let's look at ways of relaxing and dealing with specific anxiety disorders. These are ideas you might want to combine with the strategies above.

Dealing with Panic Disorder

I will first lay out ways you might address panic disorder because it is the basic fight or flight reaction underlying all anxiety disorders. Because of this, most of the strategies in this section can be used to deal with the other anxiety disorders. I am working from an assumption that those worried they are suffering from such a disorder will have had a physical to rule out any medical causes of panic such as hyperthyroidism or anemia. Unless you have a panic attack that is very different from all of your other episodes, there is nothing to worry about and there are some steps that you can take. First, gradually reduce caffeine for a couple of days to see if this makes a big difference. For some people, particularly those who were in the habit of drinking large amounts of coffee, drinking fewer caffeinated drinks may be all that they need to do to eliminate panic attacks. Remember the client I mentioned previously who appeared to have Panic Disorder but was "cured" in one session after she indicated that she drank multiple cups of coffee a day.

Panic attacks are scary, but they are only so severe. Know that you are not dying. You are not having a heart attack or on the verge of losing consciousness. Also keep in mind that other people probably can't tell there is anything wrong, so you should not worry about embarrassing yourself. Remember that you aren't going crazy or having a nervous breakdown. You aren't going to end up in a psychiatric ward. In addition, your episode of panic will pass. Say to yourself, "This is just a panic attack."

Talk to your family doctor about your panic attacks for reassurance if you continue to have doubts that the panic attacks are not signaling a serious medical problem. Your doctor can also prescribe a small dose of an anti-anxiety medication that works in approximately twenty minutes. Just having this with you and knowing that it works quickly can often make you less anxious and consequently less likely to have a panic attack. You may find that you rarely need to take the medication. Additionally, your doctor may want to prescribe a low dose of an antidepressant that could reduce the likelihood of your having a panic attack in the first place. If your episodes occur daily or weekly, this option is worth considering.

It is common for a person's first panic attack to coincide with a major transition in their life. If you are prone to anxiety, you can help to prevent problems by preparing well for transitions and making them gradually. If it feels like it is too late and you're already having panic attacks, Progressive Muscle Relaxation is the most basic way of teaching your body to relax. This relaxation will make it less likely you experience episodes of panic. A therapist can teach you or you can use a recording (e.g., tape, app) or read a book. The recording is probably the easiest. The goal of Progressive Muscle Relaxation is for you to eventually be able to relax yourself within minutes (see the appendix for books on Progressive Muscle Relaxation). The technique involves learning to relax all of the muscles of your body from head to toe by first tensing each muscle and then letting go of the tension so that each muscle automatically relaxes (this begins with you wrinkling and relaxing your forehead and ends with you curling and releasing your toes). Biofeedback can enable you to learn this more quickly, however, biofeedback sessions can be expensive. Breathing exercises are another shortcut. Taking a few deep breaths can sometimes quickly reduce your level of anxiety. Although we are discussing anxiety here, you might be interested to know that the RESPeRATE corporation has developed a low-cost guided breathing technology that is FDA cleared and clinically proven to lower blood pressure. These remarkable devices are in widespread use, and you should ask your doctor if they may promote your health.

Regular massage sessions are another good way to reduce bodily tension. With Progressive Muscle Relaxation and massage addressing your bodily tension, you can also add visualization exercises to calm your mind. I often recommended that my clients picture themselves in their favorite place to relax after finishing their Progressive Muscle Relaxation exercises. Your favorite place could be lying on the beach or in warm grass or a hammock in your back yard. Use your five senses to appreciate the outdoors. Some people have had success being hypnotized or learning EMDR (Eye Movement Desensitization and Reprocessing) but there is some controversy around these two treatment approaches and they are expensive.

Yoga and meditation are among the single best ways to relax your body and mind. There are many yoga classes available that are geared toward every level of fitness. I've found that my clients reported doing best when they started with "gentle yoga" classes (see the appendix for books on yoga and meditation). You will want to find a book or class for beginners, and some videos are available for free online. When you first start meditating, you may feel relaxed during the sessions only to have your anxiety return almost the minute that you're finished. Meditating regularly can enable you to extend the relaxed feeling for increasingly longer periods of time.[4]

There are a number of websites or apps geared toward meditation, with Calm being one of the most popular and offering a suite of free audio recordings. As I mentioned, one caveat is that many of my anxious clients were too restless to meditate. Then again, they were able to achieve similar results through aerobic exercise. You might even consider an active form of mediation while out for a slow walk. Meditation guidebooks will explain how to concentrate on your five senses, the gentle wind in your hair, and environment while walking, pushing aside anxious thoughts.

Meditators are instructed to try to let go of any thoughts that come into their minds. However, allowing yourself to daydream can also be relaxing. You can even direct your daydreaming by deciding what to think about. Topics might be pleasant memories from the past or dreams for your future. Some people see daydreaming as a waste of time

---

4. Transcendental Meditation™ is a very popular technique based on an Indian tradition. A TM master gives you your own personal mantra that you are to repeat in your mind until you have eliminated distracting thoughts. The secret mantra, that you aren't supposed to divulge, is considered crucial. In his 1975 book *The Relaxation Response*, Herbert Benson tried to take the mystery out of this by instructing people to utilize a one syllable word in place of the mantra.

and try to suppress these thoughts. But daydreaming can be a source of many creative ideas.

If you have started curtailing certain activities or situations because you fear that they might bring on a panic attack, you might begin gradually introducing yourself to these activities or settings by utilizing a hierarchy like the one presented in the chapter on Agoraphobia. This technique is described in detail in the appendix. Your hierarchy needs to be completely individualized for you. You will be taking one small step at a time. For example, if you are afraid of having a panic attack at the store your hierarchy might have you driving past the store as number 1, running into the store and quickly buying one item somewhere in the middle and shopping for a week's groceries as the ultimate goal at number 20. You can enlist a friend to accompany you, and you can carry a small dose of anti-anxiety medication. Reward yourself with a small guilty pleasure after you complete each step. If you are not ready for in vivo exercises you can visualize each step after you've gotten yourself into a relaxed state with Progressive Relaxation. When you are able to visualize shopping in the store without feeling panicky, you'll be ready for the in vivo exercise which consists of performing each step in order of its difficulty.

You may remember Jill, the college coed who began to have panic attacks on her way to class the first semester of her freshman year. She ended up leaving for home without officially withdrawing from the university and received failing grades in all of her classes. Several years later, Jill came to me when I was working at the counseling center to try to get the grades expunged from her transcript. When she described what had happened, I explained Panic Disorder and the treatment for it, referred her to a therapist in her hometown, and encouraged her to work toward going back to school, starting at her community college. With the encouragement of her therapist, Jill initially took one class at a time until she built up to four classes a semester. After a few years, she was able to transfer to a four-year college that was smaller than the university where I worked. She continued to work with a counselor and was able to complete the program and graduate with good grades. You too can overcome panic attacks.

Agoraphobia

If you have developed Agoraphobia, you can utilize the suggestions above, but you want to go at a slower pace. If you are housebound, you can start very small with your initial goal being to walk out to the mailbox. Gradually you can set goals to walk farther in your immediate neighborhood. A significant other or a friend can accompany you initially when you attempt each step. You could adopt a dog to walk along with you.

Recall Nancy, the fifty-four-year-old retired attorney who was completely housebound. Nancy's sister was finally able to convince Nancy to let her schedule an appointment with a psychologist and accompanied her to the first session. The therapist taught Nancy Progressive Muscle Relaxation and had her develop a hierarchy with the goal of being able to do volunteer work. Nancy spent a month visualizing each step until she was able to attempt completing the hierarchy in real life. The therapist suggested that Nancy adopt a dog, and this enabled her to spend increasingly longer periods of time outside walking the dog. Next, Nancy's sister began driving her to the grocery store and Nancy waited in the parking lot until she was able to accompany her sister into the store. The next step was for Nancy to drive her sister to the store. During this time, Nancy started taking a low dose of an antidepressant and was very gradually reducing the anti-anxiety medication that she had been taking. The turning point came when Nancy was able to volunteer as a pro bono lawyer. She worked up to all of this so gradually that she didn't have any full-blown panic attacks and was able to "talk herself down" if she felt a twinge of panic. Nancy even met a man online and had been with him for two years the last time that I spoke to her sister. Here is the Hierarchy that worked for Nancy:

1. Take Fido into the back yard
2. Walk one third of a mile with Fido
3. Walk a mile with Fido
4. Go on a short drive with Mary (sister)
5. Accompany Mary to the grocery store and wait in the car for ten minutes
6. Accompany Mary into the store for five minutes
7. Remain in the store for ten minutes
8. Remain in the store for twenty minutes
9. Remain in the store long enough to buy groceries for a week
10. Accompany Mary downtown
11. Spend fifteen minutes walking around the downtown with Mary
12. Email an old friend

13. Talk to a friend on the phone
14. Go out to lunch with Mary and an old friend
15. Go to lunch with an old friend without Mary
16. Go out to lunch with two friends
17. Take the class on pro bono volunteer work
18. Obtain a pro bono client

Social Anxiety

If you recognized yourself in the chapter on Social Anxiety, there are many things that you can do. A sizable proportion of my friends, as well as my clients, remembered having been shy as children or at some point in their lives. Some of my clients who were in treatment to address other problems described "outgrowing" their social anxiety or having conquered it. This suggests that you, too, can overcome your fear.

If your anxiety is limited to performing or taking tests, you can address the specific issue by developing a hierarchy such as the hierarchy that I developed for one of my clients who was afraid of public speaking, with giving a lecture to a large group as his ultimate goal. We used fifteen index cards on which the client listed anxiety-arousing situations involving speaking in front of people and then arranged them from least to most anxiety arousing with giving a speech as number 15. His first step was to read a short poem to a friend. Leading a small group discussion was in the middle at number 8. Psychiatrists sometimes prescribe a blood pressure medication to take the edge off a performer's anxiety, because it doesn't make the person drowsy like anti-anxiety medication does. This can be effective for treating test anxiety as well.

What if you suffer from more generalized Social Anxiety? Every situation involving other people will be an opportunity for you to develop your social skills and become more comfortable around people. Take advantage of some of these day-to-day opportunities. For example, you can make it a point to compliment a cashier or your mail carrier. Adopt or borrow a dog and walk around your neighborhood or take your dog to a dog park. This can be an excellent way to meet your neighbors. People often strike up conversations when they see someone walking a dog and they will be focused on your pet and not you. If you prefer not to attract too much attention to yourself at this point, walk in a slightly less populated area where you are likely to encounter a more manageable number of people. You can hide behind sunglasses if this helps.

Understanding Anxiety

If you fear parties, develop a hierarchy that starts with lunch with a friend. Lunch with three or four friends or joining a book club could be somewhere in the middle of the hierarchy. Try to remember that people at these gatherings are not that focused on you, since they are often thinking about the impression they're making and what they're going to say. Some of my clients found that parties were much easier for them if they arrived early when there were fewer people. This allowed them to warm up gradually as they had time to talk with some of the guests individually.

The best and easiest thing that you can do to combat Social Anxiety is to begin with one-on-one encounters and to practice listening. If you are listening to another person, you can't also be dwelling on your own feelings and thoughts. This also makes you a much better conversationalist. If you are truly listening, questions and comments will come naturally to you. To hold a satisfactory conversation, you need to do two things: (1) reveal things about yourself and (2) ensure you are asking the other person questions. The psychological literature on conversation (e.g., Lakoff, 1990) can give you more information on conversation, but if you are not a natural conversationalist, start by keeping those two principles in mind. If you are only talking about yourself and never asking about the other person, you are hosting a one-sided conversation. Likewise, in a conversation, you are expected to share something about yourself, your own ideas and sentiments, and so forth, so it doesn't feel like an interview and gives other people fodder for conversation. If you sometimes find conversations awkward, don't be afraid to literally say to yourself, "OK, I just told them what I think; now I ask a question."

Beyond those basics, it doesn't hurt to think about a couple of interesting topics that you're excited about before you get together with people. These can serve as openers for starting conversations. If you attend a large party alone, you can find a person who doesn't seem to be engaged in a conversation to approach. Admit that you don't know many people at the party and ask how they know the host. Typically, though, you'll know at least one or two people at the party and you can start with them. Sipping a drink, even if it is nonalcoholic, gives you something to do. Don't go overboard with alcohol, as you don't want to embarrass yourself. You want to make this gathering as successful as possible so that the next one will be easier.

You might also join a group or take a class. One of my clients found that a group exercise class was perfect. Attending this class put her in a group of people that she saw three times a week, but she didn't have to interact with anyone until she was ready. Meanwhile, the aerobic exercise itself reduced her anxiety. It took almost a year, but now she has several friends in the class. Yoga classes are particularly good because everyone tends to be relaxed after the class. Be easy on yourself by making this process of joining a group gradual and giving yourself credit for accomplishing each small step. Remember to treat yourself in a supportive way as you might your best friend instead of faulting yourself when you find a social situation difficult. Counter any self-critical thoughts that cross your mind with positive "self-talk" in the form of supportive statements to yourself (resources related to Positive Self-Talk, a Cognitive Behavioral technique, are provided in the appendix). Many of us have used this self-talk for years without realizing that there was a term for it. Examples are "That conversation went well" and "She seemed to like me" instead of "I sounded so stupid" or "You're making a fool of yourself."

Peter Kramer (1993) writes that, for a subset of people, taking a serotonin reuptake inhibitor (SSRI), which is a class of antidepressants, can transform their personalities. He writes, "Prozac seemed to give social confidence to the habitually timid, to make the sensitive brash, and to lend the introvert the social skills of a salesman." If self-help techniques don't work, you might want to talk to a psychiatrist to get an opinion on taking a small dose of an SSRI antidepressant.

Understand Your Shyness

Sometimes it can help to get a better understanding of your Social Anxiety in its various forms. Try to remember your earliest memories of being shy. Was there an incident that triggered it? In my case, I was born shy as evidenced in my approach to kindergarten that I described earlier. But I can trace my lack of confidence in certain social situations back to an incident from grade school. My seven-year-old friends were going door to door selling their artwork. I told my parents that I wanted to sell something, and my father suggested that I put some of the vegetables from our huge garden in a wagon and sell them to neighbors. One of the first houses that I approached belonged to an eighth-grade teacher who lived across the street from us. When she opened the door and I announced why I was there, she stared at me with a look of pity, assuming that my parents had sent me out to bring in money for the family. This was the first time that I felt complete and utter shame.

This incident made me hesitant to sell anything, especially myself. A crafty salesman could have told me to use her misunderstanding to my advantage! However, a seven-year-old doesn't think that way. If you can remember an incident that triggered your shyness, you may be better able to combat your anxiety. Know that you are a different person now. Also, you can think about settings in which you feel confident. How do these differ from those you find difficult? Setting up a hierarchy can also give you insight into the exact nature of your shyness.

Remember Mary Ellen from the chapter on Social Anxiety? Her situation was greatly complicated by her addiction to anti-anxiety medications and alcohol. Things began to turn around for Mary Ellen when a new psychiatrist suspected the addictions were masking Social Anxiety and that she didn't have Bipolar Disorder. After he explained Mary Ellen's actual problem to her parents, they were able to give her the support and encouragement that she needed. Mary Ellen agreed to stay away from her friends who took drugs and drank excessively. Under her doctor's direction and her parents' supervision, she was able to wean off of the medications for Bipolar Disorder and to gradually reduce and eliminate her anti-anxiety medication (she remained on a small dose of an antidepressant). The psychiatrist helped Mary Ellen to address her Social Anxiety by setting up a hierarchy with her. With his help, she began taking courses at the community college and developed a passion for animal science. She was able to reestablish some of her friendships from middle school and start dating. The last that I heard, Mary Ellen was living with a roommate, working at a veterinarian's office, and involved in a serious relationship with a young man whom she met at college.

Specific Phobia

If you have a phobia, the first thing to do is to acknowledge how common phobias are. Many high achieving people suffer from phobias much stranger than yours. If you are afraid of something that can easily be avoided without restricting your life in any way, don't even worry about it. It is of no consequence if it doesn't impact your life in a negative way. If you're afraid of heights, don't push yourself to climb ladders. If you fear elevators and don't live in a big city and are in good shape, climbing stairs is a healthy alternative to using an elevator. If a phobia is impacting your life (i.e., you're a professional painter who has been afraid of ladders), make a hierarchy and utilize all of the ideas that I've presented under Panic Disorder. You can ask your doctor if she thinks a small dose of an anti-anxiety medication might be indicated when you first start working on the hierarchy. Remember, at some point, just having the medication with you may be enough to progress through the hierarchy. If you are not ready to confront your fears in vivo, begin with Progressive Muscle Relaxation. After you are in a relaxed state, picture yourself confronting your particular phobia. Then begin imagining taking small steps to approach the feared object or situation. You will need to eventually face your fear. Remember the young woman who conquered her fear of death by working with a hospice. If you are afraid of snakes, for example, you can begin by looking at a picture book about snakes and then visiting a snake exhibit at a museum or zoo. This is how my snake phobic client was able to conquer her fear and resume gardening. You may remember Maureen who sold her historic home because of her fear of spiders. She became so unhappy living in a new house in a generic subdivision that she returned to treatment. By mastering Progressive Relaxation and visualizing spiders until she could remain comfortable, Maureen was able to start looking at picture books on spiders and to desensitize herself. She visited a spider exhibit at a museum twice a week for several months until she was no longer panicky and eventually started vacationing at historic B&Bs again. She was even able to buy and restore another historic home. Maureen now had two things to be proud of: her charming historic home and the fact that she overcame her phobia. Grace, the young mother who feared that her daughter would become car sick, never got over her disgust of vomit, but she was able to drive her daughter to activities by repeatedly reassuring herself that her daughter had never thrown up in the car and that the chances of her getting sick were extremely low. After a couple of months, Grace was able to drive her daughter around without thinking about her becoming car sick.

Obsessive Compulsive Disorder (OCD)

If obsessions or compulsions are interfering with your daily living and the suggestions in this section are not enough to enable you to live your best life, you can talk to your doctor to see if medication might be indicated. Several antidepressants have been approved by the FDA for treating Obsessive Compulsive Disorder (OCD).

Since obsessions and compulsions tend to worsen during times of stress, it will be particularly important for you to reduce the stress in your life by following the aforementioned tips. Sometimes this is enough to reduce your obsessive thinking. Remember that the thoughts are harmless because you are not going to act on them (if you're hearing voices that are telling you to harm yourself or someone else, this is another matter; you must seek professional help immediately).

First and foremost, don't attempt to fight obsessive thoughts. By allowing yourself to think these thoughts without fighting them, you can more easily let them go. Just tell yourself, "Well that was a random thought." Obsessive thoughts are just thoughts. Know that you won't follow through on the "bad" thoughts that happen to cross your mind. Remind yourself that you are not a bad person if some of your passing thoughts happen to be socially unacceptable, immoral or violent. Obsessive thoughts are typically "out of character" to the person who is experiencing them, as people generally let innocuous thoughts go without even being fully aware of them. This should go a long way toward helping you relax and eliminate any feelings of guilt, reducing your overall anxiety and the thoughts themselves. You may also be able to redirect your thoughts by taking a walk, meditating on the sights and sounds in nature around you. However, if you have actually done something wrong, you can turn your guilt into productive action by apologizing to someone you've hurt or by making restitution in some way. As I suggested in reference to dealing with anxiety in general, if you have difficulty sleeping, try spending ten minutes before bed scribbling down any thoughts that you have. This exercise is particularly helpful for people with OCD and can help you to let the thoughts go.

If you are more prone to generalized worry rather than specific obsessive thoughts, you can start out by setting aside twenty minutes a day to focus exclusively on any worries that are coming to mind. You can write out these worries if it helps. Paradoxically, you'll probably find that it will become harder and harder to actually spend the full twenty minutes worrying. You might also try to "talk back" to your thoughts when you write them. One technique for dealing with obsessions is to draw a line down the middle of a paper and list your worries on one side with the statistical probability (or just plain "likelihood") of anything that you are worrying about actually happening on the other side. Think about any productive actions you can take to address the worry. You can also think of the worst-case scenario which often helps people to realize that they aren't dealing with anything catastrophic. In *Worry* (1997),

Hallowell has a chapter laying out ways of combatting one's tendency to worry.

In the psychology literature you will find many examples of people successfully conquering obsessions and my clients were no exception. Some of my clients were able to eliminate their obsessive thoughts almost the moment that they were able to accept that the thoughts didn't mean that they were "bad" people. This was the case for Rick who feared letting his young daughter's head slip under the water while he was bathing her. Barbara improved almost overnight when she realized that she wasn't a sinful or immoral person and that she was not in danger of actually shouting obscenities in church. She was able to go back to church by first sitting in the back row in case she felt the need to leave. This never actually happened after she understood that her thoughts were harmless. In both cases lessening overall stress also made a big difference. Rick and his wife reduced their hectic work hours and Barbara addressed her feelings about her marriage in therapy with me and then began couples counseling with her husband.

If your obsessive thoughts have led to compulsions, you may need to see a therapist if the compulsions are significantly interfering with your life. Targeted therapies like those employed to conquer phobias, including Exposure and Response Prevention (ERP), have been successful in treating OCD (Foa et al., 2103). There are also some self-help techniques that you can try. First think back to when the compulsive behaviors started. Remember Jason's compulsions to dot his i's in a particular way so that no harm would befall his mother. You will recall that after Jason's parents realized that he was under much stress due to a critical teacher and placed him in another classroom, his compulsive behavior disappeared. You may be able to get to the root of your own stressors, an important step toward reducing or eliminating them. Think about when the compulsions seem to be worse. This can help to make you aware of triggers, some of which you may be able to eliminate. Are there certain situations that are causing you more stress than you realize, making the compulsions worse? One of my clients became aware that his handwashing was more extreme whenever he was anticipating a visit to his parents' house. Another client found that her compulsive cleaning seemed completely out of control before her in-laws visited. She was able to reduce the amount of time that she spent cleaning when she admitted to herself that she felt uncomfortable being around her mother-in-law, a lovely and supportive woman who was so accomplished that my client felt inferior to her. She spent some time in therapy addressing this issue and gained confidence in her own abilities so that she felt comfortable around her husband's parents.

Greg, the anxious graduate student, was able to reduce his compulsive cleaning after he successfully requested an extension on a paper that was causing him much stress. After getting his doctorate, he has been able to recognize that when he starts cleaning excessively, it signals that he is under stress at work. He now uses his cleaning behaviors to gauge whether he has taken on too much.

If you have too much time on your hands, find some distractions so that you won't have as much time for compulsive behaviors. One of my clients had spent up to an hour or two each day checking her body for signs of skin cancer. Mary had had a small spot on her shoulder removed around the same time that a friend was diagnosed with stage four melanoma. This checking was reduced tremendously after she got a part-time job. Yet, these purposeful distractions should not be something that adds more stress to your life. You want to find the right balance between distracting yourself and taking on too much. It is also interesting that Mary realized that her compulsive checking began when she and her husband started having some conflict over his long hours at work. Six months of couple's counseling improved their relationship and reduced her anxiety so that she didn't have to fight the urge to check her skin as often.

If you have OCD and also a perfectionistic personality, you face the added stress of overworking to achieve unnecessarily difficult goals, which will often lead to disappointment and self-criticism. In their book *Perfectionistic Predicament: How to Stop Driving Yourself and Others Crazy* (1991), Miriam Elliott and Susan Meltsner quote a perfectionistic woman they call Judy who didn't know how to relax: "The minute that I sit down, I feel antsy. I feel like there's something I probably should be doing and since I'm not doing it, I feel guilty." I provide resources for perfectionists in the appendix.

Generalized Anxiety Disorder (GAD)

You will recall that like OCD, Generalized Anxiety Disorder (GAD) is characterized by worry. What distinguishes it from OCD is that the worries are usually realistic because they focus on things that could actually happen. The seemingly endless number of physical symptoms that accompany the worry can be especially problematic.

With GAD it is particularly important to reduce your overall stress by utilizing the foregoing ideas. If you are overscheduled, you will want to try to cut back. However, don't eliminate non-stressful activities that may help distract you from your worries and physical symptoms. It is important to strike a balance.

It might seem counterintuitive to a person who feels exhausted, but exercise may be the single most important thing that you can do to reduce your symptoms. It lowers your level of anxiety, allows you to sleep better, and can distract you from worrisome thoughts and bodily symptoms. The key is to start gradually and work up to around twenty minutes of aerobic exercise a day. You can continue to gradually increase this time. In a different vein, going to a massage therapist is also very helpful for those with GAD. Not only is a gentle massage extremely relaxing, it can also address your muscular aches and pains.

You can use some of the same techniques for the worry component of GAD as those listed for OCD. With the worries in GAD being realistic things that could happen to you or your family, you can take preventative action to reduce the likelihood of your worries becoming a reality. For example, if you are worried about your teenager having a car accident, go out driving with him on country roads and gradually have him work up to busier streets and highways. If you are worried about a house fire, have your wiring checked, install more smoke detectors, learn to use a fire extinguisher, and develop an escape plan for your family. If using a flag on your bicycle makes you feel safer, use one; a flag *does* make you safer, with only a tiny increase in air resistance.

When it comes to your physiological symptoms, there are a number of strategies you might use to reduce your focus on your ailments. Remember, they aren't signals that you have a serious disease. If you are scrutinizing your body for symptoms every day, reduce the time that you allow yourself to do this or try the paradoxical approach of forcing yourself to spend a half hour a day checking yourself from head to toe. Some people find that this quickly cures them of their tendency to look for something wrong.

If you are worried about a particular symptom, you can ask yourself, "What are the actual chances of this being something serious?" Then you can tell yourself, "There is only a 1 percent chance of this being...." One of my clients started noticing that it felt like she had a lump in her throat. This is not an uncommon symptom of anxiety. My client quickly consulted the *Merck Manual* and diagnosed herself with esophageal cancer! After she researched this disease, she realized that it was actually quite rare and was able to reassure herself that "there is an extremely small chance that this is cancer" until she was able to get an appointment with her doctor.

If you have a worrisome symptom that you haven't had before, it's probably best to see a doctor for reassurance that it's nothing serious. As we age, maladies naturally arise, and if they catch you by surprise or have origins mysterious to you, anxiety will follow. For example, carpal tunnel syndrome is relatively common among older adults, but the initial symptoms strike many people as perplexing. You'll do best with a seasoned doctor who won't order tests for diseases that are unlikely to be the cause of your symptoms. One who understands anxiety and won't quickly dismiss you will obviously be best. Be mindful of the doctor's time and prepare for the visit with a list of questions. Antidepressants in low doses may be particularly helpful for GAD patients both in reducing the tendency to worry and the physical symptoms. In fact, the SSRIs may even lessen pain.

If you have been spending most of your days in bed or resting on the couch, make gradual exercise a goal and take small steps each day. Remember that your goal will be to eventually be able to exercise aerobically for 20 minutes a day. Get out of bed and start moving even if you feel exhausted. People often feel better once they are up and moving around. But don't push yourself too hard. Stretching first thing in the morning can alleviate some of your aches and pains. Then start introducing some gentle exercise like walking. Try to walk a little bit farther every day. Even just walking around the block is a good start. Getting outside in nature should be reinforcing in and of itself. A dog is a great motivator to get you up and out. However, be realistic, as some dogs wake up very early and require a lot of exercise. Make sure to have a small fenced-in area so that you can let your dog out when you can't get out to walk.

The best thing that you can do is to find something to focus on besides your health! If you don't currently have any passionate interests that you can get excited about, think back to what you used to enjoy doing. Some people might have to think back to middle school or high school to come up with something. That's okay! Was there a hobby that you always wanted to try but never had the time? If you're working but are on the verge of retirement, consider just scaling back and continuing to work part-time unless your job is highly stressful. If you're retired, consider volunteering for a cause that you've always been interested in.

Many people find that volunteering at their local animal shelter can be calming.

The negative effects of stress for anyone, but especially for those with GAD, can be partially ameliorated by restorative time. In *Dancing with Fear* (2007), Foxman advocates for a Recovery Day which he conceptualizes as a day to set aside for "cleansing yourself from accumulated stress." He goes on to describe this as a quiet day: "the kind of day that you would take for yourself if you were sick and had to stay home." He recommends not even talking to anyone either in person, on the phone or by text during this day of relaxation and restoration.

EIGHT

Children, Anxiety, and Parenting Behaviors

If you recognized your son or daughter in the chapter on anxiety over the life span, there is much that you can do to address your child's heightened sensitivity. Importantly, *this chapter is not a substitute for professional medical and psychological care for your child*; please seek professional help if your child has a serious medical or behavioral problem. That said, in this chapter I will provide some strategies for parenting the anxiety-prone child. The earlier in her life that you start addressing her heightened sensitivity, the better. You can also prevent your child from developing some of the problems associated with anxiety by trying to minimize your *own* anxiety utilizing some of the strategies in the previous chapter.

To start at the very beginning, prospective mothers will want to reduce the chances of their infants being born highly reactive by doing everything possible to ameliorate stress during pregnancy. Although it seems like a cruel joke, there is evidence that mothers who were anxious during their pregnancies were more likely to end up with anxious babies (Glover, 2011), although these babies could have inherited their mother's genes for anxiety. Research in this area is ongoing. Either way, anxiety-prone mothers may have more difficult babies which in turn may certainly heighten their own anxiety.

One of the most basic things that you can do is to let go of the idea that you will be the perfect parent. This parent doesn't exist. Strive to be a "good enough" parent. The concept of the good enough mother was introduced by Donald Winnicott in the 1980s and was an important thesis in his well-read book *Babies and Their Mothers* (1992). But it seems that in each decade after that, parents have expected more of themselves. In the television hit *Downton Abbey* the family matriarch (the Dowager Countess Violet) is asked if she was one of those parents who only saw their children for an hour after tea; she replies, "Yes, but it was an hour *every* day." We all could learn a little from the Dowager Countess and still be loving and good enough parents. I will look at each stage of child development and offer strategies that parents can employ to minimize stress and help their child to cope.

Infants

Remember the airline attendant's instructions to put your own oxygen mask on before attempting to deal with your child's mask. Taking care of yourself might feel impossible when you can't even manage to sneak in a shower, but it's critical to try to find some time for *you*. A calm parent is very important in keeping the baby's environment low key and less anxiety arousing, as babies may pick up on a nervous parent's anxiety. You can try to keep calm by using the techniques that I described in the chapter on managing your anxiety.

Most importantly, try to stay rested. This is easier said than done since many new parents find sleep deprivation to be the most challenging aspect of bringing home their newborns. If you are sleep deprived, your baby's nap time isn't the time for you to clean house or prepare a gourmet meal. This precious time is best spent napping yourself. Cut yourself some slack on cooking and other household duties and welcome help from others if they can do so in a way that won't add to your stress. You do want to minimize clutter but now isn't the time to expect your house to be perfect.

There are also strategies you can use with your infant to minimize stress. If you recognized your baby in these pages, you probably have a sensitive child who reacts intensively to almost everything (Aron, 2002; Cain, 2012; Chess et al., 1965). The literature offers many suggestions you can use and adapt to raise calmer children. Your sensitive infant may need a more regular routine than the average newborn, particularly when it comes to sleeping. Sensitive babies are often more irregular in their sleeping and waking cycles. It is critical for infants to get enough sleep, especially in the first three months of their lives. Remember that these first three months are now being referred to as the fourth trimester (a contradiction in terms, but an important concept nonetheless). Thus, naptime and sleep hours need to be considered "sacred" and scheduled for approximately the same time every day. At the same time, you will need to be flexible in responding to your infant. A balance between trying to establish a routine and listening to your baby is important. You don't want to maintain such a tight schedule that your child doesn't have to learn to be flexible and to cope with changes.

Try swaddling your infant at bedtime and naptime and carrying her strapped to your chest during the day for this "fourth trimester." The warmth of your chest and your familiar heartbeat should be comforting to her. Reduce stimulation in the house by keeping it quiet with minimal artificial light. Additionally, strong smells and coarse fabrics can make sensitive babies uncomfortable. You don't need to overstimulate your infant by dangling too many toys over his head. We read so much about enriching the environment to increase your child's IQ that it can be difficult not to go overboard.

Respond to your infant at the first sign of distress, when the child is easier to soothe. Research has shown that a newborn whose parents are responsive will cry less by the time that he is a few months older and that picking your baby up does *not* reinforce crying (Tisinger, 2016). Remember that responsive parents are more likely to end up with securely attached children (Bowlby & Ainsworth, 1979). A rocking chair can be invaluable in comforting a newborn and reducing crying, since anything that rocks can simulate the rocking motions that the infant became accustomed to in the womb. Consider having your baby sleep right *next* to your bed for the first year (it is not safe for a child to sleep *in* your bed until they are older). If you are nursing, nurse your newborn whenever he seems hungry instead of nursing on a schedule. Nursing actually increases the chemical Oxytocin, which has calming effects for both you and your baby. If you are unable to nurse, you can make sure to hold your baby in the nursing position rather than propping up the bottle. It is also good to take your baby outside every day that it's possible. Start with at least twenty minutes in the beginning and work your way up. Nature is soothing. Very gradually expose your infant to family and friends.

When possible, it helps to have both parents available for the first few months. This is the period when babies cry more frequently and have more difficulty settling. Policy discussions in the United States are beginning to consider parental work leave for both parents. This policy is already in place in other countries. It is simply not realistic to expect the staff of a day care center or even an at-home nanny to be as responsive to an infant's needs as you can be. If you have a job, hopefully you can get six months of leave. However, sadly, this is currently not possible for many workers in the United States. Some mothers seem to be able to manage working from home with their child napping or playing contently nearby, but don't fault yourself if you find this impossible. I suspect anyone able to manage such an arrangement must have an easy baby.

Introduce new experiences slowly. Bath time can initially be traumatic for both parent and child. You can start with a small portable tub raised to waist height. Thereafter, a laundry basket placed in the regular bathtub offers a secure next bathtime step. When it's time to introduce solid foods, do so gradually, one new food at a time. Your sensitive child may be more likely to be a picky eater.

Once your child begins to crawl, everything changes. She may be less likely to cry because she can content herself by exploring her newly expanded world. The single best thing that you can do to reduce stress and make parenting far easier is to thoroughly childproof your entire house *before* your child starts to crawl. Not having to be constantly vigilant makes parenting considerably less stressful. Childproofing should include attention to lead hazards (in crumbling paint, in soil around the house). Lead is a powerful environmental toxin that can permanently impair cognitive development.

Toddlers

As your child grows, you will want to try to stick with a regular sleeping, napping, and eating schedule, but you don't have to be fanatical about it. Babies and toddlers can fall asleep almost anywhere, and your lifestyle may not accommodate rushing home every day at 1:00 p.m. for your toddler's nap, particularly if you have older children. Gradually expose your toddler to new things. Don't pressure them to eat something they don't want and don't push them to do something they seem to be afraid of. Let your child go at their own pace with gentle encouragement from you. But don't give in to temper tantrums. If you are consistent in never doing so, this will quickly extinguish the tantrums, eliminating one major source of stress in childrearing. At bedtime, your child may still sleep better near you. Co-sleeping is fine after your baby is a year old, when it is deemed safe to do so. Most baby mammals sleep with their mothers until they are the equivalent of four human years of age.

Ideally, you will be able to get outside for increasingly longer periods of time even if the weather isn't perfect. You can do this gently and gradually to get your child used to the outside world. Start taking your toddler to the playground, on short shopping trips, to the library for story time, or to a museum that offers programs for young children. Importantly, don't push your child to interact with other children until she is ready. She may just watch the other children for what seems like a very long time. Think of this as a necessary warming-up period. Library story hours are particularly good for preparing your child for preschool and kindergarten. Swimming lessons and exercise classes for mother and child can be good ways of introducing your toddler to other children with you there for support. Even a trip to the grocery store can be a good way of getting toddlers comfortable with the world outside of the home. At the end of the grocery run, it's OK to give your child a small treat so that she associates good things with the shopping trip and is eager to go again. It doesn't take much to satisfy a small child, so you don't have to get into the habit of spending a lot of money on large rewards.

It is important to find the right balance between encouraging your toddler to try new things and pressuring him. You don't want to expect too much, but on the other hand you don't want to treat him like a fragile orchid by overprotecting him. You need to know when to encourage your child to face his fears and when they would be overwhelming. Part of striking the right balance means accepting your child for who he is. You can't expect an introvert to behave like an extrovert. Researchers have identified distinct temperaments in children that are present from infancy (Chess et al., 1965); it is important you are attuned to your child so that you can gear your approach according to her unique needs. If you have more than one child, emphasize each of your children's strengths and talents and don't compare them to each other. There is a delicate balance between recognizing your child's personal qualities and generating "expectancy effects" by over-anticipating your child's actions and reactions. Remember, children grow and change, and avoid thinking of siblings as having exclusive traits (e.g., "Jacob is my clever one"). Finally, try to have some alone time with each of your children every day when possible.

You might want to adopt a pet if your situation allows. Pets are calming and can even help to head off a dog or cat phobia in children (remember the story of my son and his dog phobia). A good cat or dog is best as you need a tame animal that likes attention and affection. Give your pet a means of escape (e.g., a pet door that is too small for your child) so that you don't have to watch child and pet every second. This constant vigilance would inevitably increase your own stress. When your toddler encounters dogs and cats outside, teach her not to try to pet an animal unless the owner gives you the go-ahead. Some animals are truly dangerous. Big dogs tend to be frightening to children, especially if they're extremely active, and some small dogs and cats can be intimidating as well. It doesn't take much for an encounter to cause a child to fear animals. Your daily walks will give you an opportunity to desensitize your toddler to dogs by letting her approach the gentle ones first and gradually working up to the more enthusiastic and energetic dogs. If your child develops a serious phobia of dogs or cats and you can't have a pet, you might gradually expose him to a friend's pet using the desensitization techniques introduced earlier.

Don't push your toddler to interact with people outside of your family until you know they are comfortable. When you're strolling around the neighborhood you can gradually make more of an effort to let them meet your friends and neighbors. If you haven't already done so, you may want to try hiring babysitters for short periods of time. Begin by having the sitter over while you're there. You don't want to wait until you desperately need a babysitter for half a day, necessitating your leaving your toddler with a stranger. The first time that you go out, you will want to limit your time away to around an hour and leave the babysitter with a special activity that you know your child will love in order to keep them busy.

Remember that play is a child's therapy. No one knew this better than Fred Rogers of *Mr. Rogers' Neighborhood*. This is one way that children address and work through their fears. Encourage pretend play by getting a child-sized kitchen set, dress-up clothes, dolls, and a doctor's kit. Think of this as rehearsal for situations that your child will need to deal with. Playing doctor gives a child a chance to rehearse going to the doctor so that she is better prepared for something that many toddlers find especially frightening.

When both parents work, all of this careful socialization will be much more difficult to accomplish. According to Emily Oster (2019), children do best when they are raised at home for the first eighteen months to two years. I believe that this is especially true for anxious children. However, this is not always possible. If you need to place your child in day care, choose one that puts the children's needs before anything else. Such a day care center will recognize the importance of assimilating children gradually in order to make their initial transitions as painless as possible. Ideally, staff will let you and your child observe a few classes and then allow you to stay with her the first week for about twenty minutes every day. If your toddler is extremely frightened the first few days, you may want to stay the whole time (if allowed), or you and your child can leave after short visits, staying a little longer each day.

As I briefly mentioned, your toddler may be terrified of going to the doctor because they associate the doctor's office with getting a shot. Buy a doctor's kit and play doctor with your child and their stuffed animals. My children especially loved giving me shots. It may be possible to find a pediatric dentist who will do a brief checkup to desensitize your toddler to doctors' offices. In *Daniel Tiger's Neighborhood*, the excellent children's program from the Fred Rogers production company, Dr. Anna takes care of Daniel and his friends. You may find your child loves to take turns pretending to be Dr. Anna. A trip to get a haircut can also help, provided you take him to a barber or beautician who specializes in children or at least enjoys them. *Daniel Tiger's Neighborhood* uses a song that you can sing to prepare your child for new experiences. Its message is "when we do something new, let's talk about what we'll do."

You *can* allow your child to become attached to transitional objects such as blankets, stuffed animals, or a favorite shirt that provides comfort during stressful times or when you aren't together. Make sure to buy duplicates of his favorites. My daughter-in-law made dozens of little "blankies" out of a flannel sheet that was printed with animals. But won't the child be disturbed when they find out their blankie is really a set of blankies that get put in the washing machine from time to time? To the contrary! My grandson was soon walking around with three or four blankies at a time.

One of the most critical things is to make sure that your toddler gets enough "exercise" or, rather, activity, every day. It makes sense that aerobic exercise would be as beneficial to anxious children as it is for nervous adults. A study of children between six and eight years of age linked exercise to reductions of depression two years later (Zahl et al., 2016). Exercise may have similar benefits for anxious toddlers and preschoolers. Getting children out to run is much more difficult now that they want nothing more than endless screen time. You can entice a child to go outside by getting a bike earlier than you might think. As far as I'm concerned, one of the greatest inventions of this decade is the kick bike. These toddler-sized bikes without pedals can be mastered by children before they are three years old. You will be amazed to see your two-and-a-half-year-old zipping around on one. One way to get your child outdoors and to help "nip shyness in the bud" is to find a little "best" friend close in age who lives nearby and start having the friend over for play time (include this playmate's mother or father at first). You will want to make sure that this friend is a gentle, nonaggressive child.

It will be important to expose your child gradually to any things that children tend to fear. You don't want to completely avoid feared things and situations because children need to learn to face them. The longer you allow your child to avoid something, the stronger the fear is likely to become. Many toddlers are afraid of loud noises, water, the dark, and, as I've mentioned, dogs. Bath time can sometimes be a struggle so you will want to make it as enjoyable as possible. Colored bath water, bath body paint, bubble bath, cloth puppets, and bath toys can all distract a child from a fear of water. Many parents are surprised when shampooing their child's hair becomes a problem. You can pretend that your child is at a fancy spa using a "professional" voice to say: "now I'm applying ... [a special product] to make your hair shiny...." Introduce your toddler to swimming at an early age by buying an inflatable pool or encouraging him to gradually wade into a stream or lake. If he sees you enjoying a pool or lake, your toddler will probably want to try it too. Early swimming lessons can be good when he's ready to be in a small group. The small group setting can be good preparation for preschool or kindergarten.

You can play a role in helping a child feel comfortable with nature and wildlife. Take him hiking at an early age even if you don't go any farther than a neighborhood park. "Study" snakes, insects, and anything else that people sometimes fear in nature. If you don't appear to be disgusted or frightened by these creatures, they might be less likely to fear them. We were able to get my grandson an "official" ranger vest that the National Park Service sells. This motivated him to get out of the house and "hike" even if it was sometimes just in his own neighborhood. You can find plenty of insects and worms in your own back yard. Let your toddler get dirty. There are a number of nature books for toddlers which can help desensitize children to "creepy crawlies."

Darkness is an especially challenging fear. If your child fears the idea of going to bed because of the dark, you'll want to do everything that you can to avoid any struggles at bedtime. Bedtime battles raise the household stress level, making it even more difficult for a sensitive toddler to fall asleep. Help conquer a fear of the dark by making going to bed as appealing as possible. A regular ritual of cuddling up and reading bedtime stories will make bedtime something for everyone to look forward to. Perhaps they will want to pick out a "special" flashlight to use while reading in tents and "forts" made out of blankets. Toy companies have gotten more creative with flashlights and night-lights; you will be impressed.

Make your child's bedroom as welcoming as possible. An alcove can be especially cozy. When it's safe to have things in his crib, a few favorite stuffed animals are great company. I found an elephant for my grandson that he calls Mr. Heavy that can be heated in the microwave to simulate a warm-blooded animal. The elephant smells like lavender when heated, an herb thought to promote relaxation and sleep. I have also seen stuffed animals that are equipped with recordings of an adult's heartbeat to simulate the mother. White noise machines may also be comforting. You can buy special flannel sheets and, when your child is old enough, a small pillow or two and blankets that make his crib cozy. You can read the last story in a darkened bedroom with the flashlight. There is nothing wrong with using a night light to make bedtime less frightening. Some night lights even play soothing music or project stars onto the ceiling. If your toddler wants to sleep with a sibling or with you, this is fine too. SIDS is only a danger in infancy.

Preschoolers

Many of the suggestions for toddlers will continue to apply to pre-schoolers, but you will want to begin introducing your child to the wider world in even larger doses. Each time that you encourage your preschooler to try something new, remind her she can leave the situation anytime she begins to feel uncomfortable. Allowing for escape will make it more likely that your child will agree to try new experiences.

Now is the time to consider preschool. Shy children will need plenty of practice for their 12 years in school. You can work up to "school" by taking your preschooler to story hour at the library and enrolling her in small classes like swimming or gymnastics. You can start with classes that you can attend with her, such as mommy/baby yoga or small classes at a museum or zoo. These classes allow your child to get used to being in small groups of children while still having you there for support. Of course, you will want to keep going to the playground every few days for increasingly longer periods of time. You will have been encouraging your child to have plenty of play dates with that special friend. This may be the time to introduce a third child in order to form a play group with two other mothers. You can try to get the children together two or three times a week. When your child turns three, you might want to have a very small birthday party with a couple of other children.

When it is time for preschool, choose carefully. You and your child can visit several. Make sure that the classes are small and that the teachers love their jobs. Their earliest teachers are especially important for sensitive children since a bad experience can make them afraid of subsequent teachers and school itself. I have found that the preschools run by churches often seem to have the most motivated teachers. Select a school that offers half-day classes three times a week. Before the school year starts, you and your child can play on the school grounds when school isn't in session in order to get her comfortable with the building and the playground. At home you can "play school" with your child sitting in a circle with her stuffed animals. You can introduce her to the various activities offered at preschools. Hopefully, you will have been able to take your preschooler to library story hours on a regular basis since the activities during story hour are similar to those on preschool schedules. At the very least, story hours train children to sit quietly and raise their hands to talk.

If you can't afford a private or church-based preschool, you may be eligible for a free- or reduced-cost program through Head Start or a similar initiative. Each year Head Start serves nearly a million lower income children and their families (Dept. of Health and Human Services, 2019). You can start your own "school" by inviting two other children and their mothers over three mornings a week. Set up a schedule similar to a preschool schedule, including things like group activities, reading time, and some free play. Require the children to raise their hands when they have something to say to get them used to school rules. Have their mothers in attendance when possible so you only need to discipline your own child.

Some children who tend toward shyness have difficulty talking on the phone. Start getting your child comfortable with phones early using play phones and then by letting her talk with relatives on a real phone. Most children are fascinated with smart phones so this may be a way of getting yours comfortable talking with people outside of the household, like grandparents. Video calls are a wonderful development as they can be more interesting and less confusing for children.

Keeping in mind the importance of a stable peer group for your child, you'll want to put careful consideration into deciding to make a move that would put your family in a different school district. Educational scientists have long been interested in how student mobility affects outcomes in a student's academic performance and his overall well-being. Later in the chapter I will discuss the importance of thinking carefully about even the "normal" educational transitions across grades and school levels, but beyond that, it does appear that, in a variety of ways, nonpromotional school moves, the kind that occur when you move to a new city, are risky for students (Rumberger, 2003). Rumberger cites a student who said that "moving and changing schools really shattered my personality." While that may sound extreme, moving does mean starting all over again for a student. One study from Nashville found that when students moved, they lost the equivalent of about 10 days of learning (Grigg, 2012). Other losses that are more social in nature might be even greater. Aside from average effects, consider the potential effects on your *own* children carefully. Some kids who make friends easily and adjust to new environments quickly may barely be fazed by a move. For others, particularly anxious ones, it could be much more difficult, as in the case cited by Rumberger.

For families who are required to move, especially if they need to move frequently, consistent routines within the household should help to ameliorate the effects of these disruptions. If you need to move to another city or even another house in the same city, you'll want to make sure that you prepare your child for the move. Approach this as an exciting opportunity highlighting the good things about the new neighborhood (e.g., a cool playground) or city (e.g., a zoo) but empathize with your child's feelings of hesitancy. A move may actually provide you with an opportunity to get a house that better suits your family (e.g., a slightly larger house may make it easier to minimize clutter) and to improve on the neighborhood. If possible, try to pick a family-friendly neighborhood with sidewalks and parks that will allow for exercise and safely walking to friends' houses. You can take your toddler with you to look at houses and view properties online to get him interested. Remember that play is your child's therapy. You can rehearse the move through play. Have a dollhouse and move the people into another cardboard house nearby with a toy moving van. Have your child help to decorate his new bedroom, and, most important, do not insist that he part with anything that he doesn't want to leave behind.

Any time that your child begins to show signs of stress, you can start teaching him how to relax. Encourage him to remember a favorite place and to imagine that he is there. You can also teach him some basic breathing techniques, yoga postures, and stretching exercises. These are not only relaxing coping strategies, but they also serve to distract a child from an immediate worry.

School-Aged Children

Everything that applies to preschool is applicable to elementary school. Major transitions involving the unknown are especially challenging for anxious people of any age, but the first major transition is especially critical. For many, kindergarten or first grade is the first major transition that we face. Most elementary schools are considerably larger than preschools with more children milling around in the hallways, making them potentially more intimidating. Whether or not this huge transition goes well will set the stage for your child's approach to every other milestone they'll encounter in life. If your child has been to preschool, this will have served as an excellent orientation to elementary school. If not, remain optimistic; elementary school teachers are well-versed on how to make the kindergarten classroom a welcoming and safe space and they will do everything they can to help ease the transition for your student. If available, a school in your own neighborhood is desirable, as it increases the likelihood of your child knowing some of their classmates and developing lasting friendships.

What are some of the main issues of socialization as a student begins school? Robert Dreeben (1968), Phillip Jackson (1968), and others outlined some of the main differences between your child's life at home and at school many years ago which remain true today. First, at home your child is a unique individual, your special little guy. At school children are placed into categories both generic and specific. They will be treated first and foremost as a "kindergartner," as a member of the silver reading group, etc., rather than as unique. Second, at home your child gets lots of individual attention, while at school they are part of a small "crowd," competing for attention. Third, at home they are part of a family unit working together, but schools emphasize independent work and individual achievement. At home, students get lots of praise, and there is a deep well of love and goodwill. At school students receive praise but also some negative evaluations. The teacher as an authority figure offers a more professional and tenuous form of goodwill. If all this sounds harsh, keep in mind that school serves as a long and much needed transition toward adulthood and the workplace, but it can all be especially difficult for an anxious child.

Understanding Anxiety

Some parents have begun considering whether to "redshirt" their child until they are a year older. There is considerable controversy over this now fairly widespread practice. In nationally representative data, Bassok & Reardon (2013) estimate that between 4 percent and 5.5 percent of children are delayed in entering kindergarten. It is difficult for scientists to ascertain the effects of academic redshirting because those who choose to do so may be selecting a later entry for a particular reason (that the average child would not need) and because it is nearly impossible to conduct a randomized experiment on this practice. The available research does suggest that there is a short-term benefit to redshirting, particularly in children's social and behavioral skills, but that these effects largely diminish by middle school (Datar & Gottfried, 2015). Other research suggests *negative* effects, including a higher likelihood of dropping out and committing crimes, emerge later as students complete high school (Cook & Kang, 2016). Nevertheless, it's my opinion that redshirting can give an anxious child quite a few short-term advantages, including greater maturity, larger size, and increased academic readiness. For some anxious students, those early benefits may actually prevent a cycle of disengagement in school.

As this chapter is focused specifically on anxious children, I won't discuss school choice or basic school-to-school differences in great detail. But I do want to briefly encourage you to not place too much emphasis on choosing the most competitive school. What happens to your child within his classroom, and how well you as a parent support his day-to-day development and learning, is *far more important* than the school itself. Since James Coleman's (1966) landmark report on Equality of Educational Opportunity, social scientists have shown again and again, in literally hundreds of studies and with increasingly powerful research methods, that school-to-school differences in effectiveness are simply not as great as many people believe (see Kelly et al., 2020, for a recent treatment). Douglas Downey is one of the leading researchers in this area, and his 2020 book *How Schools Really Matter* will convince you that popular assumptions about schools are often wrong. You can trust your local public schools to be effective learning environments. More importantly, what your child and your family put into schooling will make the difference.

Overall, you should approach this transition to elementary school as an exciting milestone. Your child is a "big" boy or girl now. Of course, literally, a five- or six-year-old is still young and small, but because children are developing so rapidly, learning new things, and achieving milestones rapidly, *they* feel like they are getting bigger by the minute (Harter, 2015). You will want to make the most of this milestone by being generous with your praise of your child's seemingly small successes.

You will also want to celebrate this milestone by making school exciting. Prior to the first day of kindergarten, you can go on a special shopping trip with your child to buy school clothes, a special backpack and lunch box, and you can visit the barber or hair salon. Be aware of the importance of your child's fitting in and help him to pick clothes that reflect the current trends. You don't want your child to stand out too much. Any differences can be fodder for bullies. If your child is overweight, you may want to begin addressing this in a positive way by putting the whole family on a healthy diet and eliminating junk foods from the household.

As the first day of kindergarten approaches, start talking more about school in your casual conversations. Describe your own first days of kindergarten. If your child has an older sibling or a slightly older playmate who is already in school, he will probably be more eager to go to school. It will be important to familiarize your child with the building and, if possible, let them play on the school grounds when school isn't in session. If you are allowed to go inside the building before the school year starts, tour it with your child. And, of course, you will want to take advantage of the kindergarten orientation and attend with your child. You may be able to find out who your child's classmates will be and invite them to your house one at a time with a caregiver along. One of the best things that you can do is to become more familiar with the school yourself by volunteering there on a weekly basis. You will want to do this when your child is young because there will come a time when he won't want you to be anywhere near the school.

When it is time for that first day of school, try to arrive as early as possible. If you are the first to get there, your child won't be overwhelmed by too many other children all at once and the teacher can spend a few minutes with the two of you. You may be allowed to stay and observe for up to twenty to thirty minutes on the first day and for shorter periods of time for the rest of the week. When you pick your child up after school, celebrate his good day by going out for a special treat. Remember that this doesn't have to be huge. Children are satisfied with a small token or edible treat. After you get home, you can have your child dictate a story of his first day. My children enjoyed having their writing read back to them, and it seemed to help them to look forward to the next day. Taking your child shopping for school supplies that are on the teacher's list will give you another way of making school attractive. Have him pick out a special pencil case and some cool pencils, erasers, crayons, etc.

I found it was sometimes difficult to get my children to talk about their school days. The more familiar you are with the classroom, the daily schedule, and your child's classmates, the easier it will be to ask the right questions. The most ideal way to give your child an opportunity to talk about his day is to walk home from school together. If the school isn't within easy walking distance of your house, you can park a few blocks away from the school so that you'll have a chance to stroll with your child. And when you get home, you can get into the habit of serving a small snack so that you can have time to look through your kindergartner's backpack while he's sitting still in order to talk about work sheets and whatever else he brings home. Of course, you'll want to display your child's artwork from school in a prominent place in your home.

If your child needs to take a bus to school, this presents another challenge that can be especially intimidating to anxious children. If you can, wait until the second week of school before adding this element to her day. Older children will be on the bus and bullies may be a problem, particularly since the bus driver needs to focus on the road. If you have seen any Hollywood movies about childhood, you have seen a kid getting bullied on the bus. Unfortunately, that is not just a convenient plot device. You can prepare your child for the bus ride by talking about your own experiences and how you dealt with certain situations. I suggested that my children select a seat next to one of the youngest riders toward the front of the bus if possible. You can rehearse the bus ride with a toy bus and "little people."

My clinical experience has underscored the importance of nipping School Phobia in the bud by not allowing your child to miss school unless they are too sick to get out of bed or have something highly contagious. Dealing with School Phobia is very difficult, and it may be tempting to tell yourself, "It's just kindergarten," and let your child stay home from time to time. However, remember that it will only get harder the bigger he gets. You can make getting ready for school a little more exciting by timing your student to see how fast he can get dressed. Let him pick out his clothes the night before to save time and minimize arguments in the morning. There is nothing more stressful than conflict when you're under time pressure. Remind your child about something fun that is scheduled for that day based on the information that the teacher has provided. You'll want to make sure that your child has everything that's needed each day (e.g., items for show and tell, old clothes for finger painting, an extra sweater for recess). Don't hesitate to enlist a therapist if you can't get your child to school on most mornings without a stressful struggle.

Outside of school, you will want to make it easy for your child to socialize and to explore the world. If possible, you might want to update the play equipment in your yard to make it attractive to neighborhood children. A tree fort is the absolute best magnet for children, even if you don't have a suitable tree and the structure is more like a clubhouse on stilts. You can upgrade your child's kick bike to one with pedals. Biking skills will eventually give her access to the larger world and allow her to keep up with the neighborhood children. All of these measures encourage outdoor play with other children.

First grade. Some children are intimidated by starting first grade because this means that they will be in "real" school. I can still remember passing the first grade classrooms and not being able to imagine being "that grown up." This transition should, however, be far easier than starting kindergarten. After the initial adjustment to these first two grades, the rest of elementary school may be relatively smooth sailing. Like any relatively minor transition, beginning each school year will be somewhat challenging because it will involve a new teacher and a different mix of children. As I've said, empathic and supportive teachers are especially important for anxious children. Fortunately, today's teachers are specifically trained and supervised to attend to children's socio-emotional development.

Parents usually keep a close eye on their children's grades when the child is old enough to get graded report cards, but it is even more important to make sure that your child's behavior in the classroom indicates that he feels comfortable in school. Ask the teacher questions. Does he appear at ease? Does he volunteer answers or does he whisper two-word responses only when called upon? Is he able to concentrate in the classroom? Restlessness and difficulty focusing are often attributed to ADHD when anxiety could be the culprit. Does he seem anxious when it is time to take a quiz? Outside of the classroom, does he seem to have friends? Does he join in playground games?

You will also want to continue to do everything that you can to help your child to develop friendships outside of school. Of particular importance is ensuring your child isn't being bullied. Children, particularly anxious ones, often don't tell their parents about encounters with bullies. In years past, some teachers even looked the other way when they observed bullying on the playground. Fortunately, greater awareness of the problem and its far-reaching consequences has improved this situation. Unsupervised play is important to children's social development so you'll want to talk about ways to handle bullies and the importance of telling an adult if bullying is occurring.

Middle / Junior High Schoolers

Going to middle school or junior high is a difficult transition for many children because this is an age when emotions tend to run high, while at the same time many preteens have a difficult time articulating their feelings. This is especially the case for those who tend to be anxious. In addition, peers are becoming more important to children of this age. This means that there is more at stake. Most students are almost desperate to fit in and to be accepted. When I was seeing children and adolescents in therapy, the middle school years tended to be among the most challenging for children as well as their parents. Since Bachman's seminal *Youth in Transition* study (see, e.g., O'Malley & Bachman, 1983), social scientists have known that the middle school years represent a low point in the average individual's self-esteem.[1] During high school and into early adulthood, self-esteem rises, on average, but this doesn't happen "on its own." Rather, adolescents and teenagers spend a huge amount of psychic energy and effort fitting in and recovering a positive identity (Kinney, 1993).

It will be important to talk to your child as the transition to middle school or junior high approaches. Anxious children may worry about this next step but not confide in their parents. A number of things about middle school can seem threatening. The school buildings themselves tend to be larger than those in elementary school with more students roaming the halls, and each class often has a higher number of students. The smaller the school, the better. Note also that the middle and junior high schools differ in their grade configurations; some are 5–8, some 6–8, some 6–7, etc. (leaving the familiar elementary school in fifth grade would seem to me to be the least

---

1. A series of longitudinal studies in the 1970s and '80s documented basic life course patterns in self-esteem, but this is an area where modern researchers could spend more energy.

desirable of these options). They may also differ in whether students move from class to class in a cohort or pod or if they attend each class with largely different students. In rare cases, a combined school may even offer classes from kindergarten through 12th grade. Hopefully you have been able to remain in the same school district so that your child will be going off to middle school with some of her peers. Bullying can be considerably worse in middle school, so parents need to be alert to this possibility. Remember that anxious preteens often have difficulty confiding in their parents. If your child develops a fear of going to school after he has seemingly adjusted, he could be the target of bullying.

Try to help your child find an extracurricular interest that he is willing to try. This could be a sport, marching or concert band, theater group, yearbook committee, Future Farmers of America, or any number of other clubs and activities. Extracurricular activities are not just a "garnish" for the more important academic side of schooling. Instead, you should think of extracurricular activities as serving several crucial functions beyond the obvious opportunity they afford for socializing with peers. First, related to a student's identity and self-esteem, extracurricular activities offer a center of activity to build that budding sense of self. Sociologists refer to this process as an "identity project" and the beneficial effects are well documented (Crosnoe, 2011; Deluca et al., 2016). Second, extracurricular activities increase *school attachment*, making students feel more positive toward school in general and to their school in particular. By increasing school attachment, extracurricular participation improves engagement and reduces the likelihood that a student will drop out (McNeal, 1995). Finally, we live in a diverse society, and extracurricular activities may be the very best way for students from diverse backgrounds to get to know one another in the context of a shared goal and identity (Kelly & Collett, 2008). Of no less importance, extracurricular activities can sometimes lead a child to developing a lifelong passion.

Extracurriculars will give your student a group of potential friends outside of the classroom. This is particularly important for children who aren't academically inclined. And let's be honest: few teenagers center their identity on academic pursuits. Thinking about sports in particular, an aerobic team sport may be best since aerobic exercise may reduce anxiety and teams provide an excellent opportunity for socializing. But more skill-based sports (e.g., tennis, gymnastics, etc.) can build self-esteem by increasing an adolescent's sense of accomplishment. Any hobby that your child loves is good, though, particularly if he can enjoy it with other children.

It is important not to pressure your child to sign up for a particular activity, and once he has decided to try something, to let him "wade in" gradually. For example, you could start taking him to watch soccer games or gymnastics lessons to determine whether he may be interested in a particular activity. You can encourage your preteen to do something that comes naturally to him, considering his level of coordination and strength. You don't want him to feel that he has failed at his first attempt at a sport. Early failures could discourage him from trying other sports. Many parents find that soccer is an especially good sport to start with; the learning curve isn't at all steep and it involves enough different positions to suit all body types. Even a child who can't run fast can make a good goalie. If your shy preteen is intimidated by a team sport, running, private tennis lessons, or hiking with the family are good options to begin with. Running and tennis will eventually involve peers if your child sticks with these sports. A self-conscious child may not enjoy a sport like baseball, gymnastics or diving in which attention is centered on him at certain points.

Overall, your job as a parent is to be a good sport and encourage and support your child, especially when they don't win. You are your child's first role model. The point is to try to make those earlier experiences positive ones. This will make your child open to trying more activities. But it's also especially important that your child not be overscheduled with too many outside activities when he has more homework from school. Here again, it can be difficult to achieve a balance. Overscheduling has become all too common.

Beyond formal extracurriculars, at this age, informal play dates are now your child's responsibility. Your pre-adolescent will be capable of exploring farther on foot or by bike and you may want to update your house and yard to make your space a continuing attraction for other children. This is the age when children can start building their own club houses so you can provide plenty of raw materials. Also, a basketball hoop and ping pong table can be a draw for neighborhood preteens. Remember that a self-conscious child won't want you to "hover" when his friends come over.

Finally, within the last few years, there have been several incidents that have made the national news. Parents have been reprimanded for allowing their children to play unsupervised in parks. In my opinion, this is unfortunate for anxious children who are old enough to play alone because a parent's insistence on watching them every minute will send the message that the world is unsafe. A reliance on play dates alone doesn't give shy children the opportunity to develop all of the social skills that they need.

High Schoolers

Parents usually realize the importance of spending time with their young children but sometimes underestimate how crucial it is to continue this after their child reaches adolescence, even when they are becoming more independent and may not seem interested in spending time with you and others in the family. Research has found that the more time that teens twelve and over spend with their parents, the less time that they're likely to spend in risk taking activities that can lead to delinquency and substance abuse (Milkie et al., 2015). Anyone who has parented an adolescent knows that it can be difficult to get him to talk and that conversations usually have to be on his terms. The more time that you're able to spend with your teen, the more likely he will be to open up about what's going on in his life. I found that driving my youngest son to school, instead of having him take the bus, afforded a good time for us to talk (he might say that he had been trapped in the car). I told Tyler that I was happy to drive him to school, but that he wasn't allowed to use his phone or play video games during the twenty-minute drive. Your teen will be more likely to talk about himself if you are open with him. You can model self-disclosure by talking about your own adolescence, especially any problems that you had and how you dealt with them. Anxious teens may have many worries that they keep to themselves.

It's not just your child's immediate sphere that impacts him now. Teens begin to become more aware of the wider world around the time that they enter high school. Social media has changed everything and is causing significant stress in teens. Drawing on data from the National Survey on Drug Use and Health, Twenge et al. (2019) found that mood disorders and suicide-related outcomes rose between the mid–2000s and 2017, especially for adolescents and young adults. Twenge and colleagues speculate that digital and social media may have contributed to this rise. It was bad enough that children had to contend with bullies on the playground, but now they can be bullied 24/7 and the whole world can witness it.

Understanding Anxiety

In addition to the prospect of cyber-bullying via social media, teens may worry about a number of social problems including the future of the country, gun violence, rising suicide rates, climate change, sexual harassment, racial conflict, etc. How should parents address these large-scale problems over which they have no control? You don't want to ignore what's going on in the world, but you might be able to minimize the traumatic effect that it can have on your adolescent by not having the TV in a prominent place with the news blaring around the clock. At the same time, you will want to talk to your teen about these issues. You also may want to structure time when smart phones are set aside. Many teens sleep with their phones and even wake up in the middle of the night to respond to texts. I believe that some of the increase in anxiety and depression in teens is due to sleep deprivation. Teens still need more sleep than adults do. Try to set up nighttime phone policies and agreements.

When your teen enters high school, you will want to continue doing many of the things that you did during middle school, keeping in mind that she will now want to be more independent. Let her be instrumental in selecting the school if there is a choice to be made, remembering that smaller schools are better for anxious adolescents. Hopefully she'll have some friends who will be attending the school that she chooses. You'll want to continue encouraging her to participate in extracurricular activities that she enjoys. Here I need to emphasize activities that *she* enjoys. I had a client whose mother had wanted to take piano lessons when she was a child but hadn't been able to do so. She pushed my client into taking piano lessons and insisted that she spend several hours a day practicing. My client finally worked up the courage to tell her mother that if she (the mother) was so interested in piano, she should be the one taking lessons.

When it comes to academics, it will be important not to add stress to your student's life. Remember that people between the ages of 15 and 23 have more stress than any other age group (American Psychological Association, 2018). It is only natural to want to encourage your student to do what it takes in order to have a competitive advantage in the educational marketplace of college and beyond. But if your student already suffers from anxiety, you need to weigh the potential risks of too much pressure. How much should you encourage your student to enroll in advanced courses like physics and calculus?

It is true that coursework itself, apart from grades or test scores, is used by selective colleges and universities to determine enrollment

(Attewell, 2001). Particularly at engineering schools, having advanced math and science courses on your high school transcript is critical. While it is somewhat more difficult to get an A in honors or other advanced courses, all else being equal, teachers in advanced courses actually grade easier than less advanced courses, probably because they assume everyone in the class is academically strong to begin with (Kelly, 2008). Thus, taking rigorous academic courses is beneficial for capable students, but don't pressure your teen to take an exceedingly heavy course load.[2] You can help your student select classes, but let her make the ultimate decisions. Indeed, you should not assume that she has to continue on to college if she's not interested. If she is going to college, AP classes or dual enrollment classes in high school are extremely beneficial (Price, 2021), but these courses really are academically demanding. Be careful not to stretch your student to his limit. It is particularly important not to attempt to get your teen to participate in activities just for the sake of her college applications; the benefit of extracurriculars is predicated on the fact that the student herself is invested. Finally, keep in mind that teenagers are usually horribly embarrassed if you arrange to meet with one of their teachers or guidance counselors. Wait for the parent teacher conferences unless, of course, you have an urgent concern.

The "College for All" Mentality. You will want to have plenty of discussions about your teen's dreams for the future. Anxious adolescents often fear the future. Keep in mind that we are living in the "college for all" era. Messages about the value of college are so ubiquitous that most students get the message they are *supposed* to go to college and anything less will be considered a shortcoming. You may have seen the billboard of Nola Oachs, triumphantly graduating from college at age 95. That billboard depicts a proud accomplishment, and it also says something about America's cultural beliefs in second chances. It is never too late to pursue an education and the American community college system helps support that. But that billboard also contributes to college-for-all norms that may not work for all students.

Economists estimate that over the life course the average college graduate earns more than $800,000 more than someone without a college degree. That is even after accounting for the rising costs of college (Daly & Bengali, 2014). You should be very aware of the importance of college to labor market success. At the same time, in his book *Beyond College for All*, James Rosenbaum (2001) argues that the individual

---

2. See Kelly (2019) for a broader discussion of course taking and curriculum tracking.

benefits of going to college shouldn't overshadow how the normative environment of college-for-all can negatively affect high schools and their students. The benefits of college for the average young person may or may not apply to your particular child. Not everyone sees themselves, or needs to see themselves, as college bound. Don't get caught up in the "college for all" mentality if your teen isn't interested. You can help her to find something that she does want to do even if it isn't what you had dreamed of for her. You've had your chance. It's her turn now.

College Students

For those young people who want to go to college, there is a school to fit almost every need. You will want to start talking about potential colleges in your teen's junior year of high school. If possible, tour campuses to help her to feel familiar with campus environments so that she'll be better able to figure out what type of school she prefers and feel more comfortable when she arrives on campus in the fall. You might also broach the idea of a "gap year," a year where the graduate has a respite from the stress of high school before she has to deal with college or beginning at a community college.

Aside from the academic fit for your student, the two biggest considerations in selecting a college are size and distance from home, since these two factors are especially important for young people who tend to be anxious. As was the case with high schools, smaller colleges are usually better for anxious students. Overall, you need to take the social side of college as seriously as you do the academic. Not only are they important in their own right, but friendship networks actually influence academic success (McCabe, 2016).

Some colleges require freshmen to live on campus for the first year. While this is generally an excellent idea, living in a dorm can be problematic for shy students. If your teen has a good friend they would like to room with, and you trust this friend, you might encourage this idea. But you might also want to find out whether private rooms are available so that your student can consider this option. If you can afford it, this arrangement may be more comfortable for some shy students. Schools will make accommodations if a doctor documents that a student has been diagnosed with an anxiety disorder, but many anxious children are very hesitant to approach disability services and definitely don't want their parents to do so. If it is possible for your child to live at home, this may be the best option for the first semester so that she can tackle one thing at a time and so that you can support her in making the transition. Ideally, she will be ready to live on campus by the second semester. The dormitory experience can be an important and memorable part of college life, giving students a sense of community. If approached correctly, living among the other students can help a shy coed to become comfortable around people. However, large dorms can be utterly overwhelming, especially if there are more than two students per room. Small dorms, with only two students per room, are preferable.

If possible, attending summer school the summer before the start of college can be an excellent way for an anxious student to prepare for campus life. Summer school classes are fast paced so it is probably best for her to take only one course each session. You will also want to make sure that the class will not be difficult for her. A successful experience on the campus during the summer will make it much easier for your college-bound student to adjust in the fall when there are more students and she'll be taking more classes. If you don't live close enough to the college, a summer school class on another college campus is the next best thing. It's also important to take advantage of the orientation sessions that the college offers over the summer before classes start. This gives students a chance to experience and adjust to some of the social aspects of college before having to worry about the academic side. Usually, parents are invited to accompany their students for part of the orientation.

Another option is for your student to start at a community college, either over the summer or for her freshman year. This will allow her to live at home and gradually "wade into" the full college experience. This strategy serves double duty because the classes are sometimes easier, and good grades—or at least credit hours—can be transferred to the college to give students a head start. Importantly, though, many community college students are understandably confused to learn that many of the courses they have taken are not in fact transferable, are not even college courses but remedial pre-requisites, so be careful (Stephan & Rosenbaum, 2009)!

Once your student is at a four-year college, you might suggest that she consider registering for the minimum course load in the fall to give her a gradual start and optimize her chances of a successful semester. You might also consider suggesting that she take one additional class which would allow her to drop a class if she starts having difficulty in a particular class. It will be important not to pressure your young person to choose a particular major. I counseled many students who hated college because their major wasn't a good fit for them. Since I worked at a school that was prided for its engineering program, I saw many disgruntled engineering majors. Their parents had pushed them toward engineering although the child didn't have the aptitude or interest for engineering. Some of them ended up being suspended or dropping out of school when they could have been highly successful in a field of their own choice. You should be supportive if your college student decides that he doesn't like the major that he chose. It is not uncommon for students to try several majors before finding the best one. You can show your student statistics on available jobs and salaries for different majors, but let the statistics speak for themselves. Don't forget to suggest that he consider the "intangibles" of different occupations as well. One intangible many people overlook is how readily you can locate and relocate to the city or community of your choosing during your career. For example, every town needs a pharmacist, but an expert on how salamanders respond to climate change? Not so much. At some point your student may have the option of joining a fraternity or sorority. This can give her a smaller community within the larger campus which can be particularly helpful at a large university.

Without becoming a helicopter parent, you are going to want to keep track of your coed to the extent that she allows in order to head off potential problems. Ask her to choose a time that would be convenient for her to check in each week. That way she won't get the message that you are overly worried when you attempt to call her repeatedly. If you are close enough, you can take her to lunch, sometimes including her roommate or a friend.

Conclusion:
Revealing and Confronting
the Hidden Handicap

Research in the psychological sciences shows that anxiety disorders are pervasive in modern life. Anxiety has always been with us. Fear, arousal, and even worry are often functional and beneficial. Too often, though, anxiety works against our better selves. The vignettes and scientific studies discussed in this book show the plurality of forms Anxiety Disorder can take and its serious consequences, from panic attacks, to specific phobia, to obsessions and compulsions, and more. Of the anxiety sufferers profiled here, all were handicapped to various degrees, particularly when their fears caused them to avoid important life activities and experiences.

I am convinced that one of the reasons anxiety has such a profound effect on individuals' lives is precisely because it is more hidden than many other problems individuals confront. Anxious people themselves, their family and friends, and even health professionals often don't understand that anxiety may be at the root of their problems.

Digging deeper into the lives of anxiety sufferers, including the ones portrayed here, we see many suffer from high levels of *chronic* anxiety. This is true regardless of how their specific symptoms manifest and which anxiety disorder best characterizes them. They have an increased sensitivity to stress and an overactive fight or flight response. These anxious individuals have particular difficulty with any kind of change and experience heightened symptoms of anxiety during important life transitions. Their level of anxiety tends to wax and wane over the years depending upon what is going on in their lives, but my patients often went many years, even whole lifetimes, without understanding what was holding them back. Many of the anxious never obtain treatment.

Revealing the role of anxiety in our lives, both as individuals and as

201

a group, is the first step toward our better selves. This starts by recognizing that anxiety may begin in early childhood, when anxiety is especially hidden. Anxiety in childhood can interrupt important learning and socialization. As we have seen throughout the book, anxiety can create a kind of cumulative disadvantage or snowball effect, where a person's reactions to the anxiety itself create further problems. Thereafter, numerous educational and life transitions, from graduations to new jobs, create risks for anxiety sufferers—risks that anxiety will win out against their hopes and aspirations. As I've shown, anxiety and its effects persist even into retirement and life's later years. It is never too late to confront anxiety.

Once revealed, anxiety *can* be addressed. Panic attacks can be blunted, specific phobias can be conquered, and compulsions can be tempered. Importantly, addressing anxiety involves not just *coping* with anxiety but adopting a holistic approach to health and well-being, including reducing the very real stressors in your life. Even as the anxiety sufferers portrayed here were dealing with persistent anxiety year after year, they had tremendous agency to take active steps to improve their lives in the face of that anxiety. The flip side of cumulative disadvantage is that sometimes seemingly small adjustments can generate lasting benefits when the anxiety snowball is caught early.

This book concluded with a discussion of parenting and anxiety. Structurally, schooling is a transition from the family to the broader social world. Real sources of anxiety seem to exist around every corner. But here, as in the rest of life, an attentive, strategic approach to anxiety and its risks can make all the difference. Parents understand their obligation to be attentive to the anxious child's needs and to make those strategic decisions, to seek help, before problems of anxiety snowball. What about our larger roles as friends, loved ones, and community members? We would be well served to be similarly attentive to anxiety and its disorders.

Appendix: Resources for Further Reading

Aids for Relaxation

Progressive Muscle Relaxation:

Progressive Muscle Relaxation and Autogenic Training by Franziska Diesmann Torsten. This text describes the P&A Method.

Progressive Muscle Relaxation: Exercises for Deep Wholistic Relaxation by Carola Riss-Tafilaj.

Progressive Muscle Relaxation: From Inner Tension to Relaxation by Karl C. Mayer.

Relaxation: A Complete Guide for Body Relaxing including Aromatherapy and Massage Therapy by Jessica Thompson (audiobook).

The Relaxation Response by Herbert Benson. This is the classic book in which the author attempts to take the mystery out of meditation.

Meditation:

Meditation: Introductory Guide to Relaxation for Mind and Body by David Fontana.

Meditation for Beginners by Kevin Kockat (audiobook).

Quiet Mind: A Beginners Guide to Meditation by Sakyong Mipham, Sharon Salzberg and Larry Rosenberg.

Total Meditation by Deepak Chopra (audiobook).

Mindfulness:

Mindfulness: How to Create Inner Peace by David Clark (audiobook).

Mindfulness in Plain English by Bhante Gunaratana.

Breathing Techniques for Relaxation:

Breathe: Self Help Guide to Stress and Relaxation Management by Sue Baker.

Dancing with Fear by Paul Foxman. The chapter "Take a Deep Breath" on breathing beginning is particularly useful.

Cognitive Behavioral Techniques for Managing Stress

The Anxiety and Worry Workbook: The Cognitive Behavioral Solution by David A. Clark and Aaron T. Beck.

Cognitive Behavioral Therapy by Olivia Telford.

The Cognitive Behavioral Workbook for Anxiety by William J. Knaus.

Foods, Herbs and Supplements for Relaxation

The Chemistry of Calm by Henry Emmons.

A Doctor's Perspective on CBD: Science, Success Stories and Changed Lives by Mark Lindholm.

Food: Your Miracle Medicine by Jean Carper. See especially pages 294–301.

Food and Mood: The Complete Guide to Eating Well and Feeling Your Best by Elizabeth Somer.

Herbal Defense by Robyn Landis. See especially pages 289–312.

Secrets of Serotonin by Carol Hart.

Light Therapy

Winter Blues Fourth Edition: Everything You Need to Know to Beat Seasonal Affective Disorder by Norman E. Rosenthal.

Overall Stress Management

Don't Sweat the Small Stuff and It's All Small Stuff: Simple Ways to Keep the Little Things from Taking Over Your Life by Richard Carlson.

The Highly Sensitive Person: How to Thrive When the World Overwhelms You by Elaine N. Aron. This book is geared especially for people who have been born with a sensitive temperament. It focuses on accepting yourself and living your best life.

Natural Prozac: Learning to Release Your Body's Own Anti-Depressants by Joel Robertson.

Stress Management to Be Calm and Stop Feeling Overwhelmed by James Winters and Marc Scott (audiobook).

Why Zebras Don't Get Ulcers by Robert M. Sapolskey.

Perfectionism

The Joy of Imperfection by Damon Zarariades.

Overcoming Perfectionism: Finding the Key to Balance and Self-Acceptance by Ann W. Smith.

The Perfectionistic Predicament: How to Stop Driving Yourself and Others Crazy by Miriam Elliot and Susan Meltsner.

Raising Sensitive Children

Your Child Is a Person by Stella Chess, Alexander Thomas, and Herbert G. Birch.

The Highly Sensitive Child: Helping Our Children Thrive When the World Overwhelms Them by Elaine N. Aron.

Sleep Hygiene

Falling Asleep Deeply Relaxed: With Calm Progressive Muscle Relaxation into a Restful Sleep by Franziska Diesmann Torsten (audiobook).

A Good Night's Sleep by Lawrence Epstein with Steve Mardon.

A Guided Meditation for Healthful Sleep by Belleruth Naperstek (audiobook).

The Sleep Book: How to Sleep Well Every Night by Guy Meadows.

Organizations

Anxiety Disorders Association of America (ADAA), *www.adaa.org*, (240) 485–1001.

National Anxiety Foundation, *www.lexington-on-line.com/naf.html*, (606) 272–7166.

Social Phobics Anonymous, *www.heal socialanxiety.com*.

References

Aboujaoude, E. (2020). We All Need OCD Now. *Wall Street Journal* (March 31). https://www.wsj.com/articles/we-all-need-ocd-now-11585672342.

Acocella, J. (2014). Let It Go. *New Yorker* (December 15), 69–73.

Ainsworth, M.D.S., Blehar, M.C., Waters, E., & Wall, S.N. (1978 [2015]). *Patterns of Attachment: A Psychological Study of the Strange Situation*. Psychology Press.

Allende, I. (1994). *Paula*. Harper Perennial.

American Psychiatric Association. (1994). *Diagnostic and Statistical Manual of Mental Disorders, DSM-IV*. American Psychiatric Association.

American Psychiatric Association. (2013). *Diagnostic and Statistical Manual of Mental Disorders, DSM-5*. American Psychiatric Association.

American Psychological Association. (2018). *Stress in America: Generation Z*. Stress in America™ Survey.

Antony, M.M., & Swinson, R.P. (2000). *Phobic Disorders and Panic in Adults: A Guide to Assessment and Treatment*. American Psychological Association.

Anxiety and Depression Association of America. (2020). Facts & Statistics. https://adaa.org/understanding-anxiety/facts-statistics.

Aron, E.N. (1996). *The Highly Sensitive Person: How to Thrive When the World Overwhelms You*. Broadway Books, Birch Lane Press.

Aron, E.N. (2002). *The Highly Sensitive Child: Helping Our Children Thrive When the World Overwhelms Them*. Broadway Books.

Arum, R., & Roksa, J. (2011). *Academically Adrift: Limited Learning on College Campuses*. University of Chicago Press.

Attewell, P. (2001). The Winner-Take-All High School: Organizational Adaptations to Educational Stratification. *Sociology of Education, 74*, 267–95.

Auden, W.H. (1947). *The Age of Anxiety*. Random House.

Bandelow, B., Boerner, R.J., Siegfried, K., Linden, M., Wittchen, H.U., & Moller, H.J. (2013). The Diagnosis and Treatment of Generalized Anxiety Disorder. *DtschArztebl Int, 110*(17), 300–10.

Barlow, D.H. (1988). *Anxiety and Its Disorders: The Nature and Treatment of Anxiety and Panic*. Guilford.

Bassok, D., & Reardon, S.F. (2013). "Academic Redshirting" in Kindergarten: Prevalence, Patterns, and Implications. *Educational Evaluation and Policy Analysis, 35*, 283–97.

Beard, G. (1869). *American Nervousness, Its Causes and Consequences*. G.P. Putman's Sons.

Bech, P., & Angst, J. (1996). Quality of Life and Social Phobia. *International Clinical Psychopharmacology, 11* (Suppl 3), 97–100.

Bekker, M.H.J. (1996). Agoraphobia and Gender: A Review. *Clinical Psychology Review, 16*, 129–46.

Beltagy, M.S., Pentti, J., Vahtera, J., & Kivimaki, M. (2018). Night Work and Risk of Common Mental Disorders: Analyzing Observational Data as a Non-Randomized Pseudo Trial. *Scandinavian Journal of Work, Environment & Health, 44*, 512–20.

Bergland, C. (2016). Study: Fear of the Unknown Compounds Many Anxiety Disorders. *Psychology Today* (November

References

21). https://www.psychologytoday.com/us/blog/the-athletes-way/201611/study-fear-the-unknown-compounds-many-anxiety-disorders.

Bowlby, J. (1999 [1969]). *Attachment. Attachment and Loss (vol. 1) (2nd ed.).* Basic Books.

Bowlby, J., & Ainsworth, M.S. (1979). The Bowlby-Ainsworth Attachment Theory. *Behavioral & Brain Sciences, 2,* 637–38.

Brooks, J.L. (Director), & Andrus, M. (Screenplay) (1997). *As Good as It Gets.* Columbia TriStar Home Video.

Brown, T.A., & Tung, E.S. (2018). The Contribution of Worry Behaviors to the Diagnosis of Generalized Anxiety Disorder. *Journal of Psychopathological Behavioral Assessment, 40*(4): 636–44.

Burd, C., Burrows, M., & McKenzie, B. (2021). *Travel Time to Work in the United States: 2019 American Community Survey Reports.* U.S. Census Bureau.

Bzdok, D. (2020). *Trends in Cognitive Science.* McGill University Press.

Cain, S. (2012). *Quiet: The Power of Introverts in a World That Can't Stop Talking.* Crown.

Carducci, B.J., & Zimbardo, P.G. (1995). Are You Shy? Well, you have lots of company. *Psychology Today, 28,* 34.

Carnegie, D. (1948). *How to Stop Worrying and Start Living.* Simon & Schuster.

Chess, S., Thomas, A., & Birch, H.G. (1965). *Your Child Is a Person: A Psychological Approach to Parenthood Without Guilt.* Penguin.

Clance, P.R. (1985). *The Imposter Phenomenon: Overcoming the Fear That Haunts Your Success.* Peachtree.

Coleman, J.S., Campbell, E.Q., Hobson, C.J., McPartland, J., Mood, A.M., Weinfall, F.D., & York, R.L. (1966). *Equality of Educational Opportunity.* U.S. Department of Health, Education and Welfare.

Comoreanu, A. (2021). Credit Card Debt Study. Wallethub.com (March 8). https://wallethub.com/edu/cc/credit-card-debt-study/24400.

Cook, P.J., & Kang, S. (2016). Birthdays, Schooling, and Crime: Regression-Discontinuity Analysis of School Performance, Delinquency, Dropout, and Crime Initiation. *American Economic Journal: Applied Economics, 8,* 33–57.

Cooper, C.L., & Marshall, J. (1976). Occupational Sources of Stress: A Review of the Literature Relating to Coronary Heart Disease and Mental Ill Health. *Journal of Occupational Psychology, 49,* 11–28.

Coplan, J.D., Hodulik, S.G., Mathew, S.J., Mao, X., Hof, P.R., Gorman, J.M., & Shungu, D.C. (2012). The Relationship Between Intelligence and Anxiety: An Association with Subcortical White Matter Metabolism. *Frontiers in Evolutionary Neuroscience, 3,* 8.

Craske, M.G., Sanderson, W.C., & Barlow, D.H. (1987). The Relationship Among Panic, Fear and Avoidance. *Journal of Anxiety Disorders, 1,* 153–60.

Crosnoe, R. (2011). *Fitting In, Standing Out: Navigating the Social Challenges of High School to Get an Education* (pp. 83–113). Cambridge University Press.

Daly, M.C., & Bengali, L. (2014). Is it Still Worth Going to College? Federal Reserve Bank of San Francisco, *Economic Letter* 2014–13 (May 5).

Darwin, C.R. (1872). *Expression of Emotions in Man & Animals.* John Murray.

Datar, A., & Gottfried, M.A. (2015). School Entry Age and Children's Social-Behavioral Skills: Evidence from a National Longitudinal Study of U.S. Kindergartners. *Educational Evaluation and Policy Analysis, 37,* 333–53.

Deluca, S., Clampet-Lundquist, S., & Edin, K. (2016). *Coming of Age in the Other America.* Russell Sage Foundation.

Department of Health and Human Services (2019). *Head Start Program Fact: Fiscal Year 2019.* U.S. Department of Health and Human Services. https://eclkc.ohs.acf.hhs.gov/about-us/article/head-start-program-facts-fiscal-year-2019

Donnelly, D.A., & Murray, E.J. (1991). Cognitive and Emotional Changes in Written Essays and Therapy

References

Interviews. *Journal of Social and Clinical Psychology, 10,* 334–50.

Downey, D.B. (2020). *How Schools Really Matter: Why Our Assumption about Schools and Inequality Is Mostly Wrong.* University of Chicago Press.

Doyle, A.C. (1892). *The Great Shadow.* J.W. Arrowsmith.

Dreeben, R. (1968). *On What Is Learned in School.* Addison-Wesley.

Dugas, M.J., Buhr, K., & Ladouceur, R. (2004). *The Role of Intolerance of Uncertainty in Etiology and Maintenance.* In R.G. Heimberg, C.L. Turk, & D.S. Mennin (Eds.), *Generalized Anxiety Disorder: Advances in Research and Practice* (pp. 143–63). Guilford.

Dworkin, A.G. (1987). *Teacher Burnout in the Public School: Structural Causes and Consequences for Children.* State University of New York Press.

Feiler, B. (2020). *The Nonlinear Life: Life is in the Transitions, Mastering Change at Any Age.* Penguin.

Fields, R.D. (2015). *Why We Snap: Understanding the Rage Circuit in Your Brain.* Penguin.

Fishback, G., Chriki, L., Thayer, J.F., & Vasey, M.W. (2020). Heart Rate Variability Moderates the Association Between Beliefs about Worry and Generalized Anxiety Disorder Symptoms. *Frontiers in Neuroscience, 14,* 1034.

Floud, S., Vigna-Taglianti, F., Hansell, A., Blangiardo, M., Houthuijs, D., Breugelmans, O., Cadum E., ... & Jarup, L. (2011). Medication Use in Relation to Noise from Aircraft and Road Traffic in Six European Countries: Results of the HYENA study. *Occupational & Environmental Medicine, 68*(7), 518–24.

Foa, E.B., Simpson, H.B., Liebowitz, M.R., Powers, M.B., Rosenfield, D., Cahill, S.P., et al. (2013). Six-Month Follow-Up of a Randomized Controlled Trial Augmenting Serotonin Reuptake Inhibitor Treatment with Exposure and Ritual Prevention for Obsessive-Compulsive Disorder. *Journal of Clinical Psychiatry, 74,* 464–69.

Foxman, P. (2007). *Dancing with Fear: Overcoming Anxiety in a World of Stress and Uncertainty.* Hunter House.

Frankl, V.E. (1959). *Man's Search for Meaning: An Introduction to Logotherapy.* Simon & Schuster.

Freud, S. (2002 [1929]). *Civilization and Its Discontents.* Penguin.

Frost, R.O., & Steketee, G. (2010). *Stuff: Compulsive Hoarding and the Meaning of Things.* Houghton Mifflin Harcourt.

Glover, V. (2011). *The Effects of Prenatal Stress on Child Behavioral and Cognitive Outcomes Start at the Beginning.* Institute of Reproductive and Developmental Biology. Imperial College London, United Kingdom.

Gorka, S.M., Kreutzer, K.A., Petrey, K.M., Radoman, M., & Phan, K.L. (2020). Behavioral and Neural Sensitivity to Uncertain Threat in Individuals with Alcohol Use Disorder: Associations with Drinking Behaviors and Motives. *Addiction Biology, 25*(3), e12774.

Granovetter, M. (1973). The Strength of Weak Ties. *American Journal of Sociology, 78,* 1360–80.

Grigg, J. (2012). School Enrollment Changes and Student Achievement Growth: A Case Study in Educational Disruption and Continuity. *Sociology of Education, 85,* 388–404.

Guest, J. (1978). *Ordinary People.* Viking Press.

Hallowell, E.M. (1997). *Worry: Controlling It and Using It Wisely.* Random House.

Hamilton, M. (1960). A Rating Scale for Depression. *Journal of Neurology, Neurosurgery, and Psychiatry, 23*(1), 56.

Hanlon, H.R., & Swords, L. (2020). Adolescent Endorsement of the Weak-Not-Sick Stereotype for Generalized Anxiety Disorder: Associations with Prejudice, Discrimination and Help-Giving Intentions Toward Peers. *International Journal of Environmental Research and Public Health, 17*(15), 5415.

Harter, S. (2015). *The Construction of the Self: Developmental and Sociocultural Foundations, Second Edition.* Guilford.

Harvard Medical School. (2007). National Comorbidity Survey (NCS). Retrieved

References

from https://www.hp.med.harvard.edu/ncs/index.php. Data Table 1: Lifetime prevalence DSM-IV/WMH-CIDI disorders by sex and cohort.

Herzog, H. (2011). The Impact of Pets on Human Health and Psychological Well-Being: Fact, Fiction, or Hypothesis. *Current Directions in Psychological Science, 20*(4), 236–39.

Holland, E. (2020). *Learning to Live with Fear. Wall Street Journal* (May 16). https://www.wsj.com/articles/learning-to-live-with-fear-11589601757.

Holmes, T., & Rahe, R. (1967). Social Readjustment Rating Scale. *Journal of Psychometric Research, 11*, 213–18.

Horwath, E., Lish, J.D., & Johnson, J. (1993). Agoraphobia Without Panic: Clinical Reappraisal of an Epidemiological Finding. *American Journal of Psychiatry, 150*, 1496–1501.

Irving, J. (1976). *The World According to Garp*. Random House.

Jackson, P.W. (1968). *Life in Classrooms*. Teachers College Press.

Jewell, L. (2013). *The House We Grew Up In*. Atria, Simon & Shuster.

Kagan, J. (1994). *Galen's Prophecy: Temperament in Human Nature*. Basic Books.

Kagan, J., & Snidman, N. (2004). *The Long Shadow of Temperament*. The Belknap Press of Harvard University Press.

Kahneman, D., Krueger, A.B., Schkade, D., Schwarz, N., & Stone, A. (2004). A Survey Method for Characterizing Daily Life Experience: The Day Reconstruction Method (DRM). *Science, 306*, 1776–80.

Kampfer, S., & Mutz, M. (2013). On the Sunny Side of Life: Sunshine Effects on Life Satisfaction. *Social Indicators Research, 110*, 579–95.

Kelly, S. (2008). What Types of Students' Efforts are Rewarded with High Marks? *Sociology of Education, 81*, 32–52.

Kelly, S. (2019). Sorting Students for Learning: Eight Questions about Secondary School Tracking. In T. Domina, B. Gibbs, L. Nunn, A. Penner, & S.J. Dobrin (Eds.), *Education & Society: An Introduction to Critical Issues in the Sociology of Education* (pp. 178–91). University of California Press.

Kelly, S., & Caughlan, S. (2011). The Hollywood Teachers' Perspective on Authority. *Pedagogies, 6*, 46–65.

Kelly, S., & Collett, J. (2008). From C.P. Ellis to School Integration: The Social Psychology of Conflict Reduction. *Sociology Compass 2/5*, 1638–54.

Kelly, S., Mozenter, Z., Aucejo, E., & Fruehwirth, J. (2020). School-to-School Differences in Instructional Practice: New Descriptive Evidence on Opportunity to Learn. *Teachers College Record, 122* (11).

Kendall, J. (2013). *American Obsessives: The Compulsive Energy That Built a Nation*. Grand Central.

Kessler, R.C., & Wittchen, H.U. (2002). Patterns and Correlates of Generalized Anxiety Disorder in Community Samples. *Journal of Clinical Psychiatry, 63*, 4–10.

Kilbride, K. (2010). Man Cleans up After Years of Hoarding. *South Bend Tribune* (March 21).

Kiley, D. (1983). *The Peter Pan Syndrome: Men Who Have Never Grown Up*. Dodd, Mead & Company.

Kinney, D.A. (1993). From Nerds to Normals: The Recovery of Identity among Adolescents from Middle School to High School. *Sociology of Education, 66*, 21–40.

Kleinknecht, R.A. (1986). *The Anxious Self: Diagnosis and Treatment of Fears and Phobias*. Human Sciences Press.

Kondo, M. (2010). *The Life Changing Magic of Tidying Up: The Japanese Art of Decluttering and Organizing*. Ten Speed Press.

Kramer, P. (1993 [1997]). *Listening to Prozac: The Landmark Book About Antidepressants and the Remaking of the Self, Revised Edition*. Penguin.

Lakoff, R. (1990). *Talking Power*. Basic Books.

Lamb, W. (1998). *I Know This Much Is True*. HarperCollins.

Lang, P.J., & McTeague, L.M. (2009). The Anxiety Disorder Spectrum: Fear Imagery, Physiological Reactivity, and

References

Differential Diagnosis. *Anxiety, Stress, Coping, 22,* 5–25.

Lareau, A. (2003 [2011]). *Unequal Childhoods: Class, Race, and Family Life.* University of California Press.

Leahy, R. (2008). How Big a Problem Is Anxiety? The Anxiety Files. *Psychology Today* (April 30).

Lethem, J. (1999). *Motherless Brooklyn.* Doubleday.

Liddell, H.S. (1949). The Role of Vigilance in the Development of Animal Neurosis. *Annual Meeting of the American Psychopathological Association, 39th, June 1949, New York City, NY, US.* Grune & Stratton (1950).

Liebowitz, M.R., Gorman, J.M., Fyer, A.J., & Klein, D.F. (1985). Review of a Neglected Anxiety Disorder. *Archives of General Psychiatry, 42,* 729–36.

Littwin, S. (1986). *The Postponed Generation: Why America's Grown-Up Kids Are Growing Up Later.* William Morrow.

Lortie, D.C. (1975). *School Teacher: A Sociological Study.* University of Chicago Press.

Mantella, R.C., Butters, M.A., Amico, J.A., Mazumdar, S., Rollman, B.L., Begley, A.E., Reynolds, C.F., & Lenze, E.J. (2008). Salivary Cortisol Is Associated with Diagnosis and Severity of Late-Life Generalized Anxiety Disorder. *Psychoneuroendocrinology, 33,* 77–81.

McCabe, J.M. (2016). *Connecting in College: How Friendship Networks Matter for Academic and Social Success.* University of Chicago Press.

McNeal, R.B. (1995). Extracurricular Activities and High School Dropouts. *Sociology of Education, 68,* 62–80.

Meltsner, S., & Elliott, M. (1991). *Perfectionistic Predicament: How to Stop Driving Yourself and Others Crazy.* William Morrow.

Milkie, M.A., Nomaguchi, K.M., & Denny, K.E. (2015). Does the Amount of Time Mothers Spend with Children or Adolescents Matter? *Journal of Marriage and Family, 77,* 355–72.

Miller, A.H. (2020). *On Not Being Someone Else: Tales of Our Unled Lives.* Harvard University Press.

Morgan, W.P., Brown, D.R., Raglin, J.S., O'Connor, P.J., & Ellickson, K.A. (1987). Psychological Monitoring of Overtraining and Staleness. *British Journal of Sports Medicine, 21,* 107–14.

Murphy, K. (2020). We're All Socially Awkward Now. *New York Times* (September 1). https://www.nytimes.com/2020/09/01/sunday-review/coronavirus-socially-awkward.html.

Murphy, K. (2021). The Pandemic Shrank Our Social Circles. Let's Keep It That Way. *New York Times* (April 25). https://www.nytimes.com/2021/04/23/sunday-review/covid-friendship.html.

Newman, M.G., Zuellig, A.R., Kachin, K.E., Constantino, M.J., Przeworski, A., Erickson, T., & Cashman-McGrath, L. (2002). Preliminary Reliability and Validity of the Generalized Anxiety Disorder Questionnaire-IV: A Revised Self-Report Diagnostic Measure of Generalized Anxiety Disorder. *Behavior Therapy, 33,* 215–33.

Nikolajeva, M. (2009). Devils, Demons, Familiars, Friends: Toward a Semiotics of Literary Cats. *Marvels & Tales, 23,* 248–67.

Norton, G.R., McLeod, L., Guertin, J., Hewitt, P.L., Walker, J.R., & Stein, M.B. (1996). Panic Disorder or Social Phobia: Which Is Worse? *Behavioral Research and Therapy, 34,* 273–76.

Novaco, R.W., & Gonzales, O.L. (2009). Commuting and Well-Being. In Y. Amichai-Hamburger (Ed.), *Technology and Well-Being* (pp. 174–205). Cambridge University Press.

Olsson, L.E., Garling, T., Ettema, D., Friman, M., & Fujii, S. (2013). Happiness and Satisfaction with Work Commute. *Social Indicators Research, 111,* 255–63.

O'Malley, P.M., & Bachman, J.G. (1983). Self-Esteem: Change and Stability Between Ages 13 and 23. *Developmental Psychology, 19,* 257–68.

Orban, E., McDonald, K., Sutcliffe, R., Hoffmann, B., Fuks, K. B., Dragano, N., Viehmann, A., Erbel, R., Jöckel, K. H., Pundt, N., Moebus, S. (2016). Residential Road Traffic Noise and High

References

Depressive Symptoms after Five Years of Follow-Up: Results from the Heinz Nixdorf Recall Study. *Environmental Health Perspectives, 124*, 578–85.

Oster, E. (2019). *Cribsheet: A Data Driven Guide to Better More Relaxed Parenting from Birth to Preschool.* Random House.

Petersen, A. (2020). Colleges Brace for More Counseling. *The Wall Street Journal* (June 30). https://www.wsj.com/articles/college-counseling-centers-brace-to-help-shaken-students-11593444702.

Pollard, H.J., & Corn, K.J. (1989). Panic Onset and Major Events in the Lives of Agoraphobics: A Test of Continuity. *Journal of Abnormal Psychology, 98*, 318–21.

Price, H.E. (2021). *The Fractured College Prep Pipeline: Hoarding Opportunities to Learn.* Teachers College Press.

Prins, A., Bovin, M.J., Smolenski, D.J., Mark, B.P., Kimerling, R., Jenkins-Guarnieri, M.A., Kaloupek, D.G., Schnurr, P.P., Pless Kaiser, A., Leyva, Y.E., & Tiet, Q.Q. (2016). The Primary Care PTSD Screen for DSM-5 (PC-PTSD-5): Development and Evaluation Within a Veteran Primary Care Sample. *Journal of General Internal Medicine, 31*, 1206–11.

Quikin, F.M., Rifkin, A., Kaplan, J., & Klein, D.F. (1972). Phobic Anxiety Syndrome Complicated by Drug Dependence and Addiction. *Archives of General Psychiatry, 27*, 159–62.

Reid, J.D., & Willis, S.L. (1999). Middle Age: New Thoughts, New Directions. In S.L. Willis & J. D. Reid (Eds.), *Life in the Middle: Psychological and Social Development in Middle Age.* Academic Press.

Rodiek, S. (2002). Influence of an Outdoor Garden on Mood and Stress in Older Persons. *Journal of Therapeutic Horticulture, 13*, 13–21.

Rooney, S. (2018). *Normal People.* Penguin, Random House.

Rosenbaum, J.E. (2001). *Beyond College for All: Career Paths for the Forgotten Half.* Russell Sage Foundation.

Rumberger, R.W. (2003). The Causes and Consequences of Student Mobility.

The Journal of Negro Education, 72, 6–21.

Ruscio, A.M, Lane, M., Roy-Byrne, P., Stang, P.E., Stein, D.J., Wittchen, H-U., & Kessler, R.C. (2005). Should Excessive Worry Be Required for a Diagnosis of Generalized Anxiety Disorder? Results from the US National Comorbidity Survey Replication. *Psychological Medicine, 35*, 1761–72.

Schneier, C.E. (1974). Behavior Modification in Management: A Review and Critique. *The Academy of Management Journal, 17*, 528–48.

Schwartz, B. (2004). *The Paradox of Choice: Why More Is Less, How the Culture of Abundance Robs Us of Satisfaction.* HarperCollins.

Solomon, A. (2012). *Far From the Tree: Parents, Children and the Search for Identity.* Scribner.

Stephan, J.L., & Rosenbaum, J.E. (2009). Permeability and Transparency in the High School-College Transition. In G. Sykes, B. Schneider, & D.N. Plank (Eds.), *Handbook of Education Policy Research* (pp. 928–41). American Educational Research Association and Routledge.

Stossel, S. (2013). *My Age of Anxiety: Fear, Hope, Dread and the Search for Peace of Mind.* Alfred A. Knopf.

Straub, E. (2020). *All Adults Here.* Riverhead Books.

Stutzer, A., & Frey, B S. (2008). Stress That Doesn't Pay: The Commuting Paradox. *The Scandinavian Journal of Economics, 110*, 339–66.

Sullivan, A. (2018). What Happens in Your Body When You're Lonely? Cleveland Clinic. https://health.clevelandclinic.org/what-happens-in-your-body-when-youre-lonely/.

Taylor, C.B., Sheikh, J., Agras, W.S., Roth, W.T., Margra, F.J., Ehlers, A., Maddock, R.J., & Gossard, D. (1986). Self-Report of Panic Attacks: Agreement with Heart Rate Changes. *American Journal of Psychiatry, 143*, 478–82.

Telch, M.J., Lucas, J.A. & Nelson, P. (1989). Nonclinical Panic in College Students: An Investigation of

References

Prevalence and Symptomatology. *Journal of Abnormal Psychology, 98*(3): 300–06.

Thapamagar, S.B., Pasha, A.G., Krishnamurthy, M., & Schiavone, J.A. (2012). Atypical Presentation of the Broken Heart Syndrome Associated with Chronic Anxiety. *Journal of Nepal Health Research Council, 10*(1), 69–72.

Tisinger, S. (2016). Research Says It's OK to Pick Up Your Baby Each Time It Cries. https/www.wgad.com.

Tobar, D.A. (2012). Trait Anxiety and Mood State Responses to Overtraining in Men and Women College Swimmers. *International Journal of Sport and Exercise Psychology, 10*(2): 135–48.

Twenge, J.M., Bell Cooper, A., Joiner, T.E., Duffy, M.E., & Binau, S.G. (2019). Age, Period, and Cohort Trends in Mood Disorder Indicators and Suicide-Related Outcomes in a Nationally Representative Dataset. *Journal of Abnormal Psychology, 128*, 185–99.

Tyler, A. (1988). *A Patchwork Planet.* Random House.

Van Den Berg A.E., & Clusters, M.H. (2011). Gardening Promotes Neuroendocrine and Affective Restoration from Stress. *Journal of Health Psychology, 16*, 3–11.

Ward, S. (2020). Little Stories. *New York Times* (October 20). https://www.nytimes.com/2020/10/20/style/tiny-modern-love-stories-our-refuge-from-reality.html.

Watson, J. (1920). Is Thinking Merely the Action of Language Mechanisms? *The British Journal of Psychology, 11*, 87–104.

Wilson, K.G., Sandler, L.S., & Asmundson, G.J. (1993). Fearful and Nonfearful Panic Attacks in a Student Population. *Behavioral Research and Therapy, 31*, 407–11.

Winnicott, D. W. (1992). *Babies and Their Mothers.* Da Capo Lifelong Books.

Wittchen, H.U., & Jacobi, F.R.J. (2011). The Size and Burden of Mental Disorders and Other Disorders of the Brain in Europe 2010. *European Neuropsyhcopharmacology, 21*, 655–79.

Wolfe, B. (2005). *Understanding and Treating Anxiety Disorders.* American Psychological Association.

Yerkes, R.M., & Dodson, J.D. (1908). The Relation of Strength of Stimulus to Rapidity of Habit Formation. *Journal of Comparative Neurology and Psychology, 18*, 459–82.

Yonkers, K.A., Zlotnick, C., Allsworth, J., Warshaw, M., Shea, T., & Keller, M.B. (1998). Is the Course of Panic Disorder the Same in Women and Men. *American Journal of Psychiatry, 155*, 596–602.

Zahl, T., Steinsbekk, S., & Wichsrtrom, L. (2016). Physical Activity, Sedentary Behavior, and Symptoms of Major Depression in Middle Childhood. *Pediatrics.* 139 (2), e2016–1711.

Zimbardo, P.G. (1977). *Shyness: What It Is, What to Do About It.* Addison-Wesley.

Index

Aboujaoude, E. 101
Acocella, J. 104
adaptive behavior 20, 101, 117
addiction: adolescence, in 16; to exercise 29; to gambling 29; to love 29; to pornography 29; to prescription medications 15, 16; to sex 29; to shopping 30; to social media 29; to travel 30–31; to TV 29; to video games 29; to work 29
The Age of Anxiety 8, 9
aggression 21, 31
agoraphobia 11, 37, 43–46, 52, 55, 61, 90, 94, 104, 128, 133, 163–165
Ainsworth, M.D.S. 132, 178
alcoholism *see* substance abuse
Allende, I. 94, 119
American Psychiatric Association 10
American Psychological Association 5, 196
anger 31; gender differences in 17, 24; and PTSD 50; *see also* fight or flight response
Angst, J. 55
Annie Hall 93
anorexia 27, 90
Antony, M.M. 37, 38
Anxiety and Depression Association of America 10, 17, 25, 52, 92, 110, 111
Anxiety Sensitivity Index 127
Aron, E.N. 74, 75, 130, 140, 177, 204
Arum, R. 68
As Good as It Gets 6
attention deficit hyperactivity disorder 25, 53, 60, 114, 134, 191
Attewell, P. 197
Auden, W.H. 8
avoidance 8, 11, 20, 21–23, 61–62; agoraphobia, and 44; of feared objects or situations 8; Generalized Anxiety Disorder, and 118, 127; imposter syndrome, and 74; as natural but counterproductive response to anxiety 25, 41;Obsessive Compulsive Disorder and 93, 96;

performance anxiety and 58; phobias and 78, 87; PTSD and 50; of risk and opportunities 22–23; school phobia and 67, 135; social anxiety and 61, 63; of travel 24, 78

Bachman, J.G. 192
Bandelow, B. 7, 113
Barlow, D.H. 10, 17, 19–20, 25, 28, 41
Bassok, D. 188
Beard, G. 27
Bech, P. 55
Bekker, M.H.J. 39
Beltagy, M.S. 157
Bengali, L. 197
Bergland, C. 84
bipolar disorder 6, 25, 114
Birch, H.G. 130, 204
body dysmorphic disorder 188
borderline personality disorder 109
Bowlby, J. 132, 178
broken heart syndrome 42
Brown, T.A. 123
bullying 137, 190
Burd, C. 155
Burrows, M. 155
Bzdok, D. 57, 63

Cain, S. 57, 131, 177
cardiovascular symptoms 36, 123; heart attack 43; heart rate 20, 123
Carducci, B.J. 66
Carnegie, Dale 8
Caughlan, S. 6
celebrity anxiety 58
character flaws, perceived *see* competence
Chess, S. 130, 177, 180, 204
childhood 176–200; anxiety as especially hidden in 129; attachment 132; high reactivity 22, 74, 130; infancy 1, 33, 130–133, 176–179; level of sensory threshhold 136; sensitive temperament 20–23; snowball effect of anxiety, and

Index

12; toddlers 179–184; *see also* school; separation anxiety
chronic fatigue syndrome 24, 124–125
chronic stress, consequences of 25
chronicity *see* life course
cities: evolutionary perspective on 54; opportunity and stress of 26, 154; social anxiety 71
Clance, P.R. 73–74
Clusters, M.H. 152
Coleman, J.S. 188
college 5, 14, 15, 18, 32, 33, 198–200; ABD (all but dissertation) 139; campuses as verdant 151; community college 197–199; first-generation students 85; flounder among college students/graduates 68; graduate school 139; norms (college for all) 197; panic attacks 37–40; prevalence of anxiety in 11; returns to (value of degree) 197; transition to 138–139
Collett, J. 193
commuting 26, 155, 156
comorbidity 8; *see* also ADHD; depression
Comoreanu, A. 159
competence 3, 5, 15, 23; family perceptions of 15, 23, 31; outward appearance of normality 3; self-perceptions of 5
compulsions 100–103; *see also* compulsive behaviors; obsessive compulsive disorder
compulsive behaviors, specific: checking 103; cleaning 102, 103; shopping 30
Conan Doyle, A. 106
concentration, problems with 36, 119
confidence, lack of 138
conscientiousness, in relation to anxiety 15, 22, 34
consequences of anxiety, exacerbation of existing medical conditions: Crohn's disease 25; effect on immune system 25; long term effects 25; lupus 25; multiple sclerosis 25; *see also* addictive behaviors; depression; substance abuse
consequences of anxiety, general and other 2, 15, 28 113; *see also* avoidance; relationships; workplace
conversation, logic of (basics of) 166
Cook, P.J. 188
Cooper, C.L. 157
Coplan, J.D. 117
Corn, K.J. 55
courage, lack of 2, 5, 15, 23
Covid 19 9, 63, 101
Craske, M.G. 113
Crosnoe, R. 137, 193

Daly, M.C. 197
Daniel Tiger's Neighborhood 182
Darwin, C.R. 20, 106
Datar, A. 188
debt 158–59
Deluca, S. 193
Department of Health and Human Services 5
depression: comorbidity with anxiety 8, 13, 114, 128; exercise and 182; neuroticism 22; night-shift workers 157; in retirement 144; sleep for adolescents and 196; social understanding compared to anxiety 2, 6, 16–17, 19, 25, 31
dermatillomania *see* Obsessive compulsive disorder
desensitization 46, 47, 90, 164–165
developmental delays 134
developmental stages 84–85; *see also* lifecourse
Diagnostic And Statistical Manual IV (*DSM-IV*) 44, 50, 54, 55, 92, 93, 97, 98, 112
Diagnostic and Statistical Manual V (*DSM-V*) 54, 55
diagnostic assessment batteries *see* screening tools
divorce: as stressor contributing to anxiety 40, 142; *see also* Holmes and Rahe Life Stress Inventory
Divorce Busting 152
Dodson, J.D. 58–59
Donnelly, D.A. 160
Downey, D.B. 188
Downton Abbey 176
Dreeben, R. 187
drug use *see* substance abuse
Dugas, M.J. 112
Dworkin, A.G. 157

effort, negative perceptions by others 6, 67
Elliott, M. 172
empty nest syndrome 142
evolution (anxiety as adaptive) 19, 20–21, 79, 84, 88, 101, 114, 117; cites and 54; intelligence 21; relationships, need for 63
extraversion *see* introversion/extraversion

Failure to Launch 67, 68, 138
fear 8, 9, 11, 20–28; of change 21, 33; of darkness 81, 183; of driving 14, 33; of failure 29, 31–32; of flying 14, 33; gender and 17; of public speaking 58; self-blame 32; social anxiety disorder and 52–56,

214

62; of strangers 36; of the unknown 21; *see also* childhood; imposter syndrome; infancy; panic disorder; separation anxiety
fear, as evolutionarily adaptive *see* evolution
feelings, accompanying anxiety: embarrassment 54, 64; guilt 29–30, 68, 95, 97–98, 108–109, 124, 143, 147, 149, 170; over-reactions 22; overwhelmed 17, 22; shame 25, 45, 52, 167; *see also* survivor's guilt
Feiler, B. 40
fibromyalgia 24, 124, 125
Fields, R.D. 131
fight or flight response 11, 19, 20, 24, 53, 77, 112, 113, 120, 125; adrenaline 20; amygdala 20; autonomic nervous system 20, 37; cerebral cortex 20; freezing 21; vigilance to danger 21
film and literature, introduction to depictions of anxiety on 6
Fishback, G. 94, 116
flashbacks 99–100
Floud, S. 154
floundering *see* failure to launch
Foa, E.B. 171
Foxman, P. 28, 148, 175, 203
Frankl, V.E. 88
Freedom Writers 6
Freud, S. 88, 95
Frey, B.S. 155
Frost, R.O. 106

gastrointestinal problems 11, 24, 36, 37, 54, 123; *see also* symptoms
general practitioners 8, 24, 48, 124, 126
generalized anxiety disorder 11, 24, 84; free floating anxiety 21; genito-urinary symptoms 36, 123; self-critical thoughts and GAD 115; symptoms, multiple listed 123–124; *see also* gastro-intestinal problems; life course; physiological and mood; symptoms
geographic mobility *see* moving
Glover, V. 176
Gone with the Wind 159
Gonzales, O.L. 155
Gorka, S.M. 84
Gottfried, M.A. 188
Granovetter, M. 72
Grigg, J. 186
Guest, J. 51
guilt 30, 95–98, 119

Hallowell, E.M. 10, 21, 110, 111, 117–119, 171

Hamilton, M. 10, 35–36
Hamilton Anxiety Rating Scale 36, 37
Hanlon, H.R. 6
Harter, S. 189
Harvard Medical School 16, 17
headaches 11, 24, 123
Hearst, William Randolph 30
Henry VIII 30
heritability of anxiety 7
Herzog, H. 151
hidden handicap thesis 3, 8, 13, 15, 23, 201–202; from themselves 23; happiness and anxiety 3, 8, 15, 24, 52; *see also* underachievement
hierarchy of stressors 46, 47, 164, 165
high somatization disorder 127
Holland, E. 20
Holmes, T. 10, 40, 44, 85, 96, 142, 150
Holmes and Rahe Life Stress Inventory 40, 44, 85, 96, 158
Horwath, E. 90
How to Stop Worrying and Start Living *see* Carnegie, Dale
hyper-aroused state *see* vigilance
hypochondria 90, 127

I Know This Much Is True 119
identity theft 9
illness anxiety disorder 127
immune system, anxiety's effects on 25
imposter phenomenon/imposter syndrome 73, 74
impulse control disorders 16, 22, 24
infertility 26
insomnia 11, 15, 36, 38, 110, 123
introversion/extroversion 56, 180
irritable bowel syndrome 24, 124; *see also* symptoms
Irving, J. 141

Jackson, P.W. 187
Jacobi, F.R.J. 7
Jewell, L. 106

Kagan, J. 130–131
Kahneman, D. 155
Kampfer, S. 153
Kang, S. 188
Kelly, S. 6, 188, 193, 197
Kendall, J. 58
Kessler, R.C. 113
Kilbride, K. 104
Kiley, D. 68
Kinney, D.A. 192
Kleinknecht, R.A. 102
kleptomania 106–109; *see also* obsessive compulsive disorder

Index

Kondo, M. 105, 153
Kramer, P. 24, 167

Lakoff, R. 166
Lamb, W. 119
Lang, P.J. 48
Lareau, A. 156
laziness 15, 23
Leahy, R. 9
learning disabilities 60, 67, 134
leisure 2, 30, 156
Lethem, J. 106
Liddell, H.S. 21
Liebowitz, M.R. 55
life course 1, 8, 11, 18, 68, 128–129; late adulthood 142–145; middle age 142; retirement 1, 9, 11, 44, 142–145; self-critical thoughts 23; self-esteem 192; young adults 16, 33, 138; *see also* failure to launch
Little Albert see Watson, J.
Littwin, S. 68
Lortie, D.C. 157
Lucas, J.A. 39

Mantella, R.C. 113, 145
marriage *see* relationships
Marshall, J. 157
McCabe, J.M. 198
McKenzie, B. 155
McNeal, R.B. 193
McTeague, L.M. 48
Medici family 30
Meltsner, S. 172, 204
Milkie, M.A. 195, 209
Miller, A.H. 98 138
misdiagnoses and anxiety: lupus 126; multiple sclerosis 126
Mr. Rogers' Neighborhood 181
Morgan, W.P. 149
Motherless Brooklyn 106–107
moving (locations, to a new home or school) 26, 32, 33, 40, 144, 154–156, 186; children and 136; generalized anxiety disorder and 128; life course and 85, 140; Miriam's story in 18–19; panic attacks 145; social anxiety and 71; trends in rate of 9; *see also* school
multiple sclerosis 25, 126; *see also* consequences of anxiety; exacerbation of existing conditions; misdiagnoses and anxiety
Munch, Edvard 8
Murphy, K. 54, 63
Murray, E.J. 160
Mutz, M. 153

National Anxiety Center 57
neighborhood environments 154–156
Nelson, P. 39
nervous breakdown (non-scientific term) 1, 15, 38, 40, 41, 43
neuroticism *see* depression
Newman, M.G. 52
nightmares 48–51, 81; *see also* post traumatic stress disorder
Nikolajeva, M. 101
Normal People 38
Norton, G.R. 55
Novaco, R.W. 155

obsessive compulsive disorder 11, 28, 90, 92–109; in comparison to generalized anxiety disorder 115–116, 118, 127, 128; compulsions 100–103; dermatillomania 107, 108; on film 6; hoarding 11, 99, 100, 104, 105; life course, over the 145; obsessive thoughts 93–96; slowness 102; tourette syndrome 106, 107; treatment 169–172; trichotillomania 107, 108
Olsson, L.E. 155
O'Malley, P.M. 192
Orban, E. 154
Ordinary People 51
Oster, E. 181
overtraining 149
overwork, culture of 157

panic 1, 8, 24, 25, 128; forms of 10–11; in OCD 93; postponed adulthood, and 71; in relation to GAD 112–114, 123; in relation to PTSD 51–52; in relation to social anxiety 54; in specific phobia 77, 82; *see also* avoidance; test anxiety
panic disorder 37–39, 41–44, 45, 55, 133, 160–163; treatment 160–163
The Paradox of Choice: Why More Is Less 8
paranoid schizophrenia 96
parenting 7, 12, 141, 176–200; college students 198–200; infants 177–179; middle schoolers 195–198; pets 180; preschoolers 184–187; school-aged children 187–192; strangers, introducing 181; toddlers 179–184; your sensitive child 177; *see also* phobias; separation anxiety
A Patchwork Planet 71
performance anxiety 16, 18, 21, 22, 52, 59; athletic events 57–58; speeches/public speaking 18, 33, 58; test-taking 16, 33, 59–60
Peter Pan syndrome 68–69; *see also* failure to launch
Petersen, A. 17

Index

pets 180; *see also* prevention; treatment
phobia/specific phobia 11, 115, 116, 122, 128, 133, 168–169; animals 77; birds 81, 87; bridges 78; cats 77, 86; change 83–84; claustrophobia 79; death 88–89; dogs 77, 81; fish 86, 87; flying 78; list of 80, 81; needles 88; outdoors 83, 86–87; snakes 82, 83; speeches 32, 58; spiders 82; strangers 71, 76, 81, 84, 181
Pollard, H.J. 55
post-traumatic stress disorder (PTSD) 11, 48–52, 115, 147; generalized anxiety disorder and 128; survivor's guilt and 119
prevalence rates (scientific estimates of): animal predispositions 131; anxiety disorders 16–17, 27; binge drinking 7; Bipolar Disorder 114; commuting 155; GAD 7; GAD symptoms 113; Head Start, enrollment 185; hoarding and social anxiety 104; infant predispositions 130; mental health, overall 5; panic attacks 39–40; redshirting in school 188; school phobia 67; shyness 6; Social Anxiety 55; Specific Phobia and Agoraphobia 90; stigma 6; Tourette's and OCD 106; treatment 17, 25
prevention 8; in infants and young children 130–132, 177–184; pets, and 180; in preschoolers 184–187; promoting overall health 148–150; reducing stress 150–159; *see also* Holmes and Rahe Life Stress Inventory; parenting; school; snowball effect of anxiety; stress
Price, H.E. 197
primary care physicians *see* general practitioners, screening tools
Princess Diana 30
Prins, A. 49
progressive relaxation 163; yoga 162

Quiet 57
Quikin, F.M. 28

Rahe, R. 10, 40, 44, 85, 96, 142, 150
Reardon, S.F. 188
regret 98–99, 128
Reid, J.D. 142
relationships: anxiety effects 2, 8, 22, 24, 32; cohabitation 74, 75; dating 69, 75; marriage 30, 74, 75, 152; physiological functioning 63; *see also* avoidance; divorce; hidden handicap thesis; social anxiety; strength of weak ties; substance abuse
relaxation: exercises 159, 161–163; inability to relax 36; massage 161–162; meditation 162
remediation *see* treatment
RESPeRATE device 161
Retaliation 50
Rodiek, S. 152
Roksa, J. 68
Rooney, S. 38
Rosenbaum, J.E. 197, 199
Rumberger, R.W. 186
Ruscio, A.M. 113

Schneier, C.E. 55
school 2, 18, 23, 24, 129; college for all norms 197; day care and nursery school 185; elementary school 18, 23, 84, 187–192; extracurricular activities 93–94; extra-curriculars and identity projects 193; fitting in, problems of 137; high school 9, 18, 32, 84, 195–198; identity projects 193; junior high 136; kindergarten 18, 32, 66; middle school 32, 192–195; moving to a new school 32, 186; preschool 18, 84; quality differences 188; school phobia 168–169; transition from family to school 187
Schwartz, B 9
The Scream 8
screening tools: generalized anxiety disorder 110–111; Hamilton Anxiety Rating Scale 35–37; post traumatic stress disorder 48–49; Primary Care PTSD Screener 48–49; social anxiety 52–53
selective mutism 66
self-critical thoughts *see* generalized anxiety disorder
self-esteem 22, 32, 35; middle school years 137, 192–193; social anxiety and 54, 64, 75; social media 153
sensitivity to stress 125; in childhood 130–131, 177
separation anxiety 131–132, 135
severity, anxiety, range of 2
shame, gendered experiences of 25
shyness 22, 56, 66–76, 137
Snidman, N. 130
snowball effect of anxiety 33, 129, 202
social anxiety/social phobia 1, 11, 52–56; blushing 54; in childhood 66–67; connection to shyness 56–57; coping with 65–66; fear of the unknown 84; generalized forms of 63–64; marriage, and 74–75; performance anxiety 57–58; relation to GAD 113, 115; relation to OCD 104; relation to specific phobia 90, 133; self-consciousness 17, 22, 54; sexual apprehension 69–70; treatment

Index

165–168; in the workplace 71–73; in young adulthood 67–70, 140, 145
social media 9; addiction to 29; failure to launch and 68; high school 195–196; middle school 136; treatment and 150–153
social problem, anxiety as 8
Solomon, A. 28
specific phobia *see* phobia
spoiled identity 137; *see also* schools
startle response: generalized anxiety disorder and 113, 123; infants and 22, 36, 130; post traumatic stress disorder and 50
Steketee, G. 106
Stephan, J.L. 199
stigma 2, 6, 25, 31, 137; *see also* school; spoiled identity
Stossel, S. 9, 10, 20, 22, 28, 33, 39, 58, 77, 83, 84, 91, 130, 133
stranger anxiety 81, 82
Straub, E. 99
strength of weak ties 72
stress 1, 5, 17, 18, 26, 38, 40, 123
stress induced cardiomyopathy *see* broken heart syndrome
stress, external stressors 10, 12; commuting as 26, 155; expectations of others and 196; neighborhood environments 154–156
stress, reduction: traffic 26; travel 30, 158; *see also* prevention
Stutzer, A. 155
substance abuse 14–16, 24, 29; alcoholism 6, 8, 15, 16, 24, 31, 54, 55; binge drinking 7; marijuana 14–15, 31, 66; self-medication as 6, 15, 31; smoking 16, 66
Substance Abuse and Mental Health Services Administration 7
suicide 7, 147
Sullivan, A. 150, 154
survivor's guilt 50, 119
Swinson, R.P. 37, 38
Swords, L. 6
symptoms 8, 11, 123; *see also* generalized anxiety disorder
symptoms, mood 22 36; apprehensiveness, chronic, low grade 21; irritability 22, 36; moodiness 22
symptoms, physiological 20, 44, 112; blushing 54; breathing problems 37, 43, 123; dizziness 123; dry eye 123; dry mouth 20, 37, 123; fatigue 11, 24, 110, 123; muscle tension 20, 110; overactive bladder 24, 37, 123; pain, back and neck, muscle 24, 36, 123; perspiration 20, 37,

54, 123; queasiness 20; rapid breathing 20; restlessness 17, 36, 110, 123; skin conditions 123; sweating 20, 37, 54, 123; teeth grinding 36; tension 36; tinnitus (possible) 36, 123, 124; urinary frequency 36, 123

Taylor, C.B. 39
teenagers 9, 23, 129, 136, 137; *see also* life course; schools
Telch, M.J. 39
test anxiety *see* performance anxiety
Thapamagar S.B. 42
therapy *see* treatment
Thomas, A. 130 204
Time Magazine 8
Tisinger, S. 178
Tobar, D.A. 149
Tough Love 65
transitions and change 8; anxiety's effects on 32, 144; to college 13, 198, 199; to elementary school 187–191; GAD and 116, 126, 128; precipitating anxiety 18, 66, 84–85, 129, 157; *see also* moving
treatment 1, 8, 12, 25, 147–175, 159–175, 203–204; antianxiety medication 47, 161, 163, 164, 168–169; antidepressant medication 114, 159, 161, 164, 167, 169, 174; cognitive-behavioral therapy 167, 203; countering self-critical thoughts 167; EMDR 162; horticultural therapy 152; hypnosis 162; marital therapy 171; pets 180; play for children 181, 186; self-help books 148, 152, 203–204; systematic desensitization 46–47; writing and expressive therapy 159, 160, 170; *see also* pets; progressive relaxation; relaxation; stress reduction
Tung, E.S. 123
Twenge, J.M. 195
Tyler, A. 71, 97
Type A personality 26, 44, 144

underachievement 2, 5, 13, 25, 35, 71; in careers 8, 24; education 8, 14, 24, 135; job interviews 16; *see also* avoidance
underemployment/unemployment 42
Urbach-Wiethe disease 20

Van Den Berg, A.E. 152
Vignettes: introduction to use 2; major (Alice 14; 70–71; Barbara 96–97, 99–100, 104, 171; Doug 114, 120; Irene 75–76; Jill 11, 37–42, 163; Joanne 11, 120–125; Karen 89–90; Mark 34; Mary Ellen 53–54, 65, 168; Miriam 18–19;